# QUESTIONS & ANSWERS:
## FEDERAL ESTATE & GIFT TAXATION

# QUESTIONS & ANSWERS:
## FEDERAL ESTATE & GIFT TAXATION

*Multiple-Choice and Short-Answer Questions and Answers*

Second Edition

**Elain Hightower Gagliardi**
Professor of Law
The University of Montana School of Law

ISBN: 978–0–7698–4599–9 (print)
ISBN: 978–0–3271–8215–3 (eBook)

This publication is designed to provide authoritative information in regard to the subject matter covered. It is sold with the understanding that the publisher is not engaged in rendering legal, accounting, or other professional services. If legal advice or other expert assistance is required, the services of a competent professional should be sought.

LexisNexis and the Knowledge Burst logo are registered trademarks of Reed Elsevier Properties Inc., used under license. Matthew Bender and the Matthew Bender Flame Design are registered trademarks of Matthew Bender Properties Inc.

---

**NOTE TO USERS**

To ensure that you are using the latest materials available in this area, please be sure to periodically check the LexisNexis Law School web site for downloadable updates and supplements at www.lexisnexis.com/lawschool.

---

Editorial Offices
121 Chanlon Rd., New Providence, NJ 07974 (908) 464-6800
201 Mission St., San Francisco, CA 94105-1831 (415) 908-3200
www.lexisnexis.com

MATTHEW◆BENDER

# DEDICATION

I dedicate this book to James M. Delaney. Jim and I originally wrote this book together, and this revised edition would not have been possible without his work, scholarship, and dedication. It has been a special privilege for me to work with Jim, who is a brilliant teacher and scholar. I wish him well in his new endeavors. — Elaine Gagliardi

# TABLE OF CONTENTS

# TABLE OF CONTENTS

# QUESTIONS

# INTRODUCTION TO FEDERAL WEALTH TRANSFER TAXATION

*Unless otherwise indicated, for all questions assume that the donor or decedent is a U.S. citizen or resident and that the beneficiaries are U.S. citizens.*

*Unless otherwise indicated, all references to "IRC" or to "the Code" refer to the Internal Revenue Code, all references to "Section" refer to sections of the Internal Revenue Code, and all references to "Service" refer to the Internal Revenue Service.*

1.  The debate as to whether or not to repeal the current federal estate, gift and generation skipping transfer tax system remains unsettled in 2012. Proposals to replace the current system with a different tax structure abound. Which of the following labels best characterizes the taxation of property based on the value transferred by decedent to beneficiaries?

    **(A)**  Pick up tax

    **(B)**  Inheritance tax

    **(C)**  Succession tax

    **(D)**  Estate tax

2.  Indicate which of the following persons are subject to federal estate tax.

    **(A)**  U.S. citizens only

    **(B)**  U.S. citizens and residents only

    **(C)**  U.S. citizens and residents, and nonresident aliens with property situated in the United States

    **(D)**  U.S. citizens and residents, but only on property situated in the United States

3.  Following the 2010 Tax Reform Act, Congress once again unified certain aspects of the federal estate, gift and generation-skipping transfer taxes. Indicate which features of all three taxes have been unified as of 2011.

    **(A)**  Only the effective marginal tax rate

    **(B)**  The effective marginal tax rate, the basic exclusion amount and the generation skipping transfer tax exemption

    **(C)**  The tax rate, the applicable exclusion amount and the basic exclusion amount

**(D)**   The tax rate, the applicable exclusion amount, and the annual exclusion amount

4.   What is the maximum amount of property that a U.S. taxpayer can transfer free of federal estate, gift and generation skipping transfer taxes.

     **(A)**   $5 million

     **(B)**   Basic exclusion amount

     **(C)**   Applicable exclusion amount

     **(D)**   Deceased spousal unused exclusion amount

5.   Within three years of death, Mike transfers $10 million in trust for his niece Lois, with remainder to Lois' descendants. Indicate which of the following federal taxes might apply to Mike's transfer:

     **(A)**   Only the gift tax

     **(B)**   Only the gift tax and the generation skipping transfer tax

     **(C)**   Only the gift tax and the estate tax

     **(D)**   The gift, estate and generation skipping transfer taxes

6.   Explain why the federal gift tax and generation-skipping transfer tax are said to work as a "back-stop" to the federal estate and income taxes.

ANSWER:

7.   Barbara, who is not married and who owns assets in excess of $10 million, has decided to make gifts to her only child to minimize federal estate and gift tax. Indicate which of the following assets you would recommend that Barbara give to her child:

     **(A)**   An apartment building, which produces income that Barbara uses to pay personal expenses.

     **(B)**   Company X stock, which has recently been declining in value

     **(C)**   Lake home, which has recently begun to appreciate rapidly

     **(D)**   Residence, which Barbara intends to live in long-term

**Facts for Questions 8 through 10.**

Allan, a never married U.S. citizen and resident, made a taxable gift on January 1, 2010, of $500,000, and a taxable gift on January 1, 2011, of $5,000,000. Allan dies on February 1, 2012. Assume that the gift tax applicable exclusion amount in 2010 is $1 million, the basic exclusion amount in 2011 is $5 million, and the basic exclusion amount in 2012 is $5,120,000. Also assume that the highest marginal tax rate (which kicks in at $500,000 of transfers) is 35% for all years.

8. Based on the above facts, calculate the amount of federal gift tax owed by Allan on the 2010 taxable gift.

ANSWER:


9. Based on the above facts, calculate the amount of federal gift tax owed by Allan on the 2011 taxable gift.

ANSWER:


10. Based on the above facts, calculate the amount of federal estate tax owed, if any, by Allan's estate if Allan dies owning title to $2 million of assets.

ANSWER:

11. Which of the following interests owned by Ellen, a U.S. citizen and resident, will not be included in Ellen's gross estate pursuant to Section 2033.

    (A)  Community property interest in land.

    (B)  General power of appointment.

    (C)  Tax exempt municipal bonds.

    (D)  Tenant-in-common interest in land located in Mexico.

12. Which of the following interests owned by Ellen will not be included in her gross estate pursuant to Section 2033?

    (A)  Promissory note held by Ellen under which Ellen was not receiving payments.

    (B)  A right to a rental payment that became due to Ellen prior to her death but remained unpaid as of the date of her death.

    (C)  The value of goodwill that Ellen had built up in her business during her life.

    (D)  An interest payment which accrued on tax exempt municipal bonds after Ellen's death and which was paid after death.

13. Cindy purchases a share of Apple, Inc. stock on May 1. Assume that Cindy dies in the morning on June 1. Under which of the following circumstances would the amount of such dividend be excluded in Cindy's gross estate?

    (A)  The Board of directors of Apple, Inc. resolved to pay a dividend to the shareholders of record on May 15. Cindy's estate received the dividend proceeds on May 30.

    (B)  The Board of directors of Apple, Inc. resolved to pay a dividend to the shareholders of record on June 1. The dividend proceeds were credited to Cindy's brokerage account in the afternoon of June 1.

    (C)  On May 15, the Board of directors of Apple, Inc. resolved to pay a dividend to the shareholders of record on June 10. Cindy's estate received the dividend proceeds on June 15.

    (D)  On June 1, the Board of directors of Apple, Inc. resolved to pay a dividend to the shareholders of record on May 15. Cindy's estate received the dividend proceeds on June 15.

14. Fred holds the following interests in trust. Each of the trusts were created and funded by someone other than Fred. Fred holds only the interests indicated, and no other interest in the trust. Indicate which of the following interests will be included in Fred's gross estate pursuant to Section 2033.

    **(A)** Fred's life estate in trust 1, with Fred's interest being terminated at death and trust property passing to the named remainder person on Fred's death.

    **(B)** Fred's contingent remainder interest in trust 2, with Fred's interest being terminated at death and trust property passing to the other named remainder person.

    **(C)** Fred's vested remainder interest in trust 3, with Fred's interest surviving death, and passing to Fred's estate.

    **(D)** Fred's legal title to trust property as trustee of trust 4, with Fred's interest as trustee terminating at death, and legal title passing to the named successor trustee.

15. Geri was involved in a car accident. Recovery for losses due to the accident depends on state law. Indicate which of the following recoveries that, if provided for by state law, would result in estate tax inclusion pursuant to IRC § 2033.

    **(A)** Geri's personal representative is entitled to bring an action for Geri's wrongful death, and does so successfully.

    **(B)** Harold, a surviving spouse of Geri, is entitled to bring an action for Geri's wrongful death, and does so successfully.

    **(C)** Geri's personal representative is entitled to bring an action for Geri's pain and suffering, and does so successfully.

    **(D)** Geri's no-fault insurance policy pays a state required survivor's benefit to Harold.

16. Kathy makes a loan to her sibling, and takes back a promissory note. Kathy dies holding the promissory note. Kathy's will forgives all remaining payments due on the note. Will Kathy's gross estate include the value of the remaining payments due pursuant to Section 2033, and why?

    **(A)** Yes, because Kathy made a transfer of an interest in property held at death by forgiving the promissory note.

    **(B)** Yes, because Kathy retained an interest in property transferred during life by taking back the promissory note.

    **(C)** No, because Kathy terminated the property interest by forgiving the promissory note, and no transfer occurred.

    **(D)** No, because Kathy received adequate consideration for the note so that the forgiveness did not amount to a transfer.

17. Lance died owning a sport utility vehicle. Briefly explain how the vehicle should be valued

for inclusion in the decedent's gross estate.

ANSWER:

18. Melanie died owning stock in a publicly traded corporation. The highest reported trading price per share of stock on the date of decedent's death was $100. The lowest reported trading price was $50. Most shares traded for $80 that day. Choose the value at which the stock should be reported on Melanie's federal estate tax return.

   (A) $50

   (B) $75

   (C) $80

   (D) $100

19. Assume the same facts as in question 18, above, but that Melanie passed away on a Sunday (e.g., there were no public sales of stock on the day Melanie died). Briefly explain how the stock should be valued.

ANSWER:

20. Assume that Melanie passed away on Sunday, April 1. If sales of the stock occurred on Thursday, March 29, at a mean sales price per share of $46 and on Monday, April 2, at a mean sales price per share of $52, choose the value at which the stock should be reported on Melanie's federal estate tax return.

   (A) 46

   (B) 51

   (C) 48

   (D) 50

21. Norman died holding a vested remainder interest in a trust following a life income interest payable annually to the life tenant. Trust property as of Norman's date of death totaled $100,000. The applicable federal rate at that time was 10 percent, and the age of the life tenant was 60. The remainder factor provided by actuarial tables for the remainder interest is ".21196." Determine the value of the Norman's remainder interest for purposes of determining the gross estate.

ANSWER:

**Facts for Questions 22 through 26.**

Fiddich was a lucky man while he was alive. He operated his own business and, with the profits he earned, he invested in everything under the sun. He invested in publicly traded stocks, real estate and, in his spare time, he patented an invention which he licensed to a biotech firm. He enjoyed a real "run up" in the stock market during the mid-2000s. Unfortunately, Fiddich had a heart attack on October 10, 2007, when the Dow Jones Industrial Average hit a closing high of 14,066. On that date, his vast holdings had a fair market value of an even $1 billion. The beneficiaries of his vast fortune were euphoric. However, shortly as Fiddich's executor began to account for all of his assets, the markets crashed. By April 10, 2008, instead of being worth a cool $1 billion, Fiddich's estate was now only worth approximately $500 million.

22.    Must Fiddich's estate include in gross estate the date of death value of $1 billion or does he have an opportunity to report a lesser value? Please explain in your answer.

ANSWER:

23.    Assume instead that Fiddich's portfolio of stock was worth $1,000,000 as of the date of his death. Three months after his death the portfolio was $750,000. Six months after the date of his death the portfolio was worth $500,000. If Fiddich's estate appropriately makes a § 2032 alternate valuation election, what value in relation to his portfolio would be included in his gross estate if the whole portfolio was sold three months after Fiddich's death?

   **(A)** $1,000,000

   **(B)** $750,000

   **(C)** $500,000

   **(D)** Nothing, gain or loss on the portfolio since Fiddich's death would be included in the estate's income tax return.

24.    Assume the same facts as in question 23 (e.g., a valid § 2032 election was made) and that prior to his death, Fiddich was receiving annual royalties of $50,000 for the use of his patent. The patent still had 10 years left before it would expire. As of the date of Fiddich's death, the present value of the patent royalty stream was $480,000. Assume further that a royalty payment of $50,000 was received by the estate four months after Fiddich died and that six months after he died, the rights to the patent were sold by the executor for $430,000. What amount in relation to the patent would be included in Fiddich's gross estate?

   **(A)** $480,000

   **(B)** $50,000

   **(C)** $452,632

   **(D)** $500,000

25. Assume again that a valid IRC § 2032 election was made and that the realty owned by Fiddich was worth $75,000,000 as of the date of his death. Six months after his death, the real estate was worth $100,000,000. All other assets substantially went down in value after his death. What amount in relation to the real estate would be included in Fiddich's gross estate under these circumstances?

   **(A)** $75,000,000

   **(B)** $100,000,000

   **(C)** Nothing, because the realty went up in value, it is not included in the calculation of gross estate.

   **(D)** Nothing, the $25,000,000 gain would be included in the estate's income tax return.

26. Assume instead that due to the phenomenal investment skills of his executor, the value of all assets in Fiddich's estate increased after he passed away. Moreover, Fiddich's executor decided that she would like to get a bigger step up in the basis of his assets at death so she asks you whether she can make a valid IRC § 2032 election under these circumstances?

ANSWER:

27. Laura transferred property to a trust, with Mary as trustee. Laura retained certain rights and interests in the trust. Indicate the Code section that will most likely apply to include the entire value of the trust property on Laura's date of death in the gross estate of Laura.

   **(A)** IRC Section 2033.

   **(B)** IRC Section 2036.

   **(C)** IRC Section 2040.

   **(D)** IRC Section 2041.

28. Lance transferred property to a trust with Martin as trustee. Pursuant to the trust, Lance gave Oscar, who is a life income beneficiary of the trust, the power to determine who receives the trust principal on termination of the trust, including payment to Oscar. Indicate the Code section that will most likely apply to include the trust property in the gross estate of Oscar as beneficiary of the trust.

   **(A)** IRC Section 2033.

   **(B)** IRC Section 2036.

   **(C)** IRC Section 2038.

   **(D)** IRC Section 2041.

29. Livvy transferred property to a trust, with Max as trustee. Max is also a beneficiary. Pursuant to the trust, Max possesses the power as trustee to distribute trust income and principal among beneficiaries. Indicate the Code section that will most likely apply to include the trust property in the gross estate of Max, as trustee.

   **(A)** IRC Section 2033.

   **(B)** IRC Section 2036.

   **(C)** IRC Section 2037.

   **(D)** IRC Section 2041.

30. Lanna and Lanna's spouse, Paul, own Greenacre as joint tenants with right of survivorship. Indicate the Code section that will most likely apply to include a portion of Greenacre in the gross estate of Lanna.

    **(A)**  IRC Section 2033.

    **(B)**  IRC Section 2034.

    **(C)**  IRC Section 2040.

    **(D)**  IRC Section 2044.

31.    Lucy owns a life insurance policy on the life of her spouse. Indicate the Code section that will most likely apply to include the life insurance policy in the gross estate of Lucy.

    **(A)**  IRC Section 2033.

    **(B)**  IRC Section 2036.

    **(C)**  IRC Section 2042.

    **(D)**  IRC Section 2044.

**Facts for Questions 32 and 33.**

Any State, USA, has abolished dower and curtesy. Instead, Any State allows a surviving spouse to take an elective share amount in the event decedent fails on death to make sufficient provision for the surviving spouse. The surviving spouse is not entitled to an elective share amount unless the surviving spouse makes a timely election. In Any State the surviving spouse must make any election within nine months of the death of the first spouse to die. The law of Any State also prohibits an election after the death of the surviving spouse. This right to take an elective share amount is often referred to as a "right of election."

Anna and Barry are married and domiciled in Any State. Anna dies when Anna is married to Barry. Barry dies six months following Anna's death without having exercised his right of election.

32. Based on the above facts, will Anna's gross estate include the property owned by Anna that is subject to Barry's right of election?

    (A)   Yes, because Barry's right of election is a statutory interest created in Anna's surviving spouse as a result of her death.

    (B)   Yes, because Barry's right of election is a contingent interest that may never vest in Barry.

    (C)   No, because Barry's right of election is a general power of appointment in Barry, not Anna.

    (D)   No, because Barry's right of election amounts to a valid claim against Anna's property.

33. Based on the above facts, discuss whether Barry's gross estate includes the value of the elective share amount.

ANSWER:


**Facts for Questions 34 and 35.**

Brad and Deborah have been married for 20 years. Brad earned a degree in law and began working exorbitant hours before marrying Deborah. After marriage, they had three children one after the other and Deborah gave up her lucrative job as an investment banker to take care of the children. The two began to accumulate substantial assets over the years that they were married. During the length of their marriage, Brad and Deborah lived in a community property state and all of their assets were classified as community property. One night, while driving home late in a bad snow storm, Brad died in a car accident. Upon Brad's death, the couple's combined assets were valued at

$6,000,000. However, the combined assets had a cost basis of $2,000,000 as of the date Brad passed away.

34. Assuming no 2032 election was available, what amount of assets would be included in Brad's gross estate?

    (A) $6,000,000

    (B) $3,000,000

    (C) Answer would depend on which assets were treated under local law as owned by Brad.

    (D) None, community assets are treated as included only in the surviving spouse's gross estate.

35. Assume the same facts as in question 34, above, and that Brad bequeathed all of his assets to their daughter, Rennie. What basis would Rennie have in the assets that she received from Brad?

    (A) $1,000,000

    (B) $2,000,000

    (C) $3,000,000

    (D) $6,000,000

36. Assume the same facts as in Question 35, above. What cost basis would Brad's wife Deborah have in her one-half share of the community assets after Brad's death?

    (A) $1,000,000

    (B) $2,000,000

    (C) $3,000,000

    (D) $6,000,000

37. How, if at all, would your answer to question 36, above, change if Brad and Deborah had instead resided in a non-community property state for the complete duration of their marriage?

ANSWER:


38. Celeste and Eric enter into a prenuptial agreement. Pursuant to the agreement, Celeste gives Eric a life interest in Celeste's apartment in consideration for Eric's agreement to waive any marital or other rights upon Celeste's death. Celeste dies at a time when Celeste and Eric are happily married, and Eric enforces the agreement. The prenuptial agreement

is based on adequate consideration and is enforceable under state law. Section 2053 of the Code allows a deduction for bona fide claims against the estate supported by full and adequate consideration. Indicate whether Celeste's estate may deduct the value of Eric's life interest in Celeste's apartment pursuant to Section 2053.

**(A)** Yes, because the prenuptial agreement is supported by adequate consideration and enforceable under state law.

**(B)** Yes, because Eric has enforced Eric's claim under the prenuptial agreement, and caused a life estate in the apartment to vest in Eric.

**(C)** No, because a waiver of marital rights does not amount to full and adequate consideration for federal estate tax purposes.

**(D)** No, because Eric did not enter into the agreement within the three-year period beginning one year prior to Celeste's date of death.

# ADJUSTMENTS FOR CERTAIN GIFTS MADE WITHIN THREE YEARS OF DECEDENT'S DEATH, IRC § 2035

*IRC § 2035 generally serves two purposes. First, it acts as a stop-gap to IRC §§ 2036, 2037, 2038, and 2042. For this reason, you may wish to come back to this Topic 5 after reviewing the topics addressing these sections. Second, IRC § 2035 acts to prevent the gift tax exclusive impact of gifts made within three years of decedent's death.*

*The following questions assume the transfer at issue occurred after 1981. Prior to 1982 the reach of IRC § 2035 was much broader than it is today. (Note that, while the substance of IRC § 2035 did not materially change, the numbering of the subsections changed in 1997.)*

39. Alice transfers cash to herself as trustee of an irrevocable trust for the benefit of her adult child and grandchild. As trustee, Alice may distribute income in her discretion to her child and grandchild. On the death of Alice's child, the remainder of trust property passes to Alice's grandchild or the grandchild's estate. Alice consults with her attorney, and irrevocably resigns as trustee of the trust on March 6, 2009, in order to avoid any concern that IRC §§ 2036 and 2038 would apply to include the trust property in her gross estate. Alice dies on March 6, 2012. Indicate whether Alice successfully avoided inclusion of the trust property in her gross estate, and why.

    (A) Yes, Alice avoided inclusion in her gross estate because Alice never held any interest in or power that would have caused inclusion under IRC §§ 2036 through 2038, thereby making IRC § 2035 irrelevant.

    (B) Yes, Alice avoided inclusion in her gross estate because Alice irrevocably relinquished her power over the trust more than three years prior to her date of death, thereby avoiding application of IRC § 2035.

    (C) No, Alice's gross estate includes a portion of the trust property because Alice relinquished her power over the trust assets within three years of her date of death thereby triggering application of IRC § 2035.

    (D) No, Alice's gross estate includes a portion of the trust property because Alice originally retained a power over trust income, and relinquishment of the power, regardless of when, causes IRC § 2035 to apply.

40. Assume the same facts as in question 39 above except that Alice dies on March 4, 2012. Indicate whether Alice successfully avoided inclusion of the trust property in her gross estate, and why.

**(A)** Yes, Alice avoided inclusion in her gross estate because Alice never held any interest in or power that would have caused inclusion under IRC §§ 2036 through 2038, thereby making IRC § 2035 irrelevant.

**(B)** Yes, Alice avoided inclusion in her gross estate because Alice irrevocably relinquished her power over the trust more than three years prior to her date of death, thereby avoiding application of IRC § 2035.

**(C)** No, Alice's gross estate includes a portion of the trust property because Alice relinquished her power over the trust assets within three years of her date of death thereby triggering application of IRC § 2035.

**(D)** No, Alice's gross estate includes a portion of the trust property because Alice originally retained a power over trust income, and relinquishment of the power, regardless of when, causes IRC § 2035 to apply.

41.  Barney transfers $1 million in trust and retains the power to revoke the trust during his lifetime. The trust requires trustee to pay income and principal as directed by Barney. One month prior to his death, Barney directs trustee to transfer $100,000 cash from the trust to Barney's niece. On Barney's date of death, the trust assets total $900,000. Will Barney's gross estate include any portion of the $1 million, and, if so, why and how much?

**(A)** No, Barney's gross estate will not include any portion of the amount transferred.

**(B)** Yes, Barney's gross estate will include $900,000 per IRC § 2038, and $100,000 per IRC § 2035.

**(C)** Yes, Barney's gross estate will include only $100,000 pursuant to IRC § 2035.

**(D)** Yes, Barney's gross estate will include only $900,000 pursuant to IRC § 2038.

42.  Collin purchased a life insurance policy on his own life two years prior to his death. Collin paid the initial premium payment of $20,000, then immediately transferred ownership of the policy to his child. On Collin's death, the insurance proceeds of $1 million were paid to Collin's child as beneficiary. Will Collin's gross estate include the policy proceeds, and, if so, how much?

**(A)** No, Collin's gross estate will not include the policy proceeds because Collin did not retain any incidents of ownership over the policy as of the date of his death, nor did Collin's estate receive policy proceeds.

**(B)** Yes, Collin's gross estate will include the value of the initial premium payment of $20,000 because Collin transferred the policy during the three-year period ending on decedent's death.

**(C)** Yes, Collin's gross estate will include the $1 million of policy proceeds because Collin transferred the policy during the three-year period ending on decedent's death.

**(D)** Yes, Collin's gross estate will include both the $1 million of policy proceeds and the $20,000 premium payment because Collin transferred the policy during the three-year period ending on decedent's death.

43. Dorthea transfers $12,000 outright to her child on January 1, 2011. Child invests the cash in Public Corporation stock, and as of Dorthea's death on August 1, 2012, the Public Corporation stock has appreciated to $20,000. Indicate whether Dorthea's gross estate includes the value of the gift made by Dorthea, and, if so, why and how much.

   **(A)** Dorthea's gross estate does not include any portion of the value of the gift because the gift was an outright transfer to Dorthea's child.

   **(B)** Dorthea's gross estate includes the $12,000 date-of-gift value because the gift occurred within three years of Dorthea's death.

   **(C)** Dorthea's gross estate includes the $20,000 date-of-death value because the gift occurred within three years of Dorthea's death.

   **(D)** Dorthea's gross estate includes the stock value as of the filing of Dorthea's gift tax return because the gift occurred within three years of Dorthea's death.

44. Elise makes a cash gift to her child three years and one month prior to Elise's death. Elise and Elise's spouse choose to split the gift. Two years prior to her death, Elise pays $50,000 of gift tax with respect to the gift, and Elise's spouse also pays $50,000 of gift tax with respect to the split gift. Indicate the amount, if any, included in Elise's gross estate.

   **(A)** Elise's gross estate will not include any portion of the transfer to Elise's child or any gift tax paid on that amount.

   **(B)** Elise's gross estate will include only the $50,000 of gift tax paid by Elise during the three-year period ending on her date of death.

   **(C)** Elise's gross estate will include only the $100,000 of gift tax paid by Elise and Elise's spouse during the three-year period ending on Elise's date of death.

   **(D)** Elise's gross estate will include the value of the cash gift, and the $100,000 of gift tax paid.

45. Bono had previously used up his gift tax unified credit. In 2009, Bono made a $200,000 cash gift to his daughter Liz incurring $90,000 of gift tax which he remitted to the Treasury upon filing the appropriate gift tax return in 2010. Thereafter, in 2011, Bono passed away unexpectedly. Indicate the amount, if any, that will be included in Bono's gross estate in relation to the gift.

   **(A)** Bono's gross estate will not include any portion of the transfer to Liz or any gift tax paid on that amount.

   **(B)** Bono's gross estate will include only the $90,000 of gift tax paid by Bono during the three-year period ending on his date of death.

(C)  Bono's gross estate will include the $200,000 cash gift and the $90,000 of gift tax paid by Bono during the three-year period ending on Elise's date of death.

(D)  Bono's gross estate will include the $200,000 cash gift, the $90,000 of gift tax paid by Bono and any amount of gift tax offset by the credit he used previously.

46.  One year before his death Fred makes a taxable gift to Fred's child. The transfer is not included in Fred's gross estate under IRC§ 2035. Discuss whether the transfer would be taken into account for purposes of determining whether the estate qualifies for special use valuation under IRC § 2032A.

ANSWER:

*Unless otherwise indicated in the problems below, assume (1) any trust is irrevocable, (2) trustor and trustee are not related or subordinate to each other, and (3) all transfers of property occurred on or after June 7, 1931.*

47. Alyssa transferred her home to a trust and retained the right to use the home for a period of 10 years. At the end of the 10-year period the property passed to Bobby, Alyssa's friend. At the end of the 10-year period, Alyssa moved to an apartment. Alyssa died in year 14. Indicate whether Alyssa's gross estate will include the trust property, and the reason for your answer.

   (A) Yes, IRC § 2036 includes the trust property because Alyssa retained the right to possess the home for a period beginning upon its transfer.

   (B) Yes, IRC § 2038 includes the trust property because Alyssa retained the right to possess the home for a period beginning upon its transfer.

   (C) No, IRC § 2036 does not include the trust property because Alyssa retained the right to possess the home for a period that ended prior to her death.

   (D) No, IRC § 2038 does not include the trust property because Alyssa retained the right to possess the home for a period not ascertainable with reference to her death.

48. Assume the same facts as in Question 47, above, except that Alyssa now dies within the 10-year period during which she had the right to use the home. Indicate how your answer will change based on this new fact.

ANSWER:

49. Barry transferred stock to a corporate trustee, and retained the right to all income and dividends earned by the trust during his life. On Barry's death, the trust property passes to Barry's child Cassie or, if Cassie is not then living, to Cassie's estate. Indicate whether Barry's gross estate will include the trust property, and the reason for your answer.

   (A) IRC § 2036 includes the trust property in Barry's gross estate because Barry retained the right to income from the trust for life.

   (B) IRC § 2038 includes the trust property in Barry's gross estate because Barry retained the right to income from the trust for life.

**(C)** IRC § 2037 includes the trust property in Barry's gross estate because Barry retained the right to income from the trust for life.

**(D)** The trust property is not included in Barry's gross estate under IRC §§ 2036, 2037, or 2038 because a corporate trustee, and not Barry, possesses the right to manage the trust property.

50. Assume the same facts as in Question 49, above, except assume instead that Barry retained only the right to distribute income among Barry's children in Barry's sole discretion. Indicate how your answer will change based on this new fact.

ANSWER:

51. Hannah, a 35-year-old successful developer, transfers rental real estate to a trust. Remainder of the trust property is to be received by Hannah's longtime friend Allen. Assume Hannah passes away very wealthy many years beyond her life expectancy. Which, if any, of the following trust provisions will not cause the assets to be included in the grantor's estate under IRC § 2036?

**(A)** Hannah retains the right to receive trust income for the remainder of her life.

**(B)** Hannah retains the right to receive trust income for a term of 15 years after which income is to be distributed to Allen.

**(C)** Hannah retains the right to receive trust income and principal when needed for life.

**(D)** All of the above provisions will cause the assets to be included in Hannah's estate upon her death under IRC § 2036.

52. Daisy transfers her home and income-producing property in trust. Daisy directs trustee to hold the trust property for the benefit of Daisy's adult child, and to use the trust property for the support of her child. Even though the trust terms do not allow trustee to use trust property for the benefit of anyone other than Daisy's child, trustee (with the child's consent) allows Daisy to live rent-free in the home, and uses a portion of the income to pay Daisy's living expenses up to the time of Daisy's death. Will IRC § 2036 include any portion of the trust property in Daisy's gross estate?

**(A)** Yes, IRC § 2036 includes the trust property in Daisy's gross estate based on evidence of an implied agreement that Daisy would retain use of the property.

**(B)** Yes, IRC § 2036 includes the trust property in Daisy's gross estate because Daisy owed a duty of support to her adult child.

**(C)** No, IRC § 2036 does not apply to include the trust property in Daisy's gross estate because Daisy did not retain a legally enforceable interest in the trust.

**(D)** No, IRC § 2036 does not apply to include the trust property in Daisy's gross estate because Daisy did not retain any rights as trustee.

**53.** Eva transfers property to a corporate trustee for the benefit of Eva's child, to whom Eva owes a duty of support under state law. The trust terms direct the trustee to distribute trust income and principal for the support of Eva's child until such child attains age18, and thereafter to terminate the trust and pay over remaining trust property to Eva's child, or the child's estate. Will Eva's gross estate include any portion of the trust property pursuant to IRC § 2036 if Eva dies during the term of the trust?

  **(A)** Yes, because under the trust terms Eva, as child's parent, legally has the right to control child's income and property for a period that does not end before Eva's death.

  **(B)** Yes, because Eva receives the benefit of the trust income used to satisfy her obligation of support for a period that does not end before Eva's death.

  **(C)** No, because Eva is not entitled to any distribution of income or right to enjoy the trust property prior to Eva's death.

  **(D)** No, because Eva has transferred all power over the trust property to a corporate trustee.

**54.** Turner formed a limited liability company (the "LLC") and contributed an apartment building to the newly formed LLC in exchange for the membership interests. Thereafter, Turner transferred 10% of the LLC membership interests to his child. Under which of the following circumstances will Turner be considered to have retained interests in the LLC assets under IRC § 2036?

  **(A)** Turner sells 10% of the LLC interests to his child for 10% of the value of the underlying partnership assets.

  **(B)** Turner retains a valuation expert who, after analyzing the LLC agreement, concludes that various discounts apply. Turner sells a 10% interest to his child for 7% of the value of the underlying LLC assets.

  **(C)** Turner gifts a 10% LLC interest to his child but continues to occupy one of the apartments while paying rent to the LLC for his use of the apartment.

  **(D)** Turner gifts a 10% LLC interest to his child but continues to occupy one of the apartments without paying rent.

**55.** Assume the same facts as in question 54, above, except that the LLC agreement provided that Turner as manager could in his discretion amend the operating agreement without the consent of the other members and make equal distributions to all the members without consent of the other members. Would these provisions have an impact on whether IRC § 2036 would apply to cause inclusion of the value of the LLC assets in Turner's estate?

ANSWER:

**56.** Julius owns 25 percent of Yak Corporation stock. Yak Corporation has only one class of stock. Julius gives 20 percent of his stock in Yak Corporation to his son, but Julius makes the gift of stock subject to an agreement that Julius votes the gifted stock until he dies. Will the 20 percent of Yak stock Julius transferred to his son be included in Julius' gross estate under IRC § 2036 and, if so, why?

(A) Yes, because Julius gave at least 20 percent of the Yak Corporation stock to his son.

(B) Yes, because after the transfer Julius had the right to vote at least 20 percent of the Yak Corporation stock.

(C) No, because after the transfer Julius owned less than 20 percent of the Yak corporation stock.

(D) No, because Julius gave 20 percent of the stock outright to his son, and not in trust.

57. Zany Corporation has two classes of stock, voting and non-voting. Kristina owns 25 percent of each class of stock. Kristina transfers 25 percent of the non-voting stock to her grandchild. Will Kristina's gross estate include any portion of the non-voting stock transferred to grandchild?

ANSWER:

58. Lacey and Marik are siblings. Lacey transfers $1 million in assets to a trust for the benefit of Marik and Marik's family. The trust distributes all income to Marik for life, with remainder to Marik's child or the child's estate. One week later Marik transfers $1 million in assets to a trust for the benefit of Lacey and Lacey's family. The trust created by Marik for Lacey mirrors the terms of the earlier trust created by Lacey for Marik. Will IRC § 2036 cause inclusion of any of the trust assets in Lacey's gross estate?

(A) Yes, because the trusts are interrelated and leave Lacey and Marik in substantially the same economic position, Lacey's gross estate will include the value of the assets held in trust created by Marik for Lacey's benefit.

(B) Yes, because Lacey is the income beneficiary of the trust created by Marik and is entitled to income for life, Lacey's gross estate will include the value of the assets held in the trust created by Marik for Lacey's benefit.

(C) No, because Lacey did not retain any possession or enjoyment of, or the right to income from, the trust property transferred by Lacey, Lacey's gross estate avoids inclusion of the value of any trust assets.

(D) No, because Lacey's interest in the trust for her benefit ceases as of her death and she is unable to direct its transfer, Lacey's gross estate avoids inclusion of the value of any trust assets.

59. Nels transferred property to trustee for the benefit of Nels and Nels' child. The trust directed trustee to distribute one-half the income to Nels and one-half the income to Nels' child. On Nels' death, the remainder passes to Nels' child. What amount of the trust property is includible in Nels' gross estate under IRC § 2036?

(A) All of the trust property.

(B) One-half the trust property.

(C) The value of Nels' life interest.

(D) None of the trust property.

60. Ricky transferred assets to an irrevocable trust, income to his friend Cal for life and upon Cal's death, the remainder to his friend Carly. An independent and unrelated trustee was appointed to manage the trust assets. Assume Ricky did not otherwise retain an interest in the trust, nor any power to alter or amend the terms of the trust except as follows. Which of the following trust provisions, if any, will cause the trust property to be included in Ricky's estate?

(A) Ricky, as grantor, is authorized to exercise a power that enables him to borrow from principal or income of the trust.

(B) Ricky, as grantor, is given the power to reacquire the trust corpus by substituting other property of an equivalent value.

(C) An unrelated disinterested third party was given power to add a charitable beneficiary to the trust.

(D) None, IRC § 2036 will not operate to include the trust assets in Ricky's estate.

# REVOCABLE TRANSFERS, IRC § 2038, AND COMPARISON WITH IRC § 2036(a)(2)

*There is a great deal of overlap between IRC§§ 2036(a)(2) and 2038. In addition to focusing on the broad application of IRC § 2038, this topic explores the similarities and differences between the two sections. Unless otherwise indicated in the problems below, assume (1) the trust is irrevocable, (2) trust and trustee are not related or subordinate to each other, and (3) all transfers of property occurred on or after June 23, 1936.*

61. Andy transfers property to trustee, and retains the right to revoke the trust at any time upon giving trustee 60 days' written notice of the intent to revoke. During Andy's life, trustee, in its discretion, may pay income to Andy or Andy's child. On Andy's death, the trust property passes to Andy's child or the child's estate. Andy does not exercise the power to revoke. Will IRC § 2038 include trust property in Andy's gross estate, and on what basis?

    (A) Andy's gross estate includes all property because all property is subject to the power to revoke as of Andy's date of death.

    (B) Andy's gross estate includes only the value of the remainder interest payable to Andy's child because that is the interest returned to Andy in the event of revocation.

    (C) Andy's gross estate avoids inclusion of the property subject to the power to revoke because Andy did not in fact exercise the power.

    (D) Andy's gross estate avoids inclusion of the property subject to the power to revoke because revocation does not occur until 60 days after notice to trustee.

62. How, if at all, would your answer to question 61, above, change if Andy had relinquished his power to amend, revoke or terminate the trust two years prior to his death?

ANSWER:


63. Char transfers property to a trust. Under the terms of the trust, Char serves as trustee and she is also a beneficiary along with her two children Ben and Morgan. Under the terms of the agreement, Char, together with Ben and Morgan, have the right to revoke the trust, and upon revocation Char receives one-half of the corpus. If Char passes away without the trust having been revoked, her interest in the trust passes to Morgan and Ben. What effect, if any, will IRC § 2038 have on Char's gross estate?

    (A) Char's gross estate includes all property.

**(B)** Char's gross estate includes only half the value of the remainder interest payable to her children.

**(C)** Char's gross estate is increased only if she elects to revoke.

**(D)** Char's gross estate avoids inclusion of any of the property subject to the power to revoke.

64. Becca transfers property to herself and her spouse as trustees. The trust terms allow trustees to accumulate trust income until Becca's child attains age 25, at which time accumulated income and principal pass outright to Becca's child or the child's estate. Trustees, in their discretion, also may pay trust principal to Becca's child prior to the time the child reaches age 25. Will IRC § 2038 include trust property in Becca's gross estate, and on what basis?

**(A)** Becca's gross estate includes the value of all trust property under IRC § 2038 because Becca, with her spouse, has the power to determine when Becca's child receives trust property.

**(B)** Becca's gross estate includes the value of all trust property under IRC § 2038 because the power extends beyond the minority of Becca's child.

**(C)** Becca's gross estate avoids inclusion of the trust property under IRC § 2038 because Becca does not retain the power to alter who in fact receives the trust property.

**(D)** Becca's gross estate avoids inclusion of the trust property under IRC § 2038 because Becca cannot exercise the power alone and in all events.

65. Cindy transfers property to trustee for the benefit of Cindy's adult child. Trustee, in its discretion, may pay income to Cindy's adult child for the child's support. On Cindy's death, her child or her child's estate receives all remaining trust property outright. Cindy has the power to remove and replace trustee with another trustee, including herself. Will IRC § 2038 include the value of the trust in Cindy's gross estate, and on what basis?

**(A)** IRC § 2038 includes the value of all trust property in the gross estate because trustee may determine when child receives income and Cindy may remove and replace the trustee with herself.

**(B)** IRC § 2038 includes the value of all trust property in the gross estate because trustee may satisfy a duty of support to child and Cindy may remove and replace trustee with herself.

**(C)** Cindy's gross estate avoids inclusion under IRC § 2038 even though Cindy may remove and replace trustee because the trustee's power to alter Cindy's interest is only with respect to trust income, and not principal.

**(D)** Cindy's gross estate avoids inclusion under IRC § 2038 even though Cindy may remove and replace trustee because the trustee's power is subject to a determinable external standard.

**66.** Assume the same facts as in Question 65, above. Discuss whether the assets contributed to the trust would be included in Cindy's estate if instead distributions could be made for Cindy's child's happiness and enjoyment?

ANSWER:

**67.** Assume the same facts as in Question 65, above. Discuss how your answer would change if instead Cindy has the power to remove and replace the trustee but she could not insert herself as trustee?

ANSWER:

**68.** Assume the same facts as in Question 65, above. Discuss how your answer would change if the question was whether IRC § 2036 applies to include the trust property in the gross estate.

ANSWER:

**69.** Demetra transfers property to herself as trustee. As trustee, Demetra may distribute trust income among her nieces, Effie, Faye, and Gabriela, in her sole discretion. On Demetra's death the property passes to Mensa University. Indicate whether Demetra's estate will include the full value of all trust property under either IRC § 2036 or § 2038.

**(A)** Only IRC § 2036 includes the full value of trust property in Demetra's gross estate.

**(B)** Only IRC § 2038 includes the full value of trust property in Demetra's gross estate.

**(C)** Both IRC § 2036 and § 2038 include the full value of the trust property in Demetra's gross estate.

**(D)** Neither IRC § 2036 nor § 2038 include the full value of the trust property in Demetra's gross estate.

**70.** Hanson transfers property to trustee. Hanson does not retain any power over the trust. Trustee may, in its discretion, pay income and principal from the trust property to and among Hanson's descendants. At such time as there is no descendant of Hanson then living, the trust property passes to charity. Indicate whether Hanson's gross estate will include any portion of the trust property under either IRC § 2036 or § 2038.

**(A)** Only IRC § 2036 will include trust property in Hanson's gross estate.

**(B)** Only IRC § 2038 will include trust property in Hanson's gross estate.

**(C)** Both IRC §§ 2036 and 2038 will include trust property in Hanson's gross estate.

**(D)** Neither IRC § 2036 nor § 2038 will include trust property in Hanson's gross estate.

71.    Jaime transfers property to co-trustees. The trust directs Jaime to appoint a successor trustee if a trustee vacancy occurs because of death, resignation, or removal of trustee by a proper court for cause. During Jaime's life, a vacancy in the trusteeship occurred, and Jaime appointed a successor trustee. At Jaime's death, however, no vacancy existed. Trustee possesses discretion to pay income and principal among Kalla, Larimie, and Megan, or to the survivor of them. Indicate whether Jaime's gross estate will include any portion of the trust property under either IRC § 2036 or § 2038.

   **(A)**  Only IRC § 2036 will include trust property in Jaime's gross estate.

   **(B)**  Only IRC § 2038 will include trust property in Jaime's gross estate.

   **(C)**  Both IRC § 2036 and § 2038 will include trust property in Jaime's gross estate.

   **(D)**  Neither IRC § 2036 nor § 2038 will include trust property in Jaime's gross estate.

## REVERSIONARY INTERESTS, IRC § 2037

*Although formally titled "Transfers Taking Effect at Death," IRC§ 2037 more aptly applies to reversionary interests, whether arising under the terms of the governing instrument or by operation of law. Only on rare occasions does IRC § 2037 apply to cause inclusion in the gross estate. The infrequency of its application is due to the fact that transferors of interests rarely reserve a reversion under the narrow circumstances of IRC § 2037 application.*

*Unless otherwise indicated in the problems below, assume (1) the trust is irrevocable, (2) trustor and trustee are not related or subordinate to each other, and (3) all transfers of property occurred on or after October 8, 1949. Also, unless otherwise indicated, assume the value of any reversionary interest immediately before decedent's death exceeds 5 percent of the value of the property transferred.*

72. Anderson transferred property to trustee. The trust directs trustee to pay income to Anderson's spouse for her life, with remainder to Anderson or, if he is not living at his spouse's death, to Anderson's child or to the child's estate. Anderson predeceases his spouse and his child. Indicate whether Anderson's gross estate will include any portion of the trust property under either IRC § 2033 or § 2037.

    **(A)** Only IRC § 2033 will include trust property in Anderson's gross estate.

    **(B)** Only IRC § 2037 will include trust property in Anderson's gross estate.

    **(C)** Both IRC §§ 2033 and 2037 will include trust property in Anderson's gross estate.

    **(D)** Neither IRC § 2033 nor § 2037 will include trust property in Anderson's gross estate.

73. Assume the same facts as in question 72, above. Except, instead of directing that the remainder will go to Anderson's child if Anderson is not living at his spouse's death, the trust provides that the remainder will go to Anderson's then surviving child upon spouse's death, or if the child predeceases Anderson, then to Anderson. Indicate whether Anderson's gross estate will include any portion of the trust property under either IRC § 2033 or § 2037.

    **(A)** Only IRC § 2033 will include trust property in Anderson's gross estate.

    **(B)** Only IRC § 2037 will include trust property in Anderson's gross estate.

    **(C)** Both IRC §§ 2033 and 2037 will include trust property in Anderson's gross estate.

    **(D)** Neither IRC § 2033 nor § 2037 will include trust property in Anderson's gross estate.

**74.** Based on your answer in Question 73, indicate what amount of trust assets, if any, will be included in Anderson's gross estate.

ANSWER:

**75.** Cynthia transfers property in trust, and directs income to be accumulated for Cynthia's life. At Cynthia's death accumulated income and principal pass to Cynthia's surviving descendants, or, if none, to David or David's estate. Indicate whether Cynthia's gross estate will include any portion of the trust property under either IRC § 2033 or § 2037.

   **(A)** Only IRC § 2033 will include trust property in Cynthia's gross estate.

   **(B)** Only IRC § 2037 will include trust property in Cynthia's gross estate.

   **(C)** Both IRC §§ 2033 and 2037 will include trust property in Cynthia's gross estate.

   **(D)** Neither IRC § 2033 nor § 2037 will include trust property in Cynthia's gross estate.

**76.** Ellen transfers property in trust, and directs trustee to pay income and principal to Ellen's friend for friend's life. Ellen retained the power to designate who will receive the trust property on the death of Ellen's friend, if Ellen is then living. If Ellen is not then living, the trust property passes to Ellen's niece, or if she is not then living, to her estate. Indicate whether Ellen's gross estate will include any of the trust property under IRC § 2037 and why.

   **(A)** Ellen's gross estate will include trust property under IRC § 2037 because Ellen retained the possibility of exercising power over the trust property, and her niece could only possess the trust property by surviving Ellen.

   **(B)** Ellen's gross estate will include trust property under IRC § 2037 because Ellen retained the right to determine who will possess and enjoy the trust property, and did so for a period not in fact ending before Ellen's death.

   **(C)** Ellen's gross estate avoids inclusion of trust property under IRC § 2037 because Ellen did not retain the required reversionary interest in trust property even though Ellen's niece would benefit only upon surviving Ellen.

   **(D)** Ellen's gross estate avoids inclusion of trust property under IRC § 2037 because Ellen transferred trust property for the benefit of an unrelated person, and Ellen retained no power over the property during Ellen's friend's life.

**77.** Frances transfers property in trust, and directs that income be accumulated for her life. At her death, principal and accumulated income pass to Frances' surviving children. Frances gives her spouse an unrestricted general power of appointment. Frances' spouse survives Frances but does not exercise the power given to him under the trust instrument. Will Frances' gross estate include any portion of the trust under IRC § 2037?

   **(A)** Yes, because if Frances had survived Frances' spouse, the trust property could have reverted to Frances, and Frances' children would take only by surviving Frances.

**(B)** Yes, because the power granted to Frances' spouse is attributed to Frances, Frances retains a reversionary interest, and Frances' children must survive Frances to take.

**(C)** No, because Frances' spouse could have possessed trust property immediately before Frances' death by exercising his general power of appointment.

**(D)** No, because Frances' spouse did not, in fact, exercise the general power of appointment prior to Frances' death to prevent any reversion to Frances.

78. Greg transfers property in trust with income to Greg's niece for life, remainder to niece's child if Greg predeceases niece, but if Greg survives niece, the property reverts to Greg. Discuss the method for determining whether Greg's reversionary interest immediately before death exceeds 5 percent of the trust property.

ANSWER:

*An annuity is a financial arrangement where in exchange for consideration a person receives periodic payments for a specified period of time or until a specified event occurs. Both commercial annuities and private annuities fall within this definition. Many banks, brokerage houses, and life insurance companies provide commercial annuities. Retirement benefits are often paid in the form of an annuity. Private annuity arrangements exist between private individuals, although income tax regulations issued in 2006 have significantly diminished the income tax advantages of a private annuity.*

*The following problems assume the decedent entered into the annuity arrangement after 1986. In 1984, Congress eliminated certain exclusions that had previously applied to qualified employee retirement plans, and in 1986 it significantly amended the statute again.*

79. Indicate under which of the following scenarios the Service will likely argue that IRC § 2039 applies to include an amount in the decedent's gross estate.

   **(A)** Annuity payment paid to a beneficiary for life pursuant to a life insurance policy on decedent's life.

   **(B)** Annuity payment to the beneficiary-grantor of a grantor-retained annuity trust following decedent's death.

   **(C)** Annuity payment made to a beneficiary under a qualified retirement plan with a joint and survivor payout.

   **(D)** Annuity payments made to the beneficiary pursuant to a benefit provided under the Railroad Retirement Act.

80. Richard purchased an annuity from Great Big Annuity Company ("GBAC") under which GBAC agreed to make annual annuity payments to Richard for life. Upon Richard's death, GBAC was required to make a final lump sum payment to whomever Richard designated as his beneficiary. Assume that Richard designates his friend Robert as the beneficiary. Indicate which of the following is most correct.

   **(A)** The amount of the lump sum payment to Robert will not be included in Richard's gross estate.

   **(B)** The amount of the lump sum payment to Robert will be included in Robert's gross estate.

   **(C)** The amount of the lump sum payment to Robert will not be included in Robert's gross estate.

**(D)** The amount of the lump sum payment to Robert will be included in Richard's gross estate.

81. Alice bought a lottery ticket for $1. When Alice won the lottery, she chose to receive the proceeds in the form of an annuity payable over 20 years. On Alice's death, any annuity payments still owing continue to be paid to Alice's surviving descendants pursuant to the terms of the lottery rules. Will IRC § 2039 include the value of the annuity payments remaining to be paid as of Alice's death?

   **(A)** Yes, the value of the annuity payments as of Alice's death will be included in Alice's gross estate.

   **(B)** Yes, but only a portion of the value of the annuity as of Alice's death equal to $1 over all tickets purchased will be included in Alice's gross estate.

   **(C)** No, Alice was unable to direct transfer of the annuity to anyone other than Alice's descendants pursuant to the lottery rules.

   **(D)** No, the annuity was for a term of years and was not dependent on Alice's death.

82. Pursuant to employer's retirement fund, employer made contributions to two different funds under the terms of two different agreements. Plan 1 provided employee Clarice with an annuity for Clarice's life upon retirement at age 65. Plan 2 provided Clarice's spouse a similar annuity amount for life upon Clarice's death. Under both Plans 1 and 2, if Clarice was not employed or died prior to age 65, Clarice forfeited the benefits under the plan. Under Plan 2, if Clarice's spouse remarries after Clarice's death, payments under the plan cease. Clarice died at age 66 after receiving payments under Plan 1. Indicate whether any portion of the annuity under Plan 2 will be included in Clarice's gross estate, and why.

   **(A)** Yes, the annuity payable under Plan 2 will be included in Clarice's gross estate because pursuant to the arrangement Clarice received an annuity under Plan 1, and Clarice's spouse received the annuity on Clarice's death under Plan 2.

   **(B)** No, the annuity payable under Plan 2 will not be included in Clarice's gross estate because the payments could be forfeited by Clarice's spouse upon remarriage leaving the amount receivable by Clarice's spouse uncertain.

   **(C)** No, the annuity payable under Plan 2 will not be included in Clarice's gross estate because the payments could have been forfeited under either Plan if Clarice had not lived or been employed at age 65.

   **(D)** No, the annuity payable under Plan 2 involved a separate contract than that under Plan 1, and under Plan 2 Clarice did not have any right to receive any annuity payments.

83. Under her retirement plan, Dani elected to receive a joint and survivor annuity for the benefit of herself and her spouse for the period of their joint lives. Dani died prior to receiving any payments. Payments were made to Dani's spouse under the terms of the plan. Dani paid one-half of the value of the contributions to the retirement plan. The other one-half of the contributions were made by her employer. Indicate whether any amount will

be included in Dani's gross estate, and, if so, how much.

**(A)** The entire value of the annuity will be included in Dani's gross estate because Dani had a right to receive the benefits under the plan, and Dani and Dani's employer made all contributions to the plan.

**(B)** One-half the value of the annuity will be included in Dani's gross estate because, although Dani had a right to receive benefits under the plan, Dani only contributed one-half of the consideration for the plan.

**(C)** None of the value of the annuity is includible in Dani's gross estate because Dani never in fact received benefits under the plan, and all payments were made only to Dani's spouse.

**(D)** None of the value of the annuity is includible in Dani's gross estate because Dani did not survive for a sufficient amount of time and Dani's spouse was to receive benefits regardless of whether he survived Dani.

84.    How, if at all, would your answer to question 83, above, change if the other one-half of the contributions were not made by her employer. Assume instead that the other half of the contributions to the retirement plan were made by Dani's spouse.

ANSWER:

# JOINT WITH RIGHT OF SURVIVORSHIP PROPERTY, IRC § 2040

*Because of the unique characteristics of joint with right of survivorship property, Congress enacted IRC § 2040 to specifically deal with its inclusion in the gross estate. Congress enacted simplified rules in 1981 to deal with joint tenancies held between spouses. Unless otherwise indicated, the problems below address joint tenancy with right of survivorship property after 1981.*

85. Individuals may hold property either as a tenancy in common, joint tenancy with right of survivorship, tenancy by the entirety, or community property. For purposes of determining inclusion in a decedent's gross estate, indicate the tenancies governed by IRC § 2040.

    (A) Community property.

    (B) Joint tenancy with right of survivorship.

    (C) Tenancy in common and joint with right of survivorship property.

    (D) Tenancy by the entirety and joint with right of survivorship property.

86. Abbey and Bob are married. Abbey contributed 70 percent of the funds to purchase an apartment building, and Bob contributed 30 percent of the funds to purchase the building. Abbey and Bob took title to the apartment building as joint tenants with right of survivorship. Indicate the portion of the apartment building includible in Abbey's gross estate on her death.

    (A) The entire value of the apartment building will be included in her gross estate because a joint tenant may enjoy the entire property subject to use of the other tenant.

    (B) Seventy percent of the value of the property will be included in her gross estate because that is the portion of the purchase price contributed by Abbey.

    (C) Fifty percent of the value of the property will be included in her gross estate because Abbey and Bob are married, and are the sole joint tenants.

    (D) None of the property will be included in Abbey's gross estate because the entire value of the property will be included in Bob's gross estate.

87. Carl, David, and Ellie received a gift of land from their mother as joint tenants with right of survivorship. Mom provided the entire consideration for the land. When Ellie dies and is survived by Carl and David, what portion of the land, if any, will be included in her gross estate?

(A) The entire value of the land will be included in her gross estate because none of the tracing rules regarding contributions apply to property received by gift.

(B) One-third the value of the land will be included in her gross estate because a fractional portion of joint tenancy with right of survivorship interests received by gift is included.

(C) One-half the value of the land will be included in her gross estate because Carl and David each receive a one-half interest in the joint tenancy with right of survivorship property on Ellie's death.

(D) None of the value of the land will be included in her gross estate because Ellie did not provide any consideration toward the purchase of the land received by gift.

88. Fred opened a brokerage account, and provided the entire contribution to the account. Fred then named Gavin as joint tenant with right of survivorship on the account. With Fred's consent, Gavin withdrew two-thirds of the dividends from the account each year. Gavin dies and is survived by Fred. On Gavin's death, indicate the proportionate amount of the brokerage account, if any, included in Gavin's gross estate.

(A) The entire value of the brokerage account is included in Gavin's gross estate because Gavin had access to the entire amount held in the account during his life.

(B) One-half of the value of the brokerage account is included in Gavin's gross estate because he received his interest in the brokerage account by gift from Fred.

(C) Two-thirds of the value of the brokerage account is included in Gavin's gross estate because he annually received from Fred two-thirds of the dividend income earned on the brokerage account.

(D) None of the value of the brokerage account is included in Gavin's gross estate because the estate can show he did not contribute any of the funds held in the brokerage account.

89. Heidi made a gift to her daughter of land valued at $50,000 on the date of gift. At a time when the land was worth $100,000, Heidi's daughter and Heidi decided to build a home on the land. The home was built with $100,000 contributed by Heidi. At the time the home was built, Heidi and her daughter decided to hold title to the land and home worth $200,000 as joint tenants with right of survivorship. Heidi dies and is survived by her daughter. Indicate what portion of the home, if any, is included in Heidi's gross estate.

(A) The entire value of the land and home is included in Heidi's gross estate because all consideration can be traced to Heidi.

(B) One-half the value of the land and home is included in Heidi's gross estate because each contributed one-half the value of the land and home.

(C) Three-fourths the value of the land and home is included in Heidi's gross estate because only the $50,000 appreciation is traceable to daughter.

**(D)** None of the value of the land and home is included in Heidi's gross estate because title automatically passes to Heidi's daughter under state law.

**Facts for questions 90–93.**

Dolph's father, Charles, gifted him an apartment building #1 that was filled with quality tenants. On the date of the gift, apartment building #1 had a fair market value of $2,000,000. Dolph sold the property four years later for a $1,000,000 gain and responsibly put the gains in his bank account #1. At that point in time, Dolph's father approached him and inquired as to whether Dolph would be interested in investing in another apartment building. Dolph agreed and he and his father acquired a second apartment building held between them as joint tenants with rights of survivorship for $2,000,000 with each contributing half of the consideration to purchase the new building. Charles and Dolph collected rents from apartment #2 and deposited the rents in a bank account as joint tenants with rights of survivorship. By the time Dolph's father passed away, Dolph's bank account #1 (in which he had deposited only the sale proceeds from apartment building #1) had $5,000,000. Bank account #2 (in which they had deposited only rents from apartment building #2) had $6,000,000. Building #2 had a value of $4,000,000.

90. Indicate what portion, if any, of the value of Dolph's bank account #1 is included in his father Charles' gross estate and why.

   **(A)** The entire value of account #1 is included in Charles' gross estate because all consideration paid for apartment #1 can be traced to Charles.

   **(B)** One-half the value of account #1 is included in Charles' gross estate because Dolph's bank account represents one-half of the contribution to purchase apartment building #1.

   **(C)** One-third of the value of account #1 is included in Charles' gross estate because $1,000,000 is one-third of the aggregate value of the account #1 plus the $2,000,000 value of apartment building #1.

   **(D)** None of the value of account #1 is included in Charles' gross estate because Dolph is the sole owner of the account under state law.

91. For purposes of this question only, assume Charles died prior to the sale of building #1. Indicate what portion, if any, of the value of apartment building #1 would have been included in his father Charles' gross estate and why.

   **(A)** The entire value of apartment building #1 is included in Charles' gross estate because all consideration paid for apartment #1 can be traced to Charles.

   **(B)** One-half the value of apartment building #1 is included in Charles' gross estate because Charles contributed the apartment building and Dolph contributed his management skills.

   **(C)** One-third of the value of apartment building #1 is included in Charles' gross estate because $1,000,000 is one-third of the aggregate value of building #1 at its appreciated value.

**(D)** None of the value of apartment building #1 is included in Charles' gross estate because Dolph is the owner of the apartment building #1 under state law.

92. Indicate what portion, if any, of the value of bank account #2 is included in his father Charles' gross estate and why.

    **(A)** The entire value of account #2 is included in Charles' gross estate because all consideration paid for apartment #2 can be traced to Charles.

    **(B)** One-half the value of account #2 is included in Charles' gross estate because Dolph's bank account represents one-half of the contribution to purchase apartment building #2.

    **(C)** One-fourth of the value of account #2 is included in Charles' gross estate because $1,000,000 is one-fourth of the $4,000,000 value of apartment building #2.

    **(D)** None of the value of account #2 is included in Charles' gross estate because Dolph is the owner of the account under state law.

93. Indicate what portion, if any, of the value of apartment building #2 is included in his father Charles' gross estate and why.

    **(A)** The entire value of apartment building #2 is included in Charles' gross estate because all consideration paid for apartment #2 can be traced to Charles.

    **(B)** One-half the value of apartment building #2 is included in Charles' gross estate because Dolph's bank account represents one-half of the contribution to purchase apartment building #2.

    **(C)** One-third of the value of apartment building #2 is included in Charles' gross estate because $1,000,000 is one-third of the aggregate value of the account #1 plus the $2,000,000 value of apartment building #2.

    **(D)** None of the value of apartment building #2 is included in Charles' gross estate because Dolph owns apartment building #2 on Charles' death.

94. Ingrid and her sister Joan own an apartment building as joint tenants with right of survivorship. Ingrid contributed the funds for the entire purchase price of the apartment building. Ingrid and Joan die simultaneously in a car accident. Pursuant to state law, one-half the apartment building passes through each of their estates. Indicate the portion of the apartment building included in each of their gross estates.

    **(A)** The entire date-of-death value is included in Ingrid's gross estate, and none of the value is included in Joan's gross estate.

    **(B)** The entire date-of-death value is included in Ingrid's gross estate, and one-half the value is included in Joan's gross estate.

    **(C)** One-half the date-of-death value is included in each of Ingrid's and Joan's gross estates.

**(D)** One-half of the date-of-death value is included in Ingrid's gross estate, and the entire date-of-death value is included in Joan's gross estate.

*A third party may grant decedent powers over property owned or transferred by the third party, including powers to determine who will receive income and principal of a trust, and powers to determine who will receive ultimate ownership of property held in trust or otherwise. IRC § 2041 may apply when decedent holds a power over property that is equivalent to ownership, and when decedent was not the transferor of the property subject to the power. In other words, IRC §§ 2036 through 2038 apply when decedent transfers property and retains powers over or interests in the property transferred by decedent. IRC § 2041 applies when decedent holds a power over property that was owned or transferred by another.*

*Congress enacted IRC § 2041 to include in the gross estate powers held by a decedent that are the equivalent of ownership of property. Because powers held by a decedent do not amount to ownership of the underlying property, IRC § 2033 fails to include in the gross estate property transferred by another over which decedent held a power.*

*Different rules apply to powers of appointment created prior to October 22, 1942. For purposes of the following questions, assume the powers at issue were created after October 21, 1942.*

**Facts for problems 96 through 100.**

Cooper's mother, Shannon, created a trust and appointed Cooper as trustee. Upon creation of the trust, Cooper's mother contributed cash and marketable securities. At all times, the trust corpus contained only cash and marketable securities.

95. Assume the terms of the trust grant Cooper, as trustee, the power to appoint all trust property to any person or entity. Assume that during his life, Cooper appointed all of the cash (but not the property) to his sister Parker. Further, assume that Cooper just passed away. Which of the following most accurately describes the power held by Cooper, and the estate tax consequences therefrom.

   (A) The power is a general power of appointment and all property held in trust upon his death will be included in Cooper's gross estate under IRC § 2041(a)(2).

   (B) The power is a general power of appointment but none of the trust property will be included in Cooper's gross estate under § 2041(a)(2).

   (C) The power is a general power of appointment and only the value of the money that Cooper appointed to his sister will be included in Cooper's estate under IRC § 2041(a)(2).

   (D) The power is a limited power of appointment and as such none of the trust property will be included in Cooper's gross estate under IRC § 2041(a)(2).

**96.** Assume pursuant to the terms of the trust that Cooper is only authorized to exercise his power to appoint trust property to his creditors. Assume further that he did not appoint any of the trust property to any creditor prior to his death and that he has just passed away. Which of the following most accurately describes the power held by Cooper and the estate tax consequences therefrom?

(A) The power is a general power of appointment and all of the trust property will be included in Cooper's gross estate under IRC § 2041(a)(2).

(B) The power is a general power of appointment but none of the trust property will be included in his gross estate under § 2041(a)(2).

(C) The power is a limited power of appointment and all of the trust property will be included in Cooper's estate under IRC § 2041(a)(2).

(D) The power is a limited power of appointment and as such none of the trust property will be included in Cooper's gross estate under IRC § 2041(a)(2).

**97.** Assume instead that the terms of the trust provide that Cooper may appoint trust property only to his sister. Prior to passing away, Cooper appointed all of the cash (but not the property) to his sister Parker. Which of the following most accurately describes the power held by Cooper upon his death and the estate tax consequences therefrom?

(A) The power is a general power of appointment and all of the trust property will be included in Cooper's gross estate under IRC § 2041(a)(2).

(B) The power is a general power of appointment but none of the trust property will be included in his gross estate under § 2041(a)(2).

(C) The power is a limited power of appointment and only the value of the marketable securities will be included in Cooper's estate under IRC § 2041(a)(2).

(D) The power is a limited power of appointment and as such none of the trust property will be included in Cooper's gross estate under IRC § 2041(a)(2).

**98.** Assume instead that the terms of the trust provide that Cooper, as trustee, may distribute trust property to either himself or his sister as needed for their support, health, maintenance, and education. Which of the following most accurately describes the power held by Cooper and the estate tax consequences therefrom?

(A) The power is a general power of appointment and all of the trust property will be included in Cooper's gross estate under IRC § 2041(a)(2).

(B) The power is a general power of appointment but none of the trust property will be included in his gross estate under § 2041(a)(2).

(C) The power is a limited power of appointment and only the value of the marketable securities will be included in Cooper's estate under IRC § 2041(a)(2).

**(D)** The power is a limited power of appointment and as such none of the trust property will be included in Cooper's gross estate under IRC § 2041(a)(2).

99. Assume instead that the terms of the trust provide that Cooper, as trustee, may distribute income from trust property to himself as needed and without restriction and in the event that he does not appoint any of the trust income during his life, the taker in default would be his sister. Further, the provisions of the trust allow him to distribute the trust corpus only to his sister. Cooper never appoints any of the trust income during his life. Upon Cooper's death, which of the following most accurately describes the power held by Cooper and the estate tax consequences therefrom?

**(A)** The power is a general power of appointment and all of the trust property will be included in Cooper's gross estate under IRC § 2041(a)(2).

**(B)** The power is a general power of appointment but only accumulated income will be included in his gross estate under § 2041(a)(2).

**(C)** The power is part general and part limited and only the value of income which remains in the trust will be included in Cooper's estate under IRC § 2041(a)(2).

**(D)** The power is part general and part limited but none of the trust property will be included in Cooper's gross estate under IRC § 2041(a)(2).

100. How, if at all, would your answer to question 99, above, change if Cooper had become mentally incompetent prior to his death such that he was unable to exercise his right to appoint the trust income to himself or the beneficiaries of his estate?

ANSWER:

101. Nancy was the beneficiary of a trust created by her father in year 1. Nancy received all income and so much of the principal as necessary for her support. In addition, Nancy had the right to withdraw up to $5,000 of the trust property each year. The $5,000 withdrawal power lapsed on December 31 of each year. The power terminated on her death. Nancy never exercised the $5,000 withdrawal power. Nancy died in year 3. At her death the trust assets were worth $50,000. Indicate the amount of trust assets, if any, includible in Nancy's gross estate under IRC § 2041.

**(A)** None of the assets.

**(B)** $5,000.

**(C)** $10,000.

**(D)** $15,000.

102. Oscar was the beneficiary of a trust created by his mother in year 1. Pursuant to the trust agreement, Oscar was entitled to all income from the trust. In addition, Oscar had the right to withdraw $10,000 per year. The annual $10,000 withdrawal right lapsed on December 31 each year. Oscar dies in year 4. On Oscar's death, remaining trust assets pass to Penelope.

Trust assets remained at $60,000 from inception to termination of the trust on Oscar's death. Indicate the amount of trust assets, if any, includible in Oscar's gross estate under IRC § 2041.

**(A)** None of the assets.

**(B)** $10,000.

**(C)** $25,000.

**(D)** $31,000.

103. Assume the same facts as in Question 102, except that Oscar was not entitled to receive any income from the trust. In fact, Oscar held no beneficial interest in the trust. The only access held by Oscar to trust assets was the $10,000 annual withdrawal right. Indicate to what extent your answer to Question 102 will change based on this changed fact.

ANSWER:

104. Assume the same facts as in Question 103, except that the $10,000 annual withdrawal right can be exercised only in the month of November. Also assume for purposes of this question that Oscar dies in October of year 4. Indicate to what extent your answer to Question 103 will change based on these additional changed facts.

ANSWER:

105. Kathleen transferred property into a trust for the benefit of her brother Jim. The terms of the trust gave Jim the power to appoint trust property to anyone including himself, his creditors or the creditors of his estate. Provided, however, that in order for Jim to appoint any of the property in any manner, he was required to obtain Kathleen's consent. Indicate the portion of trust assets, if any, includible in Jim's estate.

**(A)** None of the assets.

**(B)** One-third.

**(C)** One-half.

**(D)** All.

106. Prior to her death, Bob's wife, Rose, created a testamentary trust. Under the terms of the trust, income was payable to Bob for life, and the remainder was payable equally to Bob's children or to any one of such children as Bob might direct by his will. In addition, the trust terms provided that at any time during Bob's lifetime, Bob, with the consent of one of his children, could direct the trustees to distribute all or any part of the trust property to anyone, including himself. Indicate the amount of trust assets, if any, includible in Bob's gross estate under IRC § 2041. Assume that Bob has passed away. Which of the following

most accurately describes the power held by Bob?

(A)  Bob holds a general power of appointment.

(B)  Bob holds a limited power of appointment.

(C)  Bob's power is general in part and limited in part.

(D)  Bob does not have any power of appointment.

107.  Assume the same facts as in question 106, above, except that Bob had only one child, Jim. Further that if Bob failed to appoint any taker during life, Jim would be the taker in default. Which of the following most accurately describes the power held by Bob?

(A)  Bob holds a general power of appointment.

(B)  Bob holds a limited power of appointment.

(C)  Bob's power is general in part and limited in part.

(D)  Bob does not have any power of appointment.

108. Alena owned a life insurance policy on her own life, and named her estate as beneficiary. In the aggregate she paid premiums on the policy of $35,000. On her death Alena's estate received proceeds of $500,000 on the life insurance policy. Indicate the amount, if any, of life insurance proceeds includible in Alena's gross estate under IRC § 2042.

   **(A)** None.

   **(B)** $35,000.

   **(C)** $465,000.

   **(D)** $500,000.

109. Indicate how your answer to Question 108 would change if instead Alena named her daughter as beneficiary of the policy.

ANSWER:

110. Assume instead that Hometown Bank, as trustee of an irrevocable life insurance trust, purchased a $500,000 life insurance policy under which Alena was the insured. Alena was not entitled to any benefits from the life insurance policy; however, the trust provided that trustee, in its discretion, may use trust assets to pay any estate tax owed by Alena's estate. Prior to Alena's death, trustee paid policy premiums in the aggregate of $35,000. What amount, if any, of the $500,000 life insurance proceeds would be includible in Alena's gross estate under IRC § 2042?

   **(A)** None.

   **(B)** $35,000

   **(C)** $465,000.

   **(D)** $500,000.

111. Bob owned a life insurance policy on the life of his sister. The face amount of the policy is $200,000. The value assigned to the policy by the insurance company on Bob's death was $55,000. Bob paid aggregate insurance premiums of $70,000. Indicate the amount, if any, included in Bob's gross estate under IRC § 2042.

   **(A)** None.

   **(B)**  $55,000.

   **(C)**  $70,000.

   **(D)**  $200,000.

112.  Eleni purchased an insurance policy on the life of her husband, Hayden, and she transferred the policy to her irrevocable trust. On Eleni's death, Hayden became trustee of the trust that held the policy on his life. The trust agreement made no provision for Hayden. It directed Hayden as trustee to use trust assets for the benefit of his grandchildren. As trustee of Eleni's trust, Hayden held all incidents of ownership over the policy. Indicate whether Hayden's gross estate will include any portion of the life insurance proceeds under IRC § 2042, and why.

   **(A)**  Yes, Hayden's gross estate will include all trust proceeds because as trustee he held the legal right to exercise incidents of ownership over the policy, and it does not matter that Hayden held those incidents only as a fiduciary.

   **(B)**  Yes, Hayden's gross estate will include all trust proceeds because it was within Hayden's control to resign as trustee of the trust, and he chose to continue to serve as trustee and to exercise incidents of ownership over the policy.

   **(C)**  No, the insurance proceeds avoid inclusion in Hayden's gross estate because he did not transfer the policy to the trust and he held incidents of ownership only as a fiduciary with no ability to benefit himself under the trust.

   **(D)**  No, the insurance proceeds avoid inclusion in Hayden's gross estate because the transfer to the trust was by Hayden's wife and the transfer qualifies for the marital deduction.

113.  Ingrid purchases a life insurance policy on her life, and transfers ownership of the policy to her child. Ingrid reserves only the right to cancel the policy at any time. She reserves no other rights over the policy. As owner of the policy, Ingrid's child has the right to borrow against the policy and to name the beneficiary. Six years following the transfer to her child, Ingrid dies. Discuss whether Ingrid's gross estate includes any portion of the policy proceeds.

ANSWER:

114.  Indicate how your answer to Question 113 would change if instead Ingrid could exercise the right to cancel the policy only with the consent of her child.

ANSWER:

115.  Jamie purchased a life insurance policy on her life and transferred ownership of the policy to an irrevocable life insurance trust. As trustee, National Bank holds all incidents of ownership. Jamie does not retain any right, power, or interest in the life insurance trust.

Jamie paid one $10,000 annual premium before the transfer to the trust, and Jamie continued to pay two more $10,000 annual premiums after the transfer to the trust. Jamie dies two years after the transfer of the policy to the life insurance trust. The policy proceeds are paid to the irrevocable life insurance trust as named beneficiary of the policy. Indicate the portion of the life insurance proceeds, if any, includible in Jamie's gross estate.

**(A)** None, because Jamie held no incidents of ownership as of the date of her death.

**(B)** One-third, because Jamie died within three years of the transfer and paid one-third of total premiums prior to transferring the policy to the trust.

**(C)** Two-thirds, because Jamie died within three years of the transfer and paid two-thirds of total premiums following the transfer to the trust.

**(D)** All proceeds because Jamie transferred the policy within three years of death.

116. Mary transfers $10,000 cash to an irrevocable trust of which State Bank is trustee. Mary does not retain any interest in or power over the irrevocable trust. State Bank, as trustee, purchases a life insurance policy on Mary's life with a $1 million face value, and uses the $10,000 to pay the initial annual premium. Mary pays the second annual $10,000 premium directly to the insurance company on behalf of the trust. Mary dies two years after State Bank purchased the life insurance policy. The irrevocable trust receives the policy proceeds on Mary's death as the named beneficiary. Indicate the portion of the life insurance proceeds, if any, includible in Mary's gross estate.

**(A)** None, because Mary held no incidents of ownership in the life insurance policy as of the date of her death.

**(B)** One-half the policy proceeds, because Mary paid one-half of the policy premiums directly to the insurance company within three years of her death.

**(C)** The policy proceeds less the $10,000 policy premium paid by the bank trustee when it purchased the policy within three years of Mary's death.

**(D)** All policy proceeds because trustee purchased the policy within three years of Mary's death.

117. Karen and Luke were married and lived in a community property state. Luke purchased a life insurance policy on his life with community funds. Under the policy terms, Luke had the sole power to exercise incidents of ownership. Luke named his children from a prior marriage as beneficiaries. Luke dies survived by Karen. Indicate the portion of the life insurance policy, if any, includible in Luke's gross estate under IRC § 2042.

**(A)** The entire date-of-death value of the policy.

**(B)** One-half the date-of-death value of the policy.

**(C)** The portion equal to Luke's support obligation to his children.

**(D)** None of the date-of-death value of the policy.

118. Wilma was survived by her husband Henry. On Wilma's death, her executor elected Qualified Terminable Interest Property ("QTIP") treatment pursuant to IRC § 2056(b)(7) for that property passing from Wilma to a trust for Henry's benefit. The trust provided a life income interest to Henry that met the requirements of a "qualifying income interest." On Henry's death, the trust assets pass to Wilma's daughter. As of Wilma's death, QTIP trust assets were valued at $750,000. As of Henry's later death, QTIP trust assets appreciated to $1 million. Indicate the amount of QTIP trust assets includible in Henry's gross estate under IRC § 2044.

   (A) None, because the trust assets were already included in Wilma's gross estate.

   (B) The value of Henry's life interest in the trust, because he only received income from the trust assets.

   (C) $750,000, because that was the value of QTIP trust assets for which Wilma's estate received a marital deduction.

   (D) $1 million, because that is the value of QTIP trust assets as of Henry's date of death.

119. Assume that Henry's estate incurs $450,000 additional federal estate tax due to the inclusion of the QTIP trust for his benefit created under Wilma's testamentary documents. Neither Wilma's nor Henry's testamentary documents address who will bear the burden for paying the tax incurred on the QTIP trust assets. Indicate who bears the burden of the tax and how the burden is allocated pursuant to the default rules of the Code.

   (A) Henry's estate bears the burden for the proportionate amount of estate tax attributable to the QTIP assets on Henry's death.

   (B) Wilma's estate bears the burden for the incremental amount of estate tax caused by inclusion of the QTIP assets on Henry's death.

   (C) The QTIP trust bears the burden for the proportionate amount of estate tax attributable to the QTIP assets on Henry's death.

   (D) Wilma's daughter, who is the trust remainder beneficiary, bears the burden for the incremental amount of estate tax caused by inclusion of the QTIP assets on Henry's death.

120. Ellie and Tom were married. On Ellie's death, her executor made a QTIP election for assets passing to a trust for Tom's benefit, and as a consequence of the marital deduction Ellie's estate did not have to pay any estate tax. On Tom's death, Tom's executor discovered that

the trust for which a QTIP election had been made did not meet the definition of a "qualifying income interest." As a result, Tom's executor decided not to include the assets for which a QTIP election had been made on Ellie's estate tax return. At the time of Tom's death the statute of limitations had run on the collection of estate tax from Ellie's estate. The decision of Tom's executor resulted in a substantial estate tax savings on the return. Indicate whether Tom's executor was correct in not including the trust assets in Tom's gross estate, and why.

**(A)**  Yes, Tom's executor should not have included the trust assets in his gross estate because Ellie's estate was not entitled to make the QTIP election.

**(B)**  Yes, Tom's executor should not have included the trust assets in his gross estate because the QTIP election was null and void due to the fact that it was unnecessary to make a QTIP election.

**(C)**  No, Tom's executor should have included the trust assets in Tom's gross estate because courts impose a duty of consistency requiring inclusion in the survivor's estate when the predeceased spouse's estate enjoyed the benefit of a deduction.

**(D)**  No, Tom's executor should have included the trust assets in Tom's gross estate because regardless of the QTIP election, he held an income interest in trust.

**ESTATE TAX CREDITS, IRC §§ 2010, 2012, 2013, 2014, AND STATE
DEATH TAX DEDUCTION, IRC § 2058**

121. Alfred dies in 2011 with a taxable estate of $5 million. He never married and he never made
any lifetime gifts. The basic exclusion amount in 2011 equals $5 million. Alfred's personal
representative would like to know whether an estate tax will be due and owing on Alfred's
death. Discuss.

ANSWER:


122. Assume the facts as in Question 121, above. Indicate the amount of unified credit under
IRC § 2010 available to Alfred's estate.

    (A)  $5,000,000.

    (B)  $5,000,000, as adjusted for inflation

    (C)  $1,730,800.

    (D)  $1,730,800, as adjusted for inflation.

123. Betsy and Bob were married. Betsy died in 2011 with a gross estate of $3.5 million and an
available applicable exclusion amount of $5 million. Betsy's will passes all her property to
Bob. Betsy did not make any taxable gifts and her estate took a marital deduction for the
$3.5 million of assets passing to Bob on her death, leaving a taxable estate of zero. The
personal representative of Betsy's estate filed an estate tax return and properly elected the
deceased spousal unused exclusion amount. Bob does not remarry. He dies in 2012 with a
taxable estate, which includes the property received by him under Betsy's will. The basic
applicable exclusion amount in 2012 equals $5,120,000. Indicate the applicable exclusion
amount available to Bob's estate.

    (A)  $5,120,000

    (B)  $10,120,000

    (C)  $8,620,000

    (D)  $6,620,000

124. Emily and Fred were married. Fred died in 2011 with a gross estate of $4.5 million. Fred's
will passes his entire estate to his children from a prior marriage causing his taxable estate
to be $4.5 million. Fred did not make any taxable gifts prior to his death. The personal

representative of Fred's estate filed an estate tax return and elected the deceased spousal unused exclusion amount or DSUE amount. Emily survives Fred, and never remarries. Emily dies in 2012 at a time when her basic exclusion amount equals $5,120,000. Indicate the applicable exclusion amount available to Emily's estate on her subsequent death.

(A) $500,000

(B) $5,120,000

(C) $5,620,000

(D) $10,120,000

125. Assume the same facts as in Question 124, except that Emily remarries after Fred dies. She dies in 2012 survived by her second spouse, George. Indicate the applicable exclusion available to Emily's estate.

(A) $500,000

(B) $5,120,000

(C) $5,620,000

(D) $10,120,000

126. Delores dies in 2011. Delores made a $1 million gift in 2009, and completely used her gift tax unified credit amount under IRC § 2505 available at that time. When computing estate tax on Betty's gross estate, discuss whether the executor should reduce the IRC § 2010 estate tax unified credit amount by the amount of the IRC § 2505 gift tax credit amount previously used.

ANSWER:


127. Callie dies in 2011. Callie's executor files the federal estate tax return and pays tax. One year after the date that the executor timely filed Callie's federal estate tax return, Callie's estate pays $400,000 in state estate taxes to the state of her domicile as a result of an audit of the accompanying state estate tax return filed by her executor. If Callie's executor chooses to file an amended federal return to take this additional payment into account, indicate how Callie's executor should take the state estate taxes paid into account on the federal estate tax return, if at all.

(A) Callie's executor should report a state death tax credit equal to $400,000.

(B) Callie's executor should report a state death tax deduction equal to $400,000.

(C) Callie's executor should report a state death tax deduction equal to $140,000.

(D) Callie's executor should not take a state death tax deduction on the return.

**128.** Dirk dies in 2009 survived by his brother Ed. Dirk's will devises stock to his brother Ed. After payment of federal estate tax, Ed receives $3 million of stock from Dirk's estate. The portion of Dirk's estate tax attributable to the stock received by Ed equals $600,000. Ed sells the stock and reinvests in an apartment complex. Ed dies three years after Dirk in 2012. The amount of Ed's estate tax attributable to the $3 million received from Dirk's estate equals $400,000. Indicate whether and to what extent Ed's estate will receive an IRC § 2013 tax on prior transfers credit.

**(A)** Ed's estate is not entitled to an IRC § 2013 credit because Ed sold the stock received from Dirk.

**(B)** Ed's estate is limited to an IRC § 2013 credit equal to $320,000 because Ed died three years after Dirk and must calculate the credit based on the smaller $400,000 amount.

**(C)** Ed's estate is entitled to an IRC § 2013 credit equal to $400,000 because it is the amount of Ed's estate tax attributable to the property received from Dirk.

**(D)** Ed's estate is entitled to an IRC § 2013 credit equal to $600,000 because it is the amount of Dirk's estate tax attributable to the property devised to Ed.

**129.** Clara died, and her sister Edna died eighteen months later. Clara's estate plan passed an amount equal to the applicable exclusion as of the date of her death to her sister Edna, and passed assets in excess of that amount to charity. Because of the charitable deduction, Clara's estate did not pay estate tax. If Clara's estate plan had not included the charitable gift, Clara's estate would have paid estate tax of $500,000. Edna's estate pays estate tax of $300,000 with respect to the bequest received from Clara. Indicate whether and to what extend Edna's estate is entitled to an IRC § 2013 tax on prior transfers credit.

**(A)** Edna's estate is entitled to a $500,000 IRC § 2013 credit because absent the charitable deduction that is the amount of estate tax Clara's estate would have paid.

**(B)** Edna's estate is entitled to a $300,000 IRC § 2013 credit because it is the amount of estate tax actually paid with respect to the amount received from Clara's estate.

**(C)** Edna's estate is not entitled to an IRC § 2013 credit because Clara did not die prior to the filing of Edna's estate tax return so that the charitable deduction could be redetermined.

**(D)** Edna's estate is not entitled to an IRC § 2013 credit because Clara's estate did not pay any estate tax, and both estates must pay tax on the transferred amount to receive a credit.

**130.** Fred dies in 2012. Prior to his death, Fred made a taxable gift in 2009. Fred paid gift tax of $100,000 on the 2009 gift. Fred made no other taxable gifts during his life. Because Fred retained a prohibited interest in the taxable gift, the gift is included in his gross estate. Discuss whether Fred's estate will receive an IRC § 2012 credit for gift tax paid on the 2009 transfer.

ANSWER:

**131.** Gary, a U.S. citizen, owned property in a foreign country. Gary's estate paid tax to the foreign country on the property situated there. Gary also included the property in his gross estate, and paid tax to the United States on the foreign property. Discuss whether Gary's estate will pay a double tax on the property situated in the foreign country.

ANSWER:

*Except where otherwise indicated, assume the donor is a U.S. citizen and resident, and any beneficiary also is a U.S. citizen and resident. Additionally, unless otherwise indicated, assume that the donor has no remaining gift tax credit and that all annual exclusions have been exhausted.*

132. Under which of the following sets of circumstances will the transfer from Adam to Bernice avoid being subject to the gift tax pursuant to IRC § 2501?

   (A) Adam, a U.S. citizen and resident, possesses a valuable gem, which he gifts to Bernice. Bernice is neither a citizen nor resident of the United States.

   (B) Adam, an English citizen and resident who is not a citizen of the United States, gifts a parcel of land located in Jackson Hole, Wyoming, to Bernice. Bernice is neither a citizen nor a resident of the United States.

   (C) Adam, a U.S. citizen and resident, gifts a parcel of land located in Missoula, Montana, to Bernice. Bernice is a citizen and resident of the United States.

   (D) Adam, an English citizen and resident who is not a citizen of the United States, possesses a valuable gem, which he gifts to Bernice. Bernice is a U.S. citizen and resident.

133. Alicia receives a monthly payment for support under a divorce settlement agreement for so long as she does not remarry. Harry asks Alicia to marry him, but she refuses because she does not want to lose the benefit of the monthly payments that she has come to rely on during the five years since her divorce. In response to her refusal, Harry offers to transfer an amount equal to the present value of the stream of monthly support payments to an account in Alicia's name as fair value in exchange for her promise to marry him as soon as a wedding can be arranged. After thinking it over, Alicia accepts Harry's offer and Harry immediately prior to the wedding pays a substantial amount into a bank account for Alicia. Did Harry make a transfer subject to gift tax upon making the deposit and why or why not.

   (A) Yes, because Harry did not receive full and adequate consideration in money or money's worth.

   (B) Yes, because Harry did not complete the transfer within three years of the divorce.

   (C) No, because Alicia's promise to marry constituted adequate consideration for an enforceable contract.

   (D) No, because Harry lacked any donative intent to make a gift to Alicia.

**134.** Teresa opens a bank account and transfers $500,000 to the account. Teresa names herself and her son Seth as joint tenants with right of survivorship at the time she opens the account. Under the account terms, Teresa can withdraw the entire amount of the bank account at any time, as can her son Seth. On Teresa's death the amount remaining in the account passes automatically to Seth. Seth does not withdraw any funds from the account in 2011. He does withdraw $40,000 in 2012. Indicate when, if ever, Teresa makes a gift to Seth for federal gift tax purposes.

(A) Teresa never makes a taxable gift to Seth.

(B) Teresa makes a gift of $500,000 on the date she opens the bank account and transfers the money.

(C) Teresa makes a gift of $500,000 on the date she opens the bank account, and an additional gift of $40,000 when Seth withdraws funds from the bank account in 2012.

(D) Teresa makes a gift of $40,000 to Seth when he withdraws funds from the bank account in 2012.

**135.** Geri transfers $1 million to an irrevocable trust she creates for the benefit of Shawn, her daughter. The trust terms direct the trustee to pay trust income to Shawn annually. When Shawn attains age 25, the trust terms direct the trustee to pay all remaining principal of the trust to Shawn outright. Geri reserves the right, however, to direct the trustee to accumulate trust income in any given year and distribute such accumulated income to Shawn on termination of the trust. In accordance with the trust, Shawn receives payments of income annually, and upon attaining age 25 receives all the remaining trust principal. Indicate when, if ever, Geri made a gift to Shawn for federal gift tax purposes.

(A) Geri makes a gift to Shawn when Shawn receives the trust principal on attaining age 25.

(B) Geri makes a gift to Shawn each year when the trustee distributes trust income to Shawn.

(C) Geri makes a gift to Shawn upon making the initial transfer of $1 million to the trust.

(D) Geri makes a gift to Shawn upon making the initial transfer of $1 million to the trust, and makes a gift each year of the income paid from the trust to Shawn.

**136.** Mom owns an apartment building with an appraised fair market value of $500,000. She wants to sell the apartment building, and lists it for sale. Her daughter indicates she is interested in purchasing the home, but she is only willing to pay $400,000. Mom decides to sell the apartment building to her daughter for $400,000 because she wants to encourage her daughter to make long-term investments. Characterize the transfer, and if you conclude it is a gift, indicate the amount of the gift.

(A) Mom makes a $500,000 gift on the sale of the building to daughter.

(B) Mom makes a $100,000 gift on the sale of the building to daughter.

**(C)** Mom makes a $500,000 taxable gift on the sale of the building to daughter, and daughter makes a $400,000 gift in cash to Mom.

**(D)** No gifts are made, as the transfer constitutes a purchase by daughter of the apartment building from Mom.

137. Would your answer to Question 136, above, be different if rather than the participants in the transfer being mother and daughter, they were two unrelated persons? Assume that Seller was initially asking $500,000 for the home but purchaser offered $400,000.

ANSWER:

138. Mom owns a condominium in downtown Manhattan, New York. Mom retired "young" from her position as a securities trader on Wall Street and moved to Florida to enjoy the sunnier climate. Mom kept her condo in Manhattan, now worth $2,000,000, as she was not altogether sure she was through with her career. In past years, Mom rented the Manhattan condo out on an annual basis for $120,000 per year. Mom did not intend to increase the rent in the coming year. However, this year, Mom's 27-year-old son Junior was accepted to New York University (NYU) Law School, and Mom decided that instead of renting the Manhattan condo this coming year, she would allow her son to stay in the condo rent-free beginning on January 1. Junior lived in the condo for the full year. Mom now asks you whether with respect to the condo she has made a taxable gift to Junior this past year, and, if a gift was made, the amount of the taxable gift. Indicate the most accurate response.

**(A)** Mom made a $2,000,000 taxable gift to Junior.

**(B)** Mom made a $120,000 taxable gift for the year to Junior.

**(C)** Mom has made a $2,120,000 taxable gift for the year to Junior.

**(D)** Mom has not made a taxable gift to Junior.

139. On the first day of the year, in an effort to help his son Martin get a "good start in life," Gary loaned $100,000 to Martin in exchange for a promissory note. The terms of the promissory note required that Martin pay the full $100,000 upon Gary's demand, with stated interest equal to 9 percent. Interest was payable on the note semiannually, and Martin paid Gary $4,500 in interest on June 30 and $4,500 on December 31. Assuming the loan remained outstanding at the end of the year, calculate the amount of the taxable gift for the year and explain how you arrived at the amount. For purposes of making the calculation, assume that the applicable IRC § 7872 rate (the blended annual rate) for the year was 10.45 percent and ignore any annual exclusions or gift tax credit that may exist.

ANSWER:

**GIFT TAX TREATMENT OF RETAINED POWERS, AND RETAINED INTERESTS**

140. Abby transfers $1 million in trust for the benefit of her three adult children. Trustee may pay income to Abby's children in trustee's discretion. Abby, however, retains the power to direct trustee to pay principal among one or more of her descendants. Indicate whether Abby makes a gift at the time the trust is funded, and, if so, the amount of the gift.

    (A) Yes, Abby makes a gift at the time the trust is funded equal to the value of the children's income interest.

    (B) Yes, Abby makes a gift at the time the trust is funded in the amount of $1 million.

    (C) No, Abby does not make a gift because she does not retain a general power of appointment to distribute principal.

    (D) No, Abby does not make a gift because the retained power allows her to determine who receives principal and income.

141. Madeline transfers property in trust and retains the power to revoke the trust. Several years after the initial transfer, Madeline chooses to renounce the power to revoke the trust. The trust directed trustee to pay income and principal in the trustee's discretion to Madeline's nieces and nephews. On Madeline's death the trust assets were to pass outright to her nieces and nephews then living in equal shares. Indicate when, if at all, Madeline makes a gift to the trust.

    (A) Madeline makes a gift to the trustee upon the initial transfer to the trust for the benefit of her nieces and nephews.

    (B) Madeline makes a gift upon renunciation of her power to revoke the trust and regain trust assets.

    (C) Madeline makes a gift of the entire value held in trust on the first distribution by trustee to her nieces and nephews.

    (D) Madeline does not make a gift of the trust assets until her death because the assets remain in trust until that time.

142. Chloe transfers property to trust in 2012. Trustee is required to pay income and principal as necessary for the support and health of Chloe. Upon Chloe's death, the trust assets pass to her niece. Indicate when, and to what extent, Chloe makes a taxable gift in relation to her transfer to the trust.

**(A)** Chloe makes a gift upon her 2012 transfer to the trust in the amount of the value of the remainder interest passing to her niece.

**(B)** Chloe makes a gift upon her 2012 transfer to the trust in the amount of the entire value of the property transferred to the trust.

**(C)** Chloe does not make a gift to the trust, but instead the trust assets will be includible in her gross estate due to her retained interest.

**(D)** Chloe makes a gift at her death of the value of the property held in trust at that time less the amount of the interest she retained during life.

143. Olivia transfers property to a trust in 2012 that allows trustee to pay income and principal among Olivia and her descendants in trustee's complete discretion. On Olivia's death, the remaining trust property passes to her nephew. Indicate when, and to what extent, Olivia makes a gift to the trust, if at all.

**(A)** Olivia makes a gift upon her 2012 transfer to the trust in the amount of the value of the remainder interest passing to her nephew.

**(B)** Olivia makes a gift upon her 2012 transfer to the trust in the amount of the entire value of the property transferred to the trust.

**(C)** Olivia does not make a gift to the trust because trustee is not subject to a fixed or ascertainable standard to distribute trust property.

**(D)** Olivia does not make a gift to the trust because her interest in the trust after the initial transfer is not capable of valuation in 2012.

144. Alan makes a transfer of property in trust. The terms of the trust direct trustee to distribute income to Alan's brother; provided, however, that if both Alan and Alan's brother consent to a distribution, they may direct trustee to make the distribution, including a distribution to one or both of them. On Alan's death the trust property is to pass to Alan's brother, or, if he is not then living, to Alan's brother's estate. Indicate when, if at all, Alan makes a gift with respect to the transfer of property in trust.

**(A)** Alan makes a gift at the time of the initial transfer because he does not retain an enforceable interest or power over the trust exercisable alone.

**(B)** Alan makes a gift at the time of the initial transfer because his brother possesses a substantial adverse interest with regard to Alan's power.

**(C)** Alan makes a gift at the time of the initial transfer to the extent of one-half the property transferred due to the joint power with his brother.

**(D)** Alan does not make a gift until such time as he and his brother exercise the power to direct distribution of the trust assets by trustee.

**145.** Under which of the following sets of circumstances does Ally have a general power of appointment over all of the trust property? Assume the power of appointment was created after October 21, 1942.

(A) Ally has the right to appoint any portion or the entire corpus of a trust created by her father Jim to anyone other than Ally's sister Betty.

(B) Ally and Cindy jointly have the right to appoint any portion or the entire corpus of a trust created by Ally's father Jim to anyone including themselves. Upon Ally's death, the power to appoint does not pass solely to Cindy.

(C) Ally has the right to appoint any portion or the entire corpus of a trust created by her father Jim except that Ally can exercise her power only with Jim's consent.

(D) Ally has the right to appoint any portion or the entire corpus of a trust created by her father Jim except that Ally's power can be exercised only with the consent of George who, upon Ally's death, will alone have the power to appoint the trust corpus to anyone including himself.

**146.** How, if at all, would your answer to Question 145, above, change if the power of appointment in that question had been created on or before October 21, 1942?

ANSWER:

**147.** On January 27, 2010, Dimitri created a trust for the benefit of his three children. Trust income was to be accumulated during Dimitri's life and, at his death, principal and accumulated income was to be distributed to Dimitri's then-surviving children. Under the terms of the trust, Dimitri's wife, Martine, was given unrestricted power to alter, amend, or revoke the trust. Under which of the following additional factual scenarios will Martine make a taxable gift of the entire interest in the trust?

(A) Martine survived Dimitri but did not, in fact, exercise her power of appointment during her lifetime.

(B) In July of 2012, Martine amended the trust to provide that Martine would receive trust income for life, and her sister Cindy would receive all remaining trust property upon Martine's death. Martine retained the right to alter, amend, or revoke the trust.

**(C)** In July of 2012, Martine amended the trust to provide that Martine would receive trust income for life, and her sister Cindy would receive all remaining trust property upon Martine's death. The amended trust was irrevocable.

**(D)** In July of 2012, Martine irrevocably gave up her interest in the trust.

148. After October 21, 1942, Sharon transferred property into a trust. Under the terms of the trust, the remainder of the trust property was payable to Randall upon Lisa's death. Assume that neither Lisa nor Randall has any interest in or power over the enjoyment of the property except as indicated separately in the answers below. Under which of the following additional factual scenarios will a taxable gift from Lisa to Randall result?

**(A)** Trust income is payable annually to Lisa for life. Lisa has the power under the trust to cause the income to be paid to Randall. Lisa receives an annual distribution of income from the trust.

**(B)** Trust income is payable annually to Lisa for life. For a period of 10 consecutive years, Randall has the power to cause the trustee to distribute all trust principal to Lisa. Ten years pass by, and Randall never requests that the trustee distribute the trust principal to Lisa.

**(C)** Trust income is to be accumulated for a period of 10 years. During the 10-year period, Lisa has the power to cause the trustee to distribute accumulated income to herself. Ten years pass by, and Lisa never requests that the trustee distribute the accumulated income.

**(D)** Trust income is to be accumulated for a period of 10 years. For a period of 10 consecutive years, Lisa has the power to have the income distributed to her, provided, however, that Lisa may only receive a distribution of income for reasons associated with her health, education, maintenance, or support (e.g., an ascertainable standard). Lisa never requests a distribution.

149. During 2011, Sharon transferred property to a trust for the benefit of her daughter Lisa. The terms of the trust provided that Lisa was to receive all trust income at least quarterly during each year. The trust also provided a special power of appointment to Lisa that authorized her to appoint trust assets to her daughter Taylor at any time during Lisa's life. Lisa exercises her power in 2012 by appointing half of the trust corpus to Taylor. Discuss whether Lisa has made a taxable gift in 2012.

ANSWER:

150. On January 1, 2012, Sara transfers $26,000 to an irrevocable trust for the benefit of her children Jack and Jill. Upon transfer to the trust, Jack and Jill each has the right to withdraw from the trust an amount equal to $13,000 for a period of 30 days from the date of the transfer. Neither Jack nor Jill exercises the withdrawal right. On lapse of the withdrawal right, Trustee is directed to hold property in trust until such time as Sara's death. On Sara's death, trustee shall distribute the trust property by representation to Sara's descendants. Indicate whether Jack and Jill made a taxable gift on the lapse of the

withdrawal right in 2012, and if so to what extent.

**(A)** Yes, both Jack and Jill have made a taxable gift to the trust to the extent of $13,000.

**(B)** Yes, both Jack and Jill have made a taxable gift to the trust to the extent of $8,000.

**(C)** No, neither Jack nor Jill made a taxable gift to the trust because neither exercised the general power of appointment.

**(D)** No, neither Jack nor Jill made a taxable gift to the trust because each was a beneficiary of the trust after the lapse.

*Except where otherwise indicated, assume the donor and any donee is a U.S. citizen and resident. Additionally, unless otherwise indicated, assume that the donor has no remaining gift tax credit and that all annual exclusions have been exhausted.*

151. Dad is growing old and is concerned about his health. Mom passed away some years ago and, until recently, Dad has been able to go the bank and take care of his financial matters. Lately, Dad has been forgetting to pay his bills and has spent a lot of time at the hospital receiving treatments for his advanced emphysema condition. Under which of the following additional sets of facts will Dad make a taxable gift to Barry?

   (A) Dad stuffed some money into his bed mattress and said to Barry "If I get too sick, please use this money in my mattress to pay off my bills. Whatever is left over when I die is yours." Barry takes some of the money to pay one of Dad's hospital bills.

   (B) Dad handed some money to his son Barry and said, "I am giving you this money to hold for me in case I get too sick to pay my bills. From now on, please use the money to pay my bills." Barry uses some of the money to buy a new competition ski boat for himself.

   (C) Dad added Barry as a co-signatory to his bank account. He indicated to Barry that "If I get too sick, please use the money in my account to pay off my bills. And, if you get into financial trouble you are welcome to withdraw some of the money for yourself." Barry withdrew some of the money and paid Dad's hospital bills.

   (D) Dad added Barry as a co-signatory to his bank account. He indicated to Barry that "If I get too sick, please use the money in my account to pay off my bills. And, if you get into financial trouble you are welcome to withdraw some of the money for yourself." Barry withdrew some of the money to pay off the debt balance on his sports car.

152. On January 30, 2011, Mom names Daughter as joint tenants with right of survivorship on her checking account so that Daughter can write checks on the account and make withdrawals from time to time. Either joint tenant may withdraw the entire balance of the account. The balance in the checking account on that date is $500,000. More than one year later on February 28, 2012, Daughter withdraws $100,000 from the account to make a down payment on an apartment building. Indicate when, if at all, Mom makes a gift to Daughter.

   (A) Mom makes a taxable gift on January 30, 2011 of $500,000 to Daughter.

   (B) Mom makes a taxable gift on January 30, 2011 of $250,000 to daughter.

**(C)**  Mom makes a taxable gift of $100,000 on February 28, 2012 to daughter.

**(D)**  Mom does not make a taxable gift of the bank account until she dies.

153.  Father was talking to a friend about the disadvantages of probate, and decided to follow his friend's lead and avoid probate by placing his home in the name of himself and his Son as joint tenants with right of survivorship. Father signs and records the deed to the home on January 5, 2012 when the home is valued at $1 million. Pursuant to local law, either joint tenant may unilaterally sever the survivorship interest and convert the property to a tenancy in common. Indicate when, if at all, Father makes a taxable gift to Son, and the amount of the gift.

**(A)**  Father makes a gift to Son of $1 million on January 5, 2012.

**(B)**  Father makes a gift to Son of $500,000 on January 5, 2012.

**(C)**  Father does not make a taxable transfer of any interest in his home until such time as he dies.

**(D)**  Father does not make a taxable transfer of any interest in his home until such time as Son unilaterally severs the joint interest.

154.  Jake and Craig purchase a home together as joint tenants with right of survivorship. Each contributes one-half the purchase price. Pursuant to state law, the joint tenancy is unilaterally severable. Several years later when Jake is 75, Craig is 60 and the home is worth $2 million, they decide to sever the joint tenancy, and each takes a one-half tenant-in-common interest. Indicate when, if at all, Craig makes a gift to Jake.

**(A)**  Craig makes a taxable gift at the time the home is purchased equal to the actuarial value of Craig's survivorship interest.

**(B)**  Craig makes a taxable gift at the time the joint interest is severed equal to the actuarial value of Craig's survivorship interest.

**(C)**  Craig makes a taxable gift at the time the joint interest is severed equal to $1 million less the actuarial value of Jake's survivorship interest.

**(D)**  Craig does not make a taxable gift at the time of purchase, nor does he make a gift at the time of severance of the joint interest.

155.  Michelle and Amelia purchase a home as joint tenants with right of survivorship on January 1, 2012. They each contribute one-half of the $50,000 down payment and take a mortgage for the remaining $200,000 of the purchase price. The annual mortgage payment is $24,000 per year, and Michelle makes the mortgage payments in 2012. Michelle and Amelia are jointly and severally liable for the mortgage. Michelle and Amelia agree that Michelle will not seek reimbursement for the mortgage payment from Amelia. What are the gift tax consequences of the transfer and the mortgage payment made in 2012?

**(A)**  Michelle makes a taxable gift to Amelia of $125,000.

**(B)** Michelle makes a taxable gift to Amelia of $100,000.

**(C)** Michelle makes a taxable gift to Amelia of $12,000.

**(D)** Michelle does not make a taxable gift to Amelia.

156. On January 1, 2011, Frank transfers stock in his closely held company to a trust that is revocable by him during his life. On Frank's death, the trust assets are to pass to Frank's descendants, per stripes. Frank dies on June 30, 2012, and his adult son Benson wants to disclaim the share of the trust assets he is to receive under the trust so that those assets pass to his child, and Frank's grandchild, Cathy, who is 17 years old. Pursuant to local law and the trust terms, Cathy would take Benson's interest in the event Benson disclaims. Within what time period must Benson disclaim the interest in order to qualify under IRC § 2518?

(A) Benson must disclaim within nine months following January 1, 2011.

(B) Benson must disclaim within nine months following June 30, 2012.

(C) Benson must disclaim within nine months following the date that Cathy turns age 21.

(D) Benson must disclaim within nine months of the date that Frank's federal estate tax return is filed.

157. On January 1, 2011, Jamie names her adult daughter Tamera as joint tenant with right of survivorship on the deed to her home. Local law allows a joint tenant to unilaterally sever the joint interest. Tamera succeeds to the survivorship interest on September 1, 2012 when Jamie dies. Assume Tamera would like to disclaim her interest in the home. Indicate when Tamera must make a disclaimer and the maximum amount she can disclaim.

(A) Tamera may disclaim the one-half joint tenancy interest passing to her on creation of the joint tenancy within nine months of January 1, 2011, or may disclaim the one-half survivorship interest within nine months of September 1, 2012.

(B) Tamera may disclaim the entire interest in the home within nine months of September 1, 2012, including the one-half joint tenancy interest passing on creation of the joint tenancy and the survivorship interest passing on Jamie's death.

(C) Tamera must disclaim all interests in the home within nine months of January 1, 2011, including the interest she receives on creation of the joint tenancy and the survivorship interest she is to receive on Jamie's death.

(D) Tamera must disclaim all interests in the home within nine months of the date that she begins to live in the home, including the interest she receives on creation of the joint tenancy and the survivorship interest passing on Jamie's death.

**158.** Demetra would like to disclaim the property passing to her under Sophie's will. Sophie's will directs that any disclaimed devise will pass in trust for the support of Demetra's grandchildren during their lifetimes, subject to a testamentary special power of appointment held by Demetra to pay the remainder interest as she determines among her grandchildren. Can Demetra make a qualified disclaimer of the property passing to her under Sophie's will within nine months of Sophie's death?

(A) Yes, Demetra can make a qualified disclaimer of devise under Sophie's will because she does not direct passage of the disclaimed property nor receive a property interest in the disclaimed property.

(B) Yes, Demetra can make a qualified disclaimer of the devise under Sophie's will because she does not direct passage of the disclaimed property nor does she receive a general power of appointment in the disclaimed property.

(C) No, Demetra cannot make a qualified disclaimer of the devise under Sophie's will because the disclaimed interest will pass to grandchildren, who are persons related to Demetra.

(D) No, Demetra cannot make a qualified disclaimer of the devise under Sophie's will because she holds a special power of appointment to direct passage of the disclaimed property.

**159.** Tom's will devises his lake cabin to his wife Patricia. His will provides that if Patricia disclaims the devise of the lake cabin, the cabin will pass to a trust for Patricia's support in accustomed manner of living during her life, with remainder to their descendants. Hometown Bank serves as trustee. Indicate whether Patricia can disclaim the outright devise of the lake cabin to her under Tom's will within nine months of Tom's death.

(A) Yes, Patricia can make a qualified disclaimer of the outright devise because a surviving spouse may accept an interest in the disclaimed property after the disclaimer.

(B) Yes, Patricia can make a qualified disclaimer of the outright devise because the interest she receives is subject to an ascertainable standard.

(C) No, Patricia may not make a qualified disclaimer of the outright devise because a disclaimant may not accept any interest in the disclaimed property before or after the disclaimer.

(D) No, Patricia may not make a qualified disclaimer of the outright devise because a disclaimant may not accept an interest that is not wholly within the discretion of the trustee to distribute.

*The gift tax annual exclusion pursuant to IRC § 2503(b) is $10,000, as that amount is adjusted for inflation. Because the inflation adjusted amount changes from time to time, for purposes of the following questions, assume that the gift tax annual exclusion is $10,000. Except where otherwise indicated, the answers provided assume the donor is a U.S. citizen and resident, and any beneficiary also is a U.S. citizen and resident. Additionally, unless otherwise indicated, assume that the donor has no remaining gift or estate tax credit, and assume there are no applicable deductions.*

160. John, a wealthy entrepreneur whose spouse recently passed away, has six married children and 20 minor grandchildren. He would like to maximize use of his annual exclusion amount each year, but would like to limit gifts to his children and grandchildren. What is the maximum number of annual exclusion gifts that John can make?

   (A) 6 annual exclusion gifts each year.

   (B) 26 annual exclusion gifts each year.

   (C) 26 annual exclusion gifts in total.

   (D) 32 annual exclusion gifts each year, 26 to children and grandchildren and 6 to spouses of the children, subject to the condition that each spouse will in turn make a transfer of equal value to his or her spouse who is John's child.

161. Helen wants to make annual exclusion gifts to children. Which of the following alternatives will qualify for the annual exclusion?

   (A) Outright transfer of limited partnership interests, subject to partnership distributions in discretion of the general partner and subject to restrictions on sale.

   (B) Transfer of publicly traded stock, in trust, with direction to trustee to pay all income among trustor's children as trustee deems appropriate, in equal or unequal shares.

   (C) Transfer of tenant in common interests in a leased commercial building where under state law a tenant in common has the right to request partition.

   (D) Outright transfer of the ownership of a whole life insurance policy to children as co-owners and beneficiaries.

162. Alice transfers $50,000 of publicly traded stock in trust for her child, Sam. The trust directs trustee to pay all income to Sam for Sam's life, and to pay the remainder to Sam's children. At the time of the gift, Sam's life income interest has an actuarial value of $9,000. Indicate

whether Alice can take an annual exclusion for the $50,000 transfer, and, if so, to what extent.

ANSWER:

163. Trevor decides to begin a program of annual exclusion giving to his children. Trevor would like to retain control over the transferred property to the extent possible because he is concerned about the amount of access his children will have over assets, including trust distributions. Control is as important to him as maximizing use of the annual exclusion amount. He also believes that the children are too young to receive outright gifts. He asks for advice as to what methods he has at his disposal that will allow him to limit or prevent children from having any access to the trust income and principal until they reach age 40. Of course, like all clients, Trevor would still like to obtain the maximum tax savings. Which of the following plans is most likely to effectuate Trevor's goals?

(A) Create separate trusts (one for the benefit of each child) and contribute $10,000 annually to each trust. Upon making each contribution, notify each child that he or she has the option of withdrawing up to $10,000 within a 15-day period after contribution. The trust requires the trustee to distribute net income and principal to the beneficiary for his or her maintenance, education, health, or support. The trustee is further directed to distribute any remaining income and principal to the beneficiary when the beneficiary attains the age of 40, or if the beneficiary dies before age 40, to the beneficiary's estate.

(B) Create separate trusts (one for each child) and contribute $10,000 annually to each trust. Upon making each contribution, notify each child that he or she may request that the trustee distribute the $10,000 within a 15-day period after contribution, provided, however, that the trustee may deny a child's request for annual withdrawals and make distributions in his or her uncontrolled discretion as he deems advisable. The trustee is further directed to distribute any remaining income and principal to the beneficiary when the beneficiary attains the age of 40.

(C) Create separate trusts (one for each child) and contribute $10,000 annually to each trust. Each trust provides that the trustee may distribute net income and principal to the beneficiary for maintenance, education, health, or support during the life of the beneficiary. The trustee is further directed to distribute any income and principal to the beneficiary when the beneficiary attains the age of 21 or to the beneficiary's estate if the beneficiary dies prior to attaining the age of 21.

(D) Create separate trusts (one for each child) and contribute $10,000 annually to each trust. Each trust provides that the trustee may distribute net income and principal to the beneficiary for maintenance, education, health, or support during the life of the beneficiary. The trustee is further directed to distribute any remaining income and principal to the beneficiary when the beneficiary attains the age of 40 or to the beneficiary's estate if the beneficiary dies prior to attaining the age of 21, provided, however, that the beneficiary may elect to receive any trust income and principal upon attaining the age of 21.

**164.** Angela wants to transfer property in trust for the primary benefit of her children. Trustee is to pay income and principal for the support of her children. On Angela's death, trustee is to pay remaining income and principal outright to her children in equal shares. In the event a child does not survive her, that child's share is to pass outright to the child's then living children (Angela's grandchildren) in equal shares. Angela intends to annually transfer property to the trust subject to a withdrawal power, with the goal of maximizing use of the annual exclusion amount to the extent possible without causing an adverse gift tax consequence to her children and grandchildren should the withdrawal power be allowed to lapse. Indicate which of the following withdrawal powers will best achieve Angela's goal.

**(A)** Within 15 days of a transfer to the trust, each child and grandchild of Trustor may withdraw an amount equal to the lesser of (i) the amount transferred to the trust divided by the number of children and grandchildren of Trustor and (ii) $5,000.

**(B)** Within 15 days of a transfer to the trust, each child and grandchild of Trustor may withdraw an amount equal to the lesser of (i) the amount transferred to the trust divided by the number of children and grandchildren of Trustor and (ii) the amount of the annual exclusion pursuant to IRC § 2503(b).

**(C)** Within 15 days of a transfer to the trust, each child of Trustor may withdraw an amount equal to the lesser of (i) the amount transferred to the trust divided by the number of children of Trustor and (ii) $5,000.

**(D)** Within 15 days of a transfer to the trust, each child of Trustor may withdraw an amount equal to the lesser of (i) the amount transferred to the trust divided by the number of children of Trustor and (ii) the amount of the annual exclusion pursuant to IRC § 2503(b).

**165.** Kyle meets with you and indicates he is currently making annual exclusion gifts to his minor children, nieces and nephews, but would like to make additional transfers. He says that he has heard about these so called "529" college savings plans, and he would like to start 12 accounts, one for each of his children, nieces, and nephews. He asks whether he can avoid additional gift taxes through use of such savings plans. Which of the following options would result in the most gift tax savings for Kyle?

**(A)** Kyle stops contributing to any other trusts for the benefit of the minors. Instead, he contributes $50,000 this year ($600,000 total) to 12 separate IRC § 529 qualified tuition programs for the benefit of his children, nieces, and nephews.

**(B)** Kyle contributes $120,000 per year to a *Crummey* trust for the benefit of his 12 children, nieces, and nephews. In addition, for the next five years, he contributes $10,000 per year ($120,000 total annually; $600,000 over the next 5 years) to 12 separate IRC § 529 qualified tuition programs for the benefit of each of his children, nieces, and nephews.

**(C)** Kyle contributes $120,000 per year to a *Crummey* trust for the benefit of his 12 children, nieces, and nephews. In addition, he contributes $50,000 this year ($600,000 total) to 12 separate IRC § 529 qualified tuition programs for the benefit of his children, nieces, and nephews.

**(D)** Kyle contributes $120,000 per year to a *Crummey* trust for the benefit of his 12 children, nieces, and nephews (12 total).

166. Amanda has five grandchildren, all of whom are in college. She realizes that in order to avoid paying estate tax on her death, she will need to make sizeable transfers. Amanda's goal is to help each grandchild pay for college, and at the same time minimize wealth transfer tax. Assume that tuition of each grandchild is $40,000 and room/board $20,000 per year. Amanda would like to know which of the following plans transfers the greatest amount of property without gift tax consequence.

**(A)** Amanda writes a check to each child for $60,000 per year to allow the child to pay for room and board.

**(B)** Amanda sets up a separate *Crummey* for each child, and contributes to the trust $60,000 each year. Each child is able to withdraw an amount equal to the annual exclusion amount for a period of 15 days after the date of transfer to the trust. The trustee is required to use remaining trust funds to pay each child's tuition, and room and board.

**(C)** Amanda writes a check directly to each child's university for tuition, and writes an additional check in the amount of the annual exclusion amount to each child, which the child can then use to pay room and board.

**(D)** Amanda writes a check to each child's university for $60,000 in payment of tuition, room and board.

167. Hannah has several grandchildren who need extensive orthodontic work for which there is no insurance. She currently makes annual exclusion gifts for the benefit of each of her grandchildren. Hannah asks your advice as to the best way to make transfers to pay for the orthodontic work. Please advise her.

ANSWER:

168. Georgia and Arthur are married, both are U.S. citizens and neither has previously made any taxable gifts. Georgia owns $20 million of assets and Arthur owns $2 million of assets. Assume that each has an available applicable exclusion amount of $5,120,000 in 2012, and the annual gift tax exclusion for 2012 is $13,000. After visiting with her estate planning attorney, Georgia decides to make a gift of publicly traded stock in equal amounts to each of her two children. Georgia and Art remain married during 2012. Indicate the maximum amount of stock Georgia can transfer to her two children without incurring gift tax in 2012.

   (A) Georgia may transfer up to $2,560,000 to each child.

   (B) Georgia may transfer up to $2,573,000 to each child.

   (C) Georgia may transfer $2,573,000 to each child, and transfer an additional $5,146,000 to Arthur on the condition that he make a gift of $2,573,000 to each child.

   (D) Georgia may transfer $5,133,000 to each child.

169. Assume the same facts as in the preceding Question 168, except that Georgia and Arthur elect to split gifts pursuant to IRC § 2513, and both properly make the election on the gift tax return for 2012. Indicate the maximum amount of stock Georgia can transfer to each child without incurring gift tax in 2012.

   (A) Georgia may transfer up to $2,560,000 to each child.

   (B) Georgia may transfer up to $2,573,000 to each child.

   (C) Georgia may transfer up to $5,133,000 to each child.

   (D) Georgia may transfer up to $5,146,000 to each child.

170. Heidi and Roger, who are married and now both U.S. citizens, would like to make equal gifts to their two children in 2012. Heidi has fully used her applicable exclusion amount. Roger, however, has an available applicable exclusion amount of $5 million. Each has in excess of $10 million in assets. Assume the annual gift tax exclusion amount for 2012 is $13,000. Heidi and Roger ask you to calculate the maximum gift that they can make to each child without incurring gift tax on the transfer.

   (A) $26,000 if Heidi and Roger elect to split gifts

   (B) $2,513,000 if Heidi and Roger elect to split gifts.

   (B) $2,526,000 if Heidi and Roger elect to split gifts.

(C) $5,026,000 if Heidi and Roger elect to split gifts.

171. David, a U.S. citizen, and his wife Antonia, a citizen of Mexico, were married when they were in their early twenties. They currently reside in Juarez, Mexico. They have been blessed over the last two decades with 10 children. David would like to transfer property to each of his children, and asks if it is possible to elect split gift treatment for purposes of calculating his federal gift tax. Advise him.

    (A) No, because David and Antonia currently reside in Juarez, Mexico.

    (B) No, because Antonia is not a U.S. citizen nor is she a U.S. resident.

    (C) Yes, because only one of the two spouses needs to be a U.S. citizen.

    (D) Yes, because citizenship and residence is not required to make the election.

172. Allie makes a gift of $13,000 to each of her 10 grandchildren on January 15, 2012. Her husband Tom dies on November 5, 2012. Allie then makes an additional gift of $13,000 to each of her 10 grandchildren on December 1, 2012. The gift tax annual exclusion amount is $13,000 for 2012. Allie is executor of Tom's estate, and she does not remarry. Indicate whether Allie can elect to split gifts with Tom, and, if so, the amount of the taxable gift she will be deemed to make.

    (A) Yes, Allie can split gifts and, if she does so, will not make a taxable gift.

    (B) Yes, Allie can split gifts and, if she does so, she will make a taxable gift of $6,500.

    (C) No, Allie cannot split gifts because she and Tom are not married as of December 31.

    (D) No, Allie cannot split gifts because Tom was not alive at the time of the second gift.

*Except where otherwise indicated, assume the donor and any donee is a U.S. citizen and resident. Additionally, unless otherwise indicated, assume that the donor has no remaining gift tax credit and that all annual exclusions have been exhausted.*

### General Valuation Concepts

173. Uncle Benny is a miser and always has been. He is a workaholic who has saved all his life, and he is finally beginning to relax a little. After hearing that it never rained there, he purchased himself a condominium on the beach in southern California. His nephew, Joseph, has just turned 16, and Joseph has asked his Uncle Benny what he plans to do with his old car. Uncle Benny owns a 1964 ½ Ford Mustang convertible that he drove only on the weekends. After having spent a fine afternoon watching sets roll in and the sails blow by, Uncle Benny has a rare moment and tells Joseph that he can have the Mustang so long as he takes good care of it. Uncle Benny bought the car in 1964 and paid only $2,500 for it. Assuming Uncle Benny just transferred title and turned the keys over to Joseph today, what is the value of the Mustang for gift tax purposes?

    (A) $2,500, the price that Uncle Benny paid for the Mustang.

    (B) $18,000, the amount that a reputable local auto dealer offered to pay Uncle Benny for the Mustang.

    (C) $25,000, the amount that several auto dealers in town were asking for other similar 1964 ½ Ford Mustang convertibles.

    (D) $10,000, the price that Benny sincerely believes it is worth and the price that a passerby offered him earlier in the day for the Mustang.

174. Assume the same facts as in preceding Question 173, above, except that instead of giving the Mustang to Joseph outright, Uncle Benny had shown his true colors and asked Joseph to pay him $7,000 for the car. Assume also that no gift taxes were paid on the transfer. What, if any, value must be reported as a gift from Benny to Joseph?

ANSWER:

175. Helen gave 1,000 shares of Big Inc., a publicly traded corporation on the New York Stock Exchange, to her niece Nancy. A check online to determine the high and low trading price of Big Inc. on the date the shares were transferred to Nancy reveals that at the end of trading, the highest quoted selling price was $10.00 per share and the lowest recorded selling price was $7.00. What is the value of the gift to Nancy that Helen must report on

her annual gift tax return for the year?

**(A)** $7,000.

**(B)** $8,500.

**(C)** $10,000.

**(D)** $17,000.

176. Manon is the sole owner of SVS Sporting Goods Corporation. She has never sold shares of the stock. Discuss how an appraiser might arrive at the value of the stock in the absence of comparable trades.

ANSWER:

177. Dick owns a beach home in Branford, Connecticut and a beach home in Siesta Key, Florida. Dick is tired of travelling back and forth between the two homes, not to mention paying upkeep for both homes. He prefers the year round sun of Florida, and decides to give his Connecticut home to his son. Indicate what gift tax value should be reported on Dick's gift tax return for the transfer of the home to his son.

**(A)** $350,000, the appraised value as of six months after the date of gift as arrived at by a local real estate appraiser.

**(B)** $400,000, the price that Dick originally paid for the home.

**(C)** $450,000, the assessed value of the home as reported on the county tax rolls for purposes of determining property tax.

**(D)** $600,000 the appraised date of gift value arrived at by a local real estate appraiser after taking into account comparables.

## Actuarial Concepts

178. Benny decides to move to sunnier ocean climes, and decides to give his Steamboat, Colorado home to his brother Brett to live in for the duration of his brother's life, with the remainder passing equally to his niece and nephew, Joseph and Katie, upon Brett's death. He makes the transfer on April 15, 2012. Benny does not want to pay a professional appraiser or actuary for services after already having paid to get the home itself appraised. Being a financial guru himself, Benny knows that between the life and remainder interests, he is giving 100 percent of the home away. However, he is confused about exactly what he should refer to in order to determine the appropriate actuarial factor for calculating the value of the gifts. He called the IRS helpline and they kindly referred him to IRS Publication 1457, providing example calculations, and to the IRS website for actuarial factors at: http://www.irs.gov/retirement/article/0,id=206601,00.html. He asks you which table in the publication is the most appropriate one to use for this purpose.

**(A)** Table B, Term Certain Factors.

**(B)** Table S, Single Life Remainder Factors.

**(C)** Table R(2), Two Life Last-to-Die Factors.

**(D)** Table K, Adjustment Factors for Annuities.

179. Benny locates the appropriate table and now realizes that he needs to determine his brother's age and the appropriate interest rate in order to cross-reference the appropriate factor. He knows his brother Brett is 52 years old, but he is clueless about which interest rate he should use. He again seeks your assistance and asks what the appropriate annual rate is. Assume that the date of the gift was April 15, 2012. Revenue Ruling 2012-11 indicates that the Section 7520 interest rate for April 2012 is 1.4%, and it provides the following additional interest rates:

| REV. RUL. 2012-11 TABLE 1 | | | |
|---|---|---|---|
| Applicable Federal Rates (AFR) for April 2012 | | | |
| *Period for Compounding* | | | |
| *Annual* | *Semiannual* | *Quarterly* | *Monthly* |
| **Short-term** | | | |
| AFR  .25% | .25% | .25% | .25% |
| 110% AFR  .28% | .28% | .28% | .28% |
| 120% AFR  .30% | .30% | .30% | .30% |
| 130% AFR  .33% | .33% | .33% | .33% |
| | | | |
| **Mid-term** | | | |
| AFR  1.15% | 1.15% | 1.15% | 1.15% |
| 110% AFR  1.27% | 1.27% | 1.27% | 1.27% |
| 120% AFR  1.38% | 1.38% | 1.38% | 1.38% |
| 130% AFR  1.51% | 1.50% | 1.50% | 1.50% |
| 150% AFR  1.74% | 1.73% | 1.73% | 1.72% |
| 175% AFR  2.02% | 2.01% | 2.00% | 2.00% |
| | | | |
| **Long-term** | | | |
| AFR  2.72% | 2.70% | 2.69% | 2.68% |
| 110% AFR  2.99% | 2.97% | 2.96% | 2.95% |
| 120% AFR  3.27% | 3.24% | 3.23% | 3.22% |
| 130% AFR  3.54% | 3.51% | 3.49% | 3.48% |

What is the appropriate annual interest rate?

**(A)** 0.30 percent.

**(B)** 1.38 percent.

**(C)** 1.40 percent.

**(D)** 3.27 percent.

180. Having determined the appropriate actuarial table, his brother's age, and the applicable interest rate, what is the value of Brett's life interest in Benny's Colorado home? Assume the gift was actually made on April 15, 2012, and that on that date, the home had a fair

market value of $2,000,000.

   **(A)** $2,000,000.

   **(B)** $1,442,540.

   **(C)** $721,270.

   **(D)** $557,460.

181. What is the value for gift tax purposes of Joseph and Katie's remainder interests?

   **(A)** $2,000,000.

   **(B)** $1,442,540.

   **(C)** $721,270.

   **(D)** $557,460.

182. Assume instead that Benny gives his brother a 10-year term interest in the $2 million home on April 15, 2012. After Brett's 10-year term interest has expired, the remainder interest in the home will go solely to his niece Katie. What is the value of Brett's 10-year term interest for gift tax purposes?

ANSWER:

## IRC § 2702, Gifts of Partial Interests to Family Members

183. Frank has transferred $1 million to a trust. The terms of the trust direct trustee to pay the income of the trust to Frank for 20 years, and to distribute the remainder to his son Samuel. Assume Frank's income interest as valued pursuant to the actuarial tables is $300,000. Indicate the amount of the gift to be reported by Frank for gift tax purposes.

   **(A)** 0

   **(B)** $300,000

   **(C)** $700,000

   **(D)** $1,000,000

184. Assume instead that Frank transfers $1 million to a trust for the benefit of himself and his nephew Nicholas. The terms of the trust direct trustee to pay the income of the trust to Frank for 20 years, and to distribute the remainder to his nephew Nicholas. Assume Frank's income interest is valued pursuant to the actuarial tables at $300,000. Indicate the amount of the gift to be reported by Frank for gift tax purposes.

   **(A)** 0

   **(B)** $300,000

   **(C)** $700,000

   **(D)** $1,000,000

185. Assume instead that Frank transfers $1 million to a trust for the benefit of himself and his son Samuel. The terms of the trust direct trustee to pay a fixed amount annually to Frank for 20 years, and to distribute the remainder to his son Samuel. Assume Frank's annuity interest in the trust is valued pursuant to the actuarial tables at $300,000. Indicate the amount of the gift to be reported by Frank for federal gift tax purposes.

   **(A)** 0

   **(B)** $300,000

   **(C)** $700,000

   **(D)** $1,000,000

## Valuation Premiums and Discounts

186. Ellie is pleased with the success of her company, Tech Corporation. She would like to begin to slow down and enjoy life, and has decided to involve her nephew Nate as an owner of the business because he has proved invaluable as her Senior Vice President. Ellie has engaged a reputable business appraiser who has just delivered an opinion to Ellie indicating that Tech Corporation as a whole is worth $10,000,000. Tech Corporation has 500,000 shares ($20 per share) outstanding. Ellie gives Nate 7,500 or 1.5 percent of her shares in Tech Corporation. Which of the following valuation adjustments is most likely to apply in valuing the 150,000 shares given to Nate?

   **(A)** Blockage discount.

   **(B)** Minority interest discount.

   **(C)** Control premium.

   **(D)** Subrogation discount.

187. Assume the same facts as in Question 186, above, except that instead of giving the Tech Corporation shares to Nate outright, Ellie gives the shares to Nate subject to an enforceable shareholder's agreement. The shareholder's agreement provides, among other things, that Nate's ability to sell the shares to third parties is restricted under certain circumstances. Which of the following valuation adjustments will most likely apply for purposes of valuing the 7,500 shares?

   **(A)** Blockage discount.

   **(B)** Control premium.

   **(C)** Lack of marketability.

**(D)**   Capital gains discount.

188.   Jenna, owns 20 percent of the shares of Hometown Inc. Jenna's close friend and partner
Nel's owns 40 percent of the shares of the corporation, and a third shareholder owns 40
percent. Jenna decides to gift her 20% interest to Nels. The transfer from Jenna to Nels
will bring Nel's interest to 60 percent and give him the ability to control the corporation to
extent a decision does not require a super-majority vote. Will the gift by Jenna of 20
percent of the shares be entitled to a minority discount given that the transfer will leave
Nels with owning a majority or controlling interest in Hometown Inc.?

ANSWER:

189. Patricia would like to take advantage of minority and marketability discounts. For which of the following property may she take a discount when valuing it for federal estate and gift tax purposes?

    (A) Sole proprietorship

    (B) Publicly traded stock

    (C) General partnership interests

    (D) Limited liability company membership interests

190. Teresa believes that her assets will rapidly appreciate in the future and she has decided to gift those assets to her three children and grandchildren now in order to avoid estate tax on the appreciation. She plans to make initial gifts up to her applicable exclusion amount. Her spouse recently passed away leaving her with an applicable exclusion amount of $10,000,000. Teresa's assets include publicly traded stock, stock in a family ranch, and several apartment buildings. Her goal in transferring property is to maximize use of the applicable exclusion amount, protect the assets in the event of a child's divorce and protect the assets from her children's creditors. One of her children periodically attends marriage counseling whenever her spouse threatens divorce, and the other child has a history of gambling. The third child Amanda is a financial whiz, and very adept at making excellent investments. She would like the third child to eventually manage her assets. Which of the following strategies will allow Teresa to meet these planning goals?

    (A) Outright gifts of the stock in the family ranch in equal shares to each of the three children.

    (B) Transfers to a *Crummey* trust for the three children, with distributions of income equally to the three children, and Amanda serving as trustee.

    (C) Transfers to a spendthrift trust for the three children, with distributions of income and principal wholly in the trustee's discretion, with Amanda serving as trustee.

    (D) Transfers to a limited partnership, with subsequent transfers of the limited partnership interests to the children and the general partnership interest to Amanda.

191. Carol owns membership interests in a family limited liability company. Under the terms of the operating agreement, the manager may choose whether and when to make distributions. In addition, before a member may sell his or her membership interest, the manager

must consent to the sale. Discuss whether Carol may take an annual gift tax exclusion with respect to the transfer of membership interests in the limited liability company.

ANSWER:

192. Teresa chooses to form a limited partnership for the purposes of managing her assets, and making transfers to her children. Which of the following options sets forth the best way to form the partnership and make the transfers?

   **(A)** Teresa contributes 85 percent of the property to the partnership, and each of her children contributes 5 percent of the property to the partnership. Each receives entity interests proportionate to the contribution each makes to the trust, with Amanda receiving a general partnership interest and the remaining partners receiving limited partnership interests. Six months after formation of the limited partnership, Teresa transfers limited partnership interests to her three children with an aggregate value of up to her applicable exclusion amount.

   **(B)** Teresa contributes 85 percent of the property to the partnership and each of her children contributes 5 percent of the property to the partnership. Each receives entity interests proportionate to the contribution each makes to the trust, with Amanda receiving a general partnership interest and the remaining partners receiving limited partnership interests. On the same day, Teresa transfers limited partnership interests to her three children with an aggregate value of up to her applicable exclusion amount.

   **(C)** Teresa contributes 100 percent of the property to the partnership. She receives 100 percent of the general partnership interests and the limited partnership interests. Ten days after formation of the limited partnership, Teresa transfers general partnership interests to Amanda and limited partnership interests to her other two children with an aggregate value of up to her applicable exclusion amount.

   **(D)** Teresa contributes 100 percent of the property to the partnership. She receives 100 percent of the general partnership interests and the limited partnership interests. On the same day, Teresa transfers general partnership interests to Amanda and limited partnership interests to her other two children with an aggregate value of up to her applicable exclusion amount.

193. Brianna transferred all but $100,000 of her assets to a family limited partnership formed by Brianna and her eldest child, Ed. Ed holds all general partnership interests. Over the years, Brianna transferred all but 10% of her limited partnership interests to her other children. Despite these transfers, Ed continues to distribute to Brianna 80% of the income earned by the limited partnership. On Brianna's federal estate tax return, the executor reports Brianna's 10 percent limited partnership interest after taking a substantial minority and marketability discount for her interest. As the IRS agent assigned to audit Brianna's federal estate tax return, indicate how you will treat the reporting of the limited partnership interests on Brianna's return.

**(A)** Include the full value of the assets held by the family limited partnership pursuant to IRC § 2036(a)(1).

**(B)** Include the full value of the assets held by the family limited partnership pursuant to IRC § 2036(a)(2).

**(C)** Include the limited partnership interests owned by Brianna at full undiscounted value pursuant IRC § 2036(a)(1).

**(D)** Include the limited partnership interests owned by Brianna at the discounted value reported pursuant to IRC § 2033.

194. Zach transfers his insurance business which he owns as a sole proprietor to a limited liability company (LLC). He anticipates hiring his children as employees, and wishes to avoid personal liability for the acts of employees he hires. He hires two of his children. The value of the sole proprietorship at the time of transfer constituted only about 40 percent of his total assets. After several years and the hiring of 10 more employees, Zach decides to turn over the operation of the LLC to his children, who are employed by the company. He transfers to each of his children a 20 percent membership interest in the LLC. At the same time Zach resigned as manager, and named his two children as manager of the LLC. Zach died shortly thereafter. As the IRS agent auditing Zach's estate tax return, analyze whether you would include the full undiscounted value of the LLC assets in Zach's gross estate.

ANSWER:

195. Estelle is preparing the federal estate tax return for Denise's estate. Indicate which of the following expenses may not be deducted on Denise's federal estate tax return pursuant to IRC § 2053.

   **(A)** $20,000 bill for the cemetery plot and funeral expenses incurred to bury decedent.

   **(B)** $20,000 appraiser fee incurred in determining date of death value of assets included in the gross estate.

   **(C)** $20,000 loss resulting from a reduction in the value of stock from date of death value.

   **(D)** $20,000 claim against the estate for medical expenses of decedent unpaid at death.

196. Jerry requests that he be cremated, and that a reception celebrating his life be held in Hawaii where he and his family had travelled for vacation each year to celebrate his birthday. Six months after Jerry's death, his executor purchases plane tickets for Jerry's spouse, children and grandchildren to travel to Hawaii for one last family get together celebrating Jerry's life. The state probate court affirms the travel expenses as appropriately paid funeral expenses pursuant to state law. Indicate whether the travel expenses incurred are deductible under IRC § 2053.

   **(A)** Yes, the travel expenses are deductible as reasonable funeral expenses because they were necessitated by decedent's request.

   **(B)** Yes, the travel expenses are deductible as reasonable funeral expenses because they were allowable under state law.

   **(C)** No, the travel expenses are not deductible because they are not expenses incurred in eulogizing and burying decedent.

   **(D)** No, the expenses are not deductible because they were not incurred within a reasonable time after decedent's death.

197. The executor of Sara's estate charges an executor's fee of $100,000 that exceeds the statutory maximum allowable under state law, which in the case of Sara's estate would be $80,000. The beneficiaries of the estate contest the executor's right to receive a fee in excess of the statutory maximum. They do acknowledge the executor's right to $80,000. The executor of Sara's estate takes a deduction in the amount of the $100,000 fee she claims despite the fact that she has not yet written herself a check for the fee. As the IRS agent auditing the case, should you allow the deduction?

**(A)** Yes, because $100,000 is the amount that is asserted as owed by the executor of Sara's estate.

**(B)** Yes, because the executor fee is not subject to state law limitations so long as it is justified by the executor.

**(C)** No, the deduction instead should be limited to the $80,000 amount that is ascertainable and not contested.

**(D)** No, no portion of the fee should be taken as a deduction until the fee is in fact paid to the executor.

198. The executor of Shirley's estate determines that he needs to sell Shirley's home in order to obtain sufficient liquid assets to pay federal estate tax owed by her estate. The only other asset in the probate estate is an interest in a family limited liability company for which there is no readily available market. The estate incurs a sales commission of $50,000 on the home. The expense is allowable by local law, and the executor takes the commission as a deduction on the estate tax return. As the IRS agent auditing the case, should you allow the deduction?

**(A)** Yes, because the sales commission is an allowable and necessary administration expense incurred by the estate.

**(B)** Yes, because the sales commission is an administration expense incurred with respect to the probate estate.

**(C)** No, because the sales commission is incurred for the benefit of the beneficiaries.

**(D)** No, because the executor could have avoided the expense by taking out a loan on the home to pay the estate tax.

199. Larry, a doctor, was sued for malpractice. The suit remained outstanding as of Larry's death. The complaint against Larry asked for damages in the amount of $10 million. Larry had let his malpractice coverage lapse and so any amount paid in damages would not be covered by insurance. The executor of Larry's estate is defending the estate against the suit. As of the date of filing of the federal estate tax return, the lawsuit had not been settled. An appraiser determined that the date of death value of the law suit is $5 million. Indicate whether the executor can deduct the law suit on Larry's estate tax return, and, if so, the amount of the deduction that can be taken.

**(A)** The executor may deduct $10,000,000 claimed as damages for the malpractice because that is the amount of the claim outstanding as of the date of death, and the claim is the result of a bona fide dispute.

**(B)** The executor may deduct the $5 million appraised value of the malpractice claim because that is the date of death value of the claim against the estate, and the claim is the result of a bona fide dispute.

**(C)** The executor may not deduct the amount of the claim because it is in dispute and not paid as of the date of death, but she may file a protective claim preserving the right to take the deduction when paid.

**(D)** The executor may not deduct the amount of the claim because it does not fall within the exceptions allowing deductions to the extent of any counterclaim or for claims not exceeding in the aggregate $500,000.

200. During her life, Jim's Mom promised to pay him $20 per hour, his going rate, for housekeeping and lawn services. Jim had a home repair business and he would often send one of his employees to do what his Mom needed around the house. Because his Mom was always worried about the balance in her checking account, Jim decided to bill his Mom on an annual basis immediately after she received her tax refund from the IRS each year. The check would be written to Jim's company for work rendered. As of her death the bill for the prior year's services remained outstanding. Jim timely filed the claim for payment of the bill. The executor of the estate paid the bill prior to filing the estate tax return. Indicate whether the executor should claim the deduction on the estate tax return.

**(A)** Yes, the executor should take the deduction because it is a bona fide claim against the estate.

**(B)** Yes, the executor should take the deduction because it is a reasonable expense of administration.

**(C)** No, the executor should not take the deduction because of a lack of adequate consideration in money or money's worth.

**(D)** No, the executor should not take the deduction because claims by a family member are presumed to be a bequest.

201. Within one month prior to their divorce, Imogen and Tom entered into an enforceable written agreement dividing the assets of their marital estate between them. In addition, Imogen agreed to pay Tom a monthly sum for the next ten years in satisfaction of her support obligation to Tom. After making most of the payments under the written agreement, the actual amount of the payments remaining is $13,000. The present value of the support payments remaining as of Imogen's date of death is $10,000. Tom timely files a claim for payment against the estate. Indicate whether Imogen's executor may deduct Tom's claim on the estate tax return, and, if so, the amount deductible.

**(A)** Yes, the executor may deduct the claim in the amount of $10,000 because it is a bona fide claim for full and adequate consideration in money or money's worth.

**(B)** Yes, the executor may deduct the claim in the amount of $13,000 because it is a bona fide claim for full and adequate consideration in money or money's worth.

**(C)** No, the executor may not deduct the claim because marital rights do not constitute full and adequate consideration for the claim in money or money's worth.

**(D)** No, the executor may not deduct the claim because the claim represents a satisfaction of support obligations of the decedent as opposed to a division of marital assets.

202. The executor of Mac's estate was required to pay a variety of taxes in order to close the probate estate and be relieved of duties as an executor. Mac died May 1, 2012. Which of the following taxes may the executor deduct on Mac's estate tax return?

   **(A)** Income tax due and owing by Mac for the tax year 2011.

   **(B)** State inheritance tax due and owing on Mac's estate.

   **(C)** Federal estate tax due and owing on Mac's estate.

   **(D)** Estate income tax due on income earned during estate administration.

203. Becky placed her home in a revocable trust prior to her death. As of her death there was an outstanding loan and mortgage against the home for which Becky was personally liable. The home was included in her gross estate under IRC § 2038 for $1 million. Indicate whether the executor may deduct the outstanding mortgage in the amount of $600,000 under IRC § 2053.

   **(A)** Yes, the executor may deduct the $600,000 mortgage because it is a recourse mortgage.

   **(B)** Yes, but the executor may only deduct $400,000 which represents the equity in the home.

   **(C)** No, the executor may not deduct the mortgage because the revocable trust, and not the probate estate, holds the home.

   **(D)** No, the executor may not deduct the mortgage because it is a nonrecourse mortgage.

204. John's gross estate included the value of assets held in an irrevocable trust of which he was the donor. Pursuant to state law, the trust assets were not subject to John's creditor's claims. Nevertheless, the trustee of the trust incurred administration expenses necessary to distribute assets on John's death and to terminate the trust. The expenses were allowable under state law, reasonably ascertainable and were expected to be paid within a few months of filing the return. As of the date of filing of the estate tax return nine months following John's death, however, the trustee had not yet paid the expenses. May the executor deduct the expenses incurred by the trustee under IRC § 2053?

   **(A)** Yes, the trustee may deduct the expenses incurred with respect to administration and termination of the trust because they will be paid within three years following the date the return is filed.

   **(B)** No, the trustee may not deduct the expenses incurred with respect to administration and termination of the trust because they were not paid prior to the time the estate tax return was filed.

**(C)** No, the trustee may not deduct the expenses incurred with respect to administration and termination of the trust because the trust was not part of the probate estate subject to creditor's claims.

**(D)** No, the trustee may not deduct the expenses incurred with respect to administration and termination of the trust because only probate administration expenses may be deducted.

205. Decedent's gross estate included the value of an apartment building that decedent owned as of the date of her death. As of the date of her death the apartment building and land was valued at $1 million. During the administration of the estate and prior to distribution of assets, the building burned. The building was insured and the insurance company paid the estate $700,000 in reimbursement for the value of the building, but did not pay any amount attributable to the land. Discuss whether decedent's estate can take an IRC § 2054 deduction for the loss of the apartment building, and if so to what extent.

ANSWER:

206. Decedent, an avid philanthropist during life, left a validly executed will in place. Which of the following bequests will qualify for a charitable deduction?

   **(A)** A bequest to a Catholic priest to purchase a car for himself.

   **(B)** A bequest to the University of Wyoming for educational use.

   **(C)** A bequest to the Democratic National Committee to fund a political campaign.

   **(D)** A bequest to a trust set up to fund a group that lobbies for stricter environmental laws.

207. Decedent passed away, leaving a validly executed will in place. Decedent was wealthy and always had a philanthropic mind-set. Which of the following alternative circumstances will most likely result in a $35,000 charitable deduction for the decedent's estate? Assume applicable state law does not prevent any of the following sets of circumstances from qualifying as a charitable contribution.

   **(A)** Decedent's will provided that "I give to my executor One Hundred Thousand ($100,000) Dollars, not subject to any trust, but in the hope that he will dispose of it at his absolute discretion, but giving due weight to any memoranda I may leave to him made during my life." Decedent left a memorandum indicating that he desired that $35,000 go to the United Way Charity. Consistent with the memorandum, the executor gave $35,000 to the United Way Charity.

   **(B)** Decedent's will provided that "I give $35,000 to Yale University, but this bequest will become effective only to the extent that my wife gives her express consent in writing and in the absence of such express consent the bequest shall be and is hereby revoked." Within six months after the decedent's death, the decedent's wife properly gave her express consent and the executors paid $35,000 to Yale University.

   **(C)** Decedent's will provided that "I give $35,000 to Mr. Byron T. Watson, a homeless person residing at the Helpful Homeless Shelter, 321 Hope Road, Los Angeles, CA." Within six months after the decedent's death, the executor of the decedent's estate paid $35,000 to Mr. Byron T. Watson.

   **(D)** Decedent's will provided that "I give to my executor One Hundred Thousand ($100,000) Dollars to dispose of in part or whole at his absolute discretion to one or more of the following charitable institutions: Yale University, United Way Charity, or the Roman Catholic Church. Among other distributions, the executor gave $35,000 to the United Way Charity.

**208.** Decedent passed away, survived by a son and a daughter and leaving a validly executed will in place. His estate was valued at $100,000,000 on the date of his death. While the decedent was wealthy and always had a philanthropic mind-set, he cared deeply for his two children and their financial well-being. The provisions of his will left a specific sum for his son. The rest of his assets were governed by the residuary clause, which provided that all the assets be held for the benefit of his daughter, income to her annually for life, remainder to the Red Cross (a qualified charitable organization) upon his daughter's death. Under which of the following alternative circumstances will the decedent's estate be allowed a charitable deduction in excess of the remainder interest to which the Red Cross is otherwise entitled?

    **(A)** Daughter instructed the executor to transfer to the Red Cross any income in excess of $1,000,000 that was due annually from her interest in the residuary assets.

    **(B)** Son executed a qualified disclaimer with respect to the specific bequest he received from his father.

    **(C)** Daughter instructed the executor of the decedent's estate that her share of income from the residuary should be paid to the Red Cross for the foreseeable future.

    **(D)** Daughter executed a qualified disclaimer with respect to all the decedent's property. In gratitude for her actions, the Red Cross appointed the decedent's daughter as president of the organization.

**209.** Decedent, Rose Cuadrez, passed away with a validly executed will. She was a wealthy person during life and, among other things, she owned an original Bustamante sculpture. She had purchased the sculpture for $1,000,000 in 1980 and on June 1, 2012, the date of her death, the sculpture was valued at $2,000,000 and was included in her estate. Under the provisions of her will, the sculpture was to be donated to National Museum of Art, a qualified charitable institution. On September 30, 2012, six months after the decedent's death but prior to distribution of the sculpture to the museum, the value of the Bustamante sculpture declined to $1,500,000. What amount of charitable deduction may the decedent's estate claim? Assume no IRC § 2032 election was made.

    **(A)** $2,000,000

    **(B)** $1,500,000

    **(C)** $1,000,000

    **(D)** No estate tax deduction allowed for contributions in kind

**210.** How, if at all, would your ANSWER to Question 209, above, change if the executor of the estate determined that on the aggregate it would be best if the estate made a § 2032 alternate valuation date election?

ANSWER:

211. Assume that the facts are the same as in question 209, above, except that instead of dying on June 1, 2012, Rose Cuadrez remained alive and gifted the sculpture to the National Museum of Art on that date? Assume Rose was at all times during her life a citizen and resident of the United States. What amount of gift tax deduction may Rose take?

   (A) $2,000,000

   (B) $1,500,000

   (C) $1,000,000

   (D) No gift tax deduction allowed for a gift in kind

212. Would your ANSWER to Question 211, above, change if Rose was neither a citizen nor a resident of the United States?

ANSWER:


213. During life the decedent owned a parcel of real property with a building on it, which he referred to as the "rental property." Decedent leased the property to various tenants from time to time, and tenants paid monthly rent. Upon the decedent's death in 2000, which of the following sets of circumstances will result in a charitable deduction for the decedent's estate?

   (A) In 1990, the decedent contributed the rental property to an irrevocable trust during his life, under which he was to receive the income during his life and upon his death the rental property would be distributed to a qualified charity.

   (B) Decedent's will provides that his brother will receive a life estate in the rental property and the remainder will pass to a charity.

   (C) Decedent's will provides that the rental property will be distributed to his brother if his brother survives him but if his brother is not then living, the property will pass to a qualified charity.

   (D) Decedent contributed the rental property to a trust that is to pay income to his sister for her life, remainder to the decedent's brother. Decedent's brother's will provides that all of his property will go to a qualified charity.

*Unless otherwise indicated assume that decedent and any surviving spouse are United States citizens.*

214. Hal seeks your advice as to whether his estate will receive a marital deduction for the following transfers to his spouse Sonja, who is a resident of the United States, but a citizen of Iceland. Indicate which transfers will qualify for the marital deduction.

   (A)　Hal's will gives Sonja the residue of his estate.

   (B)　Hal's will gives Sonja a limited power of appointment over his assets.

   (C)　Hal's will gives his property to the trustee of a qualified domestic trust for the benefit of Sonja.

   (D)　Hal names Sonja as life tenant of his real estate.

215. Discuss how Hal's outright gift to Sonja of $1,000,000 in cash will be treated for gift tax purposes. Again, assume Sonja is a U.S. resident and a citizen of Iceland.

ANSWER:

216. Henry and his wife Wendy were in a fatal automobile accident. Henry died at the scene. Wendy survived for 15 days before she died from her injuries. Henry's will transfers all property to Wendy, if she survives. Wendy's will transfers all property to Henry, if he survives. Indicate under which circumstance a marital deduction will be allowed for a gift to the surviving spouse.

   (A)　The wills of each spouse contain a clause requiring a beneficiary to survive the decedent by 30 days in order to take.

   (B)　Wendy's will deems Henry to survive in case of death as a result of a common accident.

   (C)　Henry's will deems Wendy to survive in the event of a simultaneous death.

   (D)　Neither will contains a survival clause. State law, however, requires a beneficiary to survive the decedent by 120 hours.

217. Samuel is survived by his wife Wylie. Indicate which of the following assets passing to Wylie as beneficiary will be deductible in full on Schedule M of Sam's estate tax return.

**(A)** Life insurance proceeds on a policy insuring Sam's life purchased and owned by Wylie and payable to her as beneficiary.

**(B)** Trust property over which Sam exercises a limited power of appointment to direct the property outright to Wylie.

**(C)** Bank account to which Samuel contributed all funds and held as joint tenants with right of survivorship.

**(D)** Property included in the gross estate that Wylie elects to receive under the state elective share statute.

218. Sara's will gives all of her property to her husband Hank. Which of the following assets is not eligible for a marital deduction?

**(A)** A patent which will continue in force for an additional 18 years from the date of Sara's death.

**(B)** The copyrights to artwork painted by Sara and owned by her as of her death.

**(C)** A life interest in undeveloped land created by Sara, with remainder passing to their children.

**(D)** The remaining payments owed to Sara on a ten year promissory note she holds after selling property on a contract for deed.

219. Cindy prefers not to pass her property outright to her spouse Sampo. Her goal is to provide for Sampo during his life, and pass any property remaining on Sampo's death to her children. She asks you to advise her as to alternatives for claiming a marital deduction. Which of the following alternatives best achieves her testamentary goals?

**(A)** A qualified terminable interest property trust.

**(B)** A general power of appointment marital trust.

**(C)** An estate trust.

**(D)** A charitable remainder unitrust.

220. Which of the following trusts can both qualify for a marital deduction and avoid triggering an estate tax on the surviving spouse's death?

**(A)** A qualified terminable interest property trust.

**(B)** A general power of appointment marital trust.

**(C)** An estate trust.

**(D)** A charitable remainder unitrust.

221. Which of the following marital deduction qualifying trusts allows surviving spouse the

greatest control over trust assets during her life?

**(A)** A qualified terminable interest property trust.

**(B)** A general power of appointment marital trust.

**(C)** An estate trust.

**(D)** A charitable remainder unitrust.

222. Which of the following marital deduction qualifying trusts best accommodates non-income producing property that decedent intends should be held by trustee and not sold or reinvested in income producing property?

**(A)** A qualified terminable interest property trust.

**(B)** A general power of appointment marital trust.

**(C)** An estate trust.

**(D)** A charitable remainder trust.

223. Indicate the reason why interests passing pursuant to a qualified terminable interest property or QTIP trust require a special exception in order to qualify for the marital deduction.

**(A)** Absent a special provision, the interest would be deemed a nondeductible terminable interest.

**(B)** Absent a special provision, the interest would be deemed not to pass from decedent to surviving spouse.

**(C)** Absent a special provision the interest would not be includible in the surviving spouse's gross estate.

**(D)** All of the above.

224. Hally wants to be certain that assets passing on her death to a qualified terminable interest property trust qualify for the marital deduction in the event her executor decides to make a QTIP election. Which of the following provisions should not be included in the trust given Hally's wishes.

**(A)** Trustee may pay all income and so much of the principal to Hally's spouse as necessary for his support.

**(B)** Hally's spouse may appoint principal to those of Hally's descendants as he desires.

**(C)** Hally's executor may choose to pass property either to a credit shelter exempt trust or to the QTIP trust on Hally's death.

    **(D)** Trustee may appoint property remaining in trust at the death of Hally's spouse among Hally's descendants.

225. Matthew intends to create a general power of appointment marital trust qualifying under IRC § 2056(b)(5) in his will for the benefit of his spouse. Assume that the trust requires all income be paid at least annually to Matthew's spouse. Which of the following powers will not meet the requirements of that section?

    **(A)** During her life, by written instrument delivered to trustee, Matthew's spouse may direct trustee to distribute to her so much of the trust property as she requests.

    **(B)** By provision in her will, Matthew's spouse may direct trustee to distribute so much of the trust income and principal remaining in trust to the executor of her estate.

    **(C)** By provision in her will, Matthew's spouse may direct trustee to distribute so much of the trust income and principal remaining in trust to or among her descendents.

    **(D)** During her life, the trustee may distribute income and or principal of the trust to or among her descendants.

226. Pam owns a policy of insurance on her life. She would like to obtain a marital deduction for life insurance proceeds payable to her husband Brent, but would like to choose a payout option that provides payment to Brent in installments. Discuss whether the proceeds will be eligible for a marital deduction on Pam's estate tax return.

ANSWER:

227. Indicate which, if any, of the following sections of the Internal Revenue Code have been enacted for the sole purpose of ensuring that the interest of the surviving spouse in a trust qualifying for the marital deduction will be included in the gross estate of the surviving spouse.

    **(A)** IRC §§ 2044 and 2519.

    **(B)** IRC §§ 2041 and 2514.

    **(C)** IRC §§ 2033 and 2513.

    **(D)** No such sections are necessary and none have been enacted.

228. Analyze whether property passing pursuant to the following clause may be eligible for the marital deduction: "All my property shall pass to my spouse provided that she survives me by six months. If my spouse does not survive me by six months, all my property shall pass to my descendants by representation."

ANSWER:

## GENERATION-SKIPPING TRANSFER TAX BASICS

229. Hank Stern has reached his fifty-seventh birthday, and he has done well for himself financially over the last half century in the oil industry. He decides this is the year to loosen up his historically tight purse strings for his family and close friends. So, he invites everyone to his house for a big banquet. After dinner Hank stands up, dings one tine of his fork on his crystal wine glass, and begins to announce various gifts to the lucky recipients. Hank announces that the following recipients will each receive $50,000, and sends his favorite niece out into the room to deliver the checks. Which of the following recipients is a "skip person" for purposes of the generation-skipping transfer (GST) tax?

   **(A)** Hank's mother, who is now 75 years old.

   **(B)** Hank's son's daughter Miley, who is now 18.

   **(C)** Hank's grandfather, who is now 95 years old.

   **(D)** Hank's daughter, who is now 40 years old.

230. Would your answer to Question 229, above, change if Hank had legally adopted his son and daughter and Hank's son had legally adopted his 18 year old daughter?

ANSWER:

231. Assume the same facts as in Question 229, above. Which of the following recipients is a "skip person" for purposes of the GST tax?

   **(A)** Hank's brother, who is now 56 years old.

   **(B)** Hank's cousin, who is now 57 years old.

   **(C)** Hank's niece, who is now 30 years old.

   **(D)** Hank's niece's daughter, who is now seven years old.

232. Hank has a stepbrother named Harley. Hank announces that he will give $1,000,000 to Harley's grandson. Is Harley's grandson a "skip person"?

ANSWER:

233. Assume the same facts as in Question 229, above. Which of the following recipients is a

"skip person" for purposes of the GST tax?

(A)  Hank's friend, who is now 43 years old.

(B)  Hank's third cousin, who is now 55 years old.

(C)  Hank's second cousin, who is now 17 years old.

(D)  Hank's friend's daughter, who is now 25 years old.

234.  How, if at all, would your answer to Question 233, above, change if answer option (D) provided that Hank's friend's daughter was 17 years old and Hank was now married to her?

ANSWER:

235.  Which of the following transfers to a trust is a transfer to a "skip person" for purposes of the generation-skipping transfer (GST) tax?

(A)  Hank's will establishes a testamentary trust with income payable to his granddaughter for a period of 10 years, remainder to Hank's wife.

(B)  During life, Hank establishes an irrevocable trust under which income is to be paid to Hank's son for life. On the death of Hank's son, principal is to be paid to Hank's granddaughter.

(C)  Hank's will establishes a testamentary trust under which the income is to be paid to Hank's wife for life and the remainder is to be paid to Hank's granddaughter.

(D)  During life, Hank establishes an irrevocable trust under which income is to be paid to his son for life, and he also gives his son power to appoint who takes the remainder. Son appoints the remainder to Hank's granddaughter.

236.  Hank asks your advice as to the maximum amount he can give to "skip persons" at the banquet without actually paying GST tax. Advise him. For purposes of this question assume Hank has not made any prior gifts or transfers that could be subject to gift or generation-skipping transfer tax.

(A)  $5 million and, in addition, the amount of the gift tax annual exclusion times the number of donees.

(B)  Up to the basic exclusion amount (as indexed for inflation).

(C)  Up to the basic exclusion amount (as indexed for inflation) and, in addition, the amount of the gift tax annual exclusion times the number of donees.

(D)  Hank's applicable exclusion amount and, in addition, the amount of the gift tax annual exclusion times the number of donees.

237.  For purposes of this question assume that in 2012 Hank makes a taxable gift of $2 million

to his granddaughter in the form of an outright cash transfer that is a direct skip. Also assume Hank has remaining $1 million of GST exemption. Hank allocates his remaining GST exemption to the direct skip. Indicate the inclusion ratio for the GST transfer.

**(A)**  Zero.

**(B)**  One-half.

**(C)**  One.

**(D)**  A direct skip does not have an inclusion ratio.

238.  Hank asks you what tax rate will apply to determine the GST tax owed on the direct skip in Question 237. Indicate the tax rate.

**(A)**  Hank's marginal gift tax rate, 35%.

**(B)**  The highest marginal estate tax rate, 35%.

**(C)**  The inclusion ratio, 50%.

**(D)**  The applicable rate, 17.5%.

239.  Determine the GST tax that Hank will owe on the direct skip to his granddaughter.

ANSWER:


240.  For purposes of this question assume that Hank has fully used his gift tax applicable exclusion amount, and that he will need to pay gift tax on the direct gift to his granddaughter. Determine the amount of gift tax that Hank will owe with respect to the gift made in Question 237.

ANSWER:


241.  Hank creates a trust during life with income payable to his daughter Mona for life with the remainder to Miley, his granddaughter. Under which of the following circumstances, if any, will a taxable termination occur?

**(A)**  Mona dies.

**(B)**  Mona receives a distribution from the trust and transfers the distribution to Miley.

**(C)**  During Mona's lifetime, Miley receives a distribution from the trustee of the trust.

**(D)**  A taxable termination does not occur under any of the above situations.

242.  Hank creates a trust during life with income payable to his daughter Mona for life and,

upon Mona's death, Mona has the power to appoint the remainder to anyone, including her own estate. Mona's will provides that all of her assets go to Miley upon Mona's death. Under which of the following circumstances, if any, will a taxable termination occur?

**(A)** Mona dies.

**(B)** During Mona's lifetime, Mona receives a distribution from the trust and transfers it to Miley.

**(C)** During Mona's lifetime, Miley receives a distribution from the trustee of the trust.

**(D)** A taxable termination does not occur under any of the above situations.

243. Hank has decided his favorite child is Mona and his favorite grandchild is Miley. Under which of the following sets of circumstances will a taxable distribution occur?

**(A)** Hank creates a trust for Miley for her life, with the remainder to be paid to Mona when Miley dies. Miley passes away, and the remainder of the trust is distributed to Mona.

**(B)** Hank creates a trust, income payable to Mona for life, remainder to be paid to Miley when Mona dies. Mona passes away, and the remainder of the trust is distributed to Miley.

**(C)** Hank creates a trust, income payable to Mona for life. When Miley turns 18, she is to receive half of the trust principal. The remaining principal is to be distributed to Miley upon Mona's death. While Mona remains alive, Miley turns 18 and receives distribution of one-half of the principal.

**(D)** None of the above qualifies as a taxable distribution.

# PRACTICE FINAL EXAM: QUESTIONS

**Facts for Questions 1 and 2.**

In 1976, Congress maintained a system in which the applicable rates, credits and amounts exempted from both estate and gift taxation were "unified" or the same. In 2001, Congress "deunified" the system which provided for declining rates and a maximum gift tax exemption of $1,000,000 but allowing the estate tax exemption to increase over time to $3,500,000 in 2009. In 2010, the estate tax rate was reduced to zero, effectively repealing the estate tax and a carryover basis system was available.

1. As of 2010, which of the following statements best describes the estate and gift taxation system?

   (A) The system is unified as to the amount of estate and gift tax exclusions, applicable credits and the rates that apply to aggregate amounts transferred during life and at death.

   (B) The system is unified as to the amount of estate and gift tax exclusions and applicable credits but the rate schedules apply separately to lifetime transfers and transfers at death.

   (C) Different applicable estate and gift tax exclusion amounts, different applicable credits, but the same progressive rate schedule based on aggregate lifetime and death time transfers.

   (D) Different applicable estate and gift tax exclusion amounts, the same applicable credit, and different progressive rate schedules based separately on aggregate lifetime transfers and aggregate death time transfers.

2. As of 2011, which of the following statements best describes the estate and gift taxation system?

   (A) The system is unified as to the amount of estate and gift tax exclusions, applicable credits and the rates that apply to aggregate amounts transferred during life and at death.

   (B) The system is unified as to the amount of estate and gift tax exclusions and applicable credits but the rate schedules apply separately to lifetime transfers and transfers at death.

   (C) Different applicable estate and gift tax exclusion amounts, different applicable credits, but the same progressive rate schedule based on aggregate lifetime and death time transfers.

**(D)** Different applicable estate and gift tax exclusion amounts, the same applicable credit, and different progressive rate schedules based separately on aggregate lifetime transfers and aggregate death time transfers.

**Facts for Questions 3 & 4.**

Clayton, an unmarried United States citizen and resident, had previous to 2009 not made any taxable gifts. Clayton made a taxable gift to his daughter on February 1, 2009 of $950,000. He also made a taxable gift to his son on June 1, 2011, of $4,050,000.

3.  Based on the above facts, calculate the amount of federal gift tax owed by Clayton on the 2009 taxable gift.

ANSWER:

4.  Based on the above facts, calculate the amount of federal gift tax owed by Clayton on the 2011 taxable gift.

ANSWER:

5.  Each year, Adeline made annual exclusion gifts of cash to her 10 grandchildren. By the time Adeline died she had transferred $2.2 million in annual exclusion gifts to her grandchildren. In addition she had made a taxable gift of $2.5 million in 2012 to an irrevocable trust. Adeline died in 2012 with a taxable estate of $3.7 million. Calculate federal estate tax owed by Adeline.

ANSWER:

6.  Ally, a successful entrepreneur, transfers real estate to a trust. Under the terms of the trust, the remainder of the trust property is to be received by Ally's long time friend Macy upon Ally's death. Ally passes away 30 years later. Which, if any, of the following trust provisions will not cause the assets to be included in Ally's estate under IRC § 2036?

    **(A)** Ally retains the right to receive trust income for the remainder of her life.

    **(B)** Ally retains the right to receive trust income for a term of 15 years after which income is to be distributed to Macy.

    **(C)** Ally retains the right to receive trust income and principle when needed for life.

    **(D)** All of the above provisions will cause the assets to be included in Ally's estate upon her death under IRC § 2036.

7.  Ellen, who is in good health, transfers all of her rental real property into a family limited partnership, the "FLP." She retains her home and sufficient assets to support herself for the remainder of her expected life. One month after formation of the FLP, Ellen transfers her 2 percent general partnership interest one-half to each of her two sons. Ellen also

transfers equal shares of limited partnership interests to her two sons up to her maximum $1 million applicable gift tax exclusion amount. She retains only a 20 percent limited partnership interest. The terms of the FLP agreement indicate that distributions will be made in proportion to the value of partnership interests held by each partner. When Ellen's sons take over management of the limited partnership, they continue to annually distribute 100 percent of the partnership income and distributions to Ellen during her life. Ellen dies survived by her two sons. Indicate the extent to which the limited partnership interests and the FLP assets will be included in Ellen's gross estate.

(A) Ellen's gross estate will include 20 percent of the value of the limited partnership interests retained by Ellen.

(B) Ellen's gross estate will include 20 percent of the value of the assets held by the FLP.

(C) Ellen's gross estate will include 100 percent of the value of all limited partnership interests held by both Ellen and her two sons.

(D) Ellen's gross estate will include 100 percent of the value of the assets held by the FLP.

8. Heidi and her sister Ingrid each paid 50 percent of the purchase price for a rental property. At the time of purchase, they took title as joint tenant with right of survivorship on the deed. Heidi dies in 2011 and is survived by Ingrid. Ingrid dies 30 days later. What portion of the rental property is included in Heidi's gross estate, and what portion is included in Ingrid's gross estate?

(A) Fifty percent of the rental property value is included in each of Heidi's and Ingrid's gross estates.

(B) Fifty percent of the rental property value is included in Heidi's gross estate and 100 percent of the rental property value is included in Ingrid's gross estate.

(C) Fifty percent of the rental property value is included in Heidi's gross estate and 75 percent of the rental property value is included in Ingrid's gross estate.

(D) Fifty percent of the rental property value is included in Heidi's gross estate and none of the rental property value is included in Ingrid's gross estate.

9. Assume the same facts as in Question 8 preceding. Also assume that both Heidi and Ingrid die with a taxable estate. After required adjustments under IRC § 2013, the portion of Heidi's estate tax attributable to inclusion of 50 percent of the rental property value in her gross estate equals $50,000. Also, after required adjustments under IRC § 2013, the portion of Ingrid's estate tax attributable to inclusion of the 50 percent rental property interest received from Heidi equals $30,000. Indicate the amount of tax on prior transfers credit, if any, allowable to Ingrid's estate.

(A) None.

(B) $30,000.

    **(C)**   $50,000.

    **(D)**   $60,000.

**10.**   Kyle is trustee of a trust created by his mother. As trustee, Kyle may use trust property for his support in reasonable comfort. On his death, Kyle may appoint any remaining property held in trust among his surviving descendants. In the absence of an exercise of the power of appointment, the remaining trust property passes to named charities. Kyle dies without exercising the power of appointment to direct property at death to his surviving descendants. Will Kyle's gross estate include any of the trust property, and why or why not?

    **(A)**   Yes, Kyle's gross estate will include trust property because Kyle may use property to satisfy a legal obligation of support to himself.

    **(B)**   Yes, Kyle's gross estate will include trust property because Kyle holds a general power of appointment to distribute trust property at his death among his descendants.

    **(C)**   No, Kyle's gross estate will not include trust property because Kyle did not exercise the power of appointment held at his death.

    **(D)**   No, Kyle's gross estate will not include trust property because Kyle's lifetime power was subject to an ascertainable standard, and at death Kyle could not direct property to his estate or his creditors.

**11.**   In 2011, Lannie purchases $1,000,000 of life insurance on her own life, and names her child as beneficiary of the policy. The policy is a whole life policy. Later that year Lannie transfers ownership of the policy to her child at a time when the policy's cash surrender value is $15,000 and the policy's terminal interpolated reserve value is $12,000. Lannie does not retain any rights to the policy following its transfer. Lannie dies in 2012. Indicate whether any portion of the policy proceeds will be included in Lannie's gross estate, and why.

    **(A)**   None of the policy proceeds will be included in Lannie's gross estate because the proceeds are not payable to her estate, and Lannie could not exercise any incidents of ownership over the policy proceeds at her death.

    **(B)**   $3,000 of the proceeds are included in Lannie's gross estate because the value of taxable gifts made within three years of Lannie's death must be included in her gross estate.

    **(C)**   $15,000 of the proceeds are included in Lannie's gross estate because the full value of gifts made within three years of Lannie's death must be included in her gross estate.

    **(D)**   $1,000,000 of the proceeds are included in Lannie's gross estate because Lannie transferred the policy within three years of her death, and in absence of the transfer the proceeds would have been included in her gross estate.

**12.** Discuss whether Lannie could have avoided application of IRC § 2035 by structuring the purchase of the policy in a different manner.

ANSWER:

**13.** The following claims and expenses were incurred following Marvin's death. Indicate which of the following claims and expenses are deductible by Marvin's estate.

(A) Expenses incurred for a reception held one month after Marvin's death to thank friends for their efforts in assisting Marvin during his bout with cancer.

(B) The maximum statutorily allowed personal representative fee allowable under state law, even though Marvin's brother, who was personal representative of Marvin's estate, declined to take the full allowable fee.

(C) Claim timely filed against the probate estate by Marvin's child for payment of an outstanding $5,000 promissory note, payable by Marvin to child in exchange for child's promise to attend college.

(D) Past due property tax that had become due and payable by Marvin prior to his date of death on property owned by him and included in his gross estate.

**14.** Nancy owned patent rights that paid substantial royalties, but were scheduled to expire under federal law in 10 years. On Nancy's death, the patent rights passed to a trust for the benefit of her spouse Omar if he survived her by 30 days. Pursuant to the trust, Omar was to receive all trust income at least annually. On Omar's death, any remaining trust property was to pass as Omar appoints among Nancy's children, and in absence of appointment, to a named charity. Can Nancy's estate claim a marital deduction for the patent rights passing to the trust for the benefit of Omar, and, if so, how?

(A) Yes, Nancy's estate can claim a marital deduction for the value of property passing in trust for the benefit of Omar by electing to treat the trust as a qualified terminable interest property (QTIP) trust.

(B) Yes, Nancy's estate can claim a marital deduction for the value of property passing in trust for the benefit of Omar by electing to treat the trust as a general power of appointment trust.

(C) No, Nancy's estate cannot claim a marital deduction for the value of property passing in trust because Omar's interest is dependent on whether or not he survives Nancy for 30 days.

(D) No, Nancy's estate cannot claim a marital deduction for the value of property passing in trust because the property is a nondeductible terminable interest.

**15.** Indicate which of the following constitutes a taxable gift by Peter:

**(A)** Peter transfers $7 million of property to an irrevocable trust for his four nieces, and retains the right as trustee to make discretionary distributions of income and principal among his nieces as he sees fit.

**(B)** Peter transfers $7 million of property to an irrevocable trust for the benefit of his nephew. The nephew is to receive all income from the trust until he attains age 25, at which time remaining trust property is to be paid to the nephew, or if he is not then living, to his estate. Peter retains discretion to pay income to nephew prior to the date that the nephew attains age 25.

**(C)** Peter transfers $7million of property to his revocable trust. The trust directs trustee to pay income and principal, in its discretion, for the benefit of Peter and his children.

**(D)** Peter names his child as beneficiary of a $7 million life insurance policy.

16.    Will Quincy have made a completed gift if Quincy transfers property to an irrevocable trust, and retains the power as trustee to pay income and principal to his friend Opal for her support, with any remaining trust property passing to Opal's children upon her death? Explain your answer.

ANSWER:

17.    On November 10, 2011, Penelope transfers $10,000 to Bank as trustee of an irrevocable trust. The trust terms grant her 25-year-old son Rylan the right to annually withdraw up to the lesser of the annual transfer to the trust or $10,000. Rylan's withdrawal right terminates 30 days following the date that Penelope makes the transfer to the trust. The trust terms require Bank to notify Rylan of his withdrawal right immediately upon receipt of any transfer to the trust. To the extent Rylan does not exercise his withdrawal right, the trust requires Bank to hold the property for the benefit of Rylan for his life, and upon his death to terminate the trust and distribute remaining trust property to Rylan's then-living descendants, per stirpes. During Rylan's life, Bank has discretion to pay income and principal for Rylan's support in reasonable comfort. Is the $10,000 transfer by Penelope to the trust a taxable gift, and why or why not?

**(A)** Yes. The $10,000 transfer to the trust is a taxable gift by Penelope because Rylan's withdrawal right exceeds the greater of $5,000 or 5 percent of the trust assets.

**(B)** Yes. The $10,000 transfer to the trust is a taxable gift because a substance-over-form analysis negates the availability of an annual exclusion where it is anticipated the power holder will never exercise the withdrawal right.

**(C)** Perhaps. The $10,000 transfer to the trust is a taxable gift by Penelope only if Rylan fails to exercise his withdrawal right because the property subject to the lapsed withdrawal right would then be a future and not a present interest in Rylan's hands.

**(D)** No. The $10,000 transfer to the trust is not a taxable gift because the withdrawal right, regardless of its exercise, provides Rylan a present interest in the transferred money sufficient to qualify for the gift tax annual exclusion.

18. Assume the same facts as in the preceding Question 17. If Rylan allows the withdrawal right to lapse, will Rylan make a taxable transfer, and, if so, in what amount?

   (A) Yes. Rylan will be deemed to make a taxable transfer of $10,000.

   (B) Yes. Rylan will be deemed to make a taxable transfer of $5,000.

   (C) Yes. Rylan will be deemed to make a taxable transfer of $500.

   (D) No. Rylan will not be deemed to make a taxable transfer.

19. Jerry, who is 37 years old, gives $20,000 to each of the below listed persons. Which of the following recipients is a "skip person" for purposes of the generation skipping transfer (GST) tax?

   (A) Jerry's mother, who is now 55 years old.

   (B) Jerry's nephew's son Jason, who is now 27.

   (C) Jerry's grandfather, who is now 75 years old.

   (D) Jerry's daughter, who is now 20 years old.

20. Mary is 60 years old. Mary creates a trust during life with income payable to her daughter Nancy for life with the remainder to Judy, her granddaughter. Under which of the following circumstances, if any, will a taxable termination occur?

   (A) Nancy receives a distribution from the trust and transfers the distribution to Judy.

   (B) During Nancy's lifetime, Judy receives a distribution from the trustee of the trust.

   (C) Nancy dies.

   (D) A taxable termination does not occur under any of the above situations.

21. Frank seeks to set up a trust for the benefit of his daughter, Martine, and his grandson Einer. Under which of the following sets of circumstances will a taxable distribution occur?

   (A) Frank creates a trust for Martine for her life with the remainder to be paid to Einer when Martine dies. Martine passes away and the remainder of the trust is distributed to Einer.

   (B) Frank creates a trust income to Einer for life, remainder to be paid to Martine when Einer dies. Einer passes away and the remainder of the trust is distributed to Martine.

   (C) Frank creates a trust income payable to Martine for life. When Einer turns 18, he is to receive half of the trust principal. The remaining principal is to be distributed to Einer upon Martine's death. While Martine remains alive, Einer turns 18 and receives distribution of one-half of the principal.

**(D)** None of the above qualifies as a taxable distribution.

# ANSWERS

*Except where otherwise indicated, the answers provided assume the donor or decedent is a U.S. citizen or resident, and any beneficiary also is a U.S. citizen. Subject to applicable treaties, federal wealth transfer taxes apply to all property owned worldwide by a U.S. citizen. Separate wealth transfer tax rules apply to nonresident aliens.*

1.      **Answer (D) is the correct answer.** The federal estate tax focuses on the transfer of property owned by the decedent. The tax is imposed on the transfer of the "taxable estate" of a deceased U.S. citizen or resident. IRC § 2001(a). Taxable estate is the aggregate value of all property included in the gross estate less applicable deductions. IRC § 2051. Generally, a federal estate tax is paid only to the extent that the aggregate value of property transferred by decedent, including that transferred during life and at death, exceeds a specified amount, called the applicable exclusion amount. Beginning in 2011 the applicable exclusion amount is comprised of the basic exclusion amount as indexed by inflation plus the deceased spousal unused exclusion amount. The basic exclusion amount is $5 million, indexed for inflation beginning in 2012. The deceased spousal unused exclusion amount is essentially the unused exclusion amount of the last deceased spouse. Thus, the amount a taxpayer may pass tax free will fluctuate from year to year. Because the estate tax focuses on the amount transferred from decedent, Answer (D) is correct.

     **Answers (B) and (C) are incorrect.** An inheritance tax, also sometimes called a succession tax, focuses instead on the right to receive property by a beneficiary. The rate of inheritance tax depends on the relationship of a beneficiary to decedent, and the amount of property received by the beneficiary. Typically, inheritance tax exempts property received by a surviving spouse. It taxes at a lower rate that property received by children, and at a higher rate that property received by more remote relatives and friends. Inheritance, legacy, and succession taxes are often imposed by the various states and the District of Columbia.

     **Answer (A) is incorrect.** It refers to the tax imposed by states prior to repeal of the state death tax credit under former IRC § 2011. For estates of decedents dying prior to 2005, the federal estate tax allowed for a state death tax credit up to an amount as calculated under IRC § 2011(b) provided that amount was paid to the state as an estate, inheritance, legacy or succession tax. States, thus, enacted state estate taxes in the amount of the federal credit for state death taxes. The state estate tax picked up or soaked up the amount of the federal credit.

2.      **Answer (C) is the correct answer.** IRC § 2001(a) imposes a tax on the "taxable estate of every decedent who is a citizen or resident of the United States." Nonresidents, who are not U.S. citizens, are subject to tax on that part of the gross estate "situated in the United States." IRC §§ 2101, 2203. The specific estate tax rules applicable to nonresident aliens are beyond the scope of the book. The gross estate of a U.S. citizen or resident includes the value of all property of the decedent "wherever situated." IRC § 2031(a); Treas. Reg. 20.0-2(a)(2). **For this same reason, Answers (A), (B), and (D) are incorrect.**

3. **Answer (B) is the correct answer.** The generation skipping transfer tax exemption is equal to the basic exclusion amount for purposes of the federal estate tax. IRC § 2631(c). The federal estate tax applicable exclusion amount, which determines the amount of taxable transfers an individual may make in the aggregate during life and at death, beginning in 2011 is comprised of two amounts: (1) the basic exclusion amount and (2) the deceased spousal unused exclusion (DSUE) amount. IRC § 2010(c). The basic exclusion amount is $5 million as that amount is indexed for inflation beginning in 2012. *Id.* As of 2012, the DSUE amount is the amount of the last deceased spouse's unused basic exclusion amount. *Id.* The applicable exclusion amount, thus, differs from the generation skipping transfer tax exemption. The rate schedule for the federal estate and gift tax is the same, and reaches a flat effective rate of 35% after an initial progressive rate schedule up to $500,000 in assets. The GST tax rate for purposes of determining the applicable rate of tax for GST purposes is the highest marginal estate tax rate, which is 35%. Thus, the best answer is Answer (B) in light of the fact that the basic exclusion amount and the generation skipping transfer exemption are the same amount, and the effective marginal tax rate is the same for all three taxes. **For that same reason, Answer (A) is incorrect. Answers (C) and (D) are incorrect** because the applicable exclusion amount can differ from the generation skipping transfer tax exemption. In addition, the annual exclusion amount is not applied in the same manner for generation skipping transfer tax purposes as for gift tax purposes.

4. **Answer (B) is correct.** The question asks what amount can pass free of all three taxes — gift, estate, and generation skipping transfer. As explained in Question 3 preceding, the GST exemption is limited to the basic exclusion amount, as indexed for inflation beginning in 2012. Under the federal estate and gift taxes, an individual can pass free of tax at least the basic exclusion amount. Because the basic exclusion amount of $5 million is indexed for inflation, **Answer (A) is incorrect.** The applicable exclusion amount can exceed the basic exclusion amount when the surviving spouse is entitled to a DSUE amount. Thus, **Answers (C) and (D) are incorrect.**

5. **Answer (D) is the best answer.** The transfer made by Mike to a trust for his niece Lois during his life will be subject to gift taxation, and likely will fully use his applicable exclusion amount, and as a result his unified credit.

   One of the respects in which the gift and estate tax are not unified is the tax exclusive nature of the gift tax (where the assets used to pay gift tax owed are not subject to gift tax) and the tax inclusive nature of the estate tax (where estate tax is paid on the assets used to pay the estate tax). In order to avoid death bed gifts for the purpose of taking advantage of the tax exclusive nature of the gift tax, Congress enacted IRC § 2035(b) which includes in the gross estate gift tax paid on certain gifts made within three years of death. Thus, because Mike made the gift to Lois within three years of death, IRC § 2035(b) will include in the gross estate the gift tax paid on the transfer to the trust. Thus, the estate tax will also be implicated.

   Finally, there is the potential for property to skip payment of estate tax on Lois' death, and pass to Lois' descendants. The generation skipping transfer tax, however, generally prevents this from occurring at least to the amount in excess of any allocated generation skipping transfer tax exemption. The generation skipping transfer tax ensures that a tax on the transfer of property is assessed at each generation to the extent a transferor makes transfers in excess of the applicable exclusion amount.

Thus, all three taxes — gift, estate, and generation skipping transfer — potentially apply to Mike's $10 million transfer to the trust for Lois' benefit; therefore, **Answer (D) is the best answer,** and **Answers (A), (B), and (C) are incorrect.**

6.    The gift tax is said to work as a "backstop" to the estate tax because, absent a gift tax, taxpayers who are able to anticipate the moment of death could transfer all assets during life and completely avoid payment of estate tax. The GST tax also works as a "backstop" to the estate tax by ensuring that transfer of property in excess of the GST exemption will incur transfer tax at each generational level. It is designed to avoid the ability to skip a "generation" of tax. Absent the GST tax, assets could be held in trust for many generations and escape any type of transfer tax following taxation of the initial transfer to trust. These taxes also work as a "backstop" to the income tax by discouraging transfers to persons in lower income tax brackets.

7.    **Answer (C) is the best answer.** One of the principal reasons for encouraging a taxpayer to make significant life time transfers of property is the possibility of excluding appreciation inhering in the asset following the transfer from estate taxation in the transferor's hands. Thus, the lake home which will rapidly appreciate in value should be the choice of asset to give. **For this same reason, Answer (B) is incorrect.**

If the donor anticipates the need to retain use of an asset, the asset should not be transferred for the purpose of achieving transfer tax savings. For example, if the donor must use income from the assets, such as the rents from the apartment building, or will need to continue to use the assets, such as Barbara's need to occupy the home, the donor will not be able to relinquish all rights to income and enjoyment of the assets as is necessary to escape inclusion in the donor's gross estate for estate tax purposes. IRC § 2036 would require such inclusion if the donor either expressly retained the right to income or to use the transferred asset, or if the donor impliedly retained such right as evidenced by the fact that she continued to avail herself of the income or continued to occupy the asset. **For this reason, Answers (A) and (D) are incorrect.**

**Questions 8 through 10.** Questions 8 through 10 demonstrate the interaction between the federal estate and gift taxes. The federal gift tax applies on an annual basis. Section 2502(a) of the Code provides the formula for calculation of federal gift tax. Based on 2010 taxable gifts of $500,000, Allan does not owe any gift tax for 2010 gifts. Note that taxable gifts do not include transfers subject to the gift tax annual exclusion amount of $10,000, as that amount is indexed for inflation. The 2010 federal gift tax is determined as follows pursuant to the calculation set forth in IRC § 2502(a).

8.    **Calculation of gift tax for 2010:**

| | | |
|---|---|---|
| Taxable gifts for current year: | $500,000 | |
| *Plus*, sum of taxable gifts for all prior years: | 0 | |
| *Equals*, sum of all taxable gifts: | $500,000 | |
| Tentative tax on aggregate taxable gifts | | $155,800 |
| Sum of taxable gifts for all prior years | $0 | |
| *Less*, Tentative tax on gifts for all prior years | | $0 |
| Applicable gift tax credit: | $330,800 | |

| | | |
|---|---:|---:|
| *Less*: Amount of credit used in prior years | 0 | |
| *Equals*: Allowable credit for current year | $330,800 | |
| *Less*, Allowable credit for current year: | | $155,800 |
| *Equals*,Gift tax owed for current year: | $0 | |

*Explanation of Calculation*: IRC § 2502(a) first computes a tentative tax on all taxable gifts, including the current-year gifts and all prior-year gifts. It then computes a tentative tax only on all prior-year gifts. The difference between the two amounts reflects the tentative gift tax attributable to gifts for the current year prior to application of the gift tax applicable credit. This calculation ensures the current year's gift bears tax at the highest applicable tax rate based on cumulative lifetime transfers. Note that the tax rate schedule set forth under IRC § 2001(c) applies to determine the gift tax, and that it is based on current rates. Also note that with the 2010 amendments, this manner of calculating the gift tax is no longer in fact necessary because gifts once taxable are all taxed at the same marginal rate. Congress nevertheless preserved the prior method used for calculation of gift tax.

The gift tax calculation also keeps track of the amount of credit used in prior years, so that only the amount of unused credit is available to offset current year's gift tax. IRC § 2505(a). The maximum gift tax credit allowable equals the amount of tax that would be imposed on the applicable exclusion amount based on current gift tax rates.

*Note on Payment of Gift Tax:* Taxpayers determine any gift tax owed on an annual basis. Gift tax returns must be filed by April 15 following the calendar year for which the gift tax is due. IRC § 6075(b)(1). An automatic extension of time to file may be granted for up to six months. IRC § 6081. The donor bears liability for the tax. IRC § 2502(c). However, if the donor fails to pay the tax, the donee becomes liable for payment under a theory of transferee liability. IRC § 6324(b).

9. **Calculation of Gift Tax for 2011.**

| | | |
|---|---:|---:|
| Taxable gifts for current year: | $5,000,000 | |
| *Plus*, sum of taxable gifts for all prior years: | 500,000 | |
| *Equals*, sum of all taxable gifts: | $5,500,000 | |
| Tentative tax on aggregate taxable gifts | | $1,905,800 |
| Sum of taxable gifts for all prior years | $500,000 | |
| *Less*, Tentative tax on gifts for all prior years | | $155,800 |
| Tentative tax owed on current gifts | | $1,750,000 |
| Applicable gift tax credit: | $1,730,800 | |
| *Less*: Amount of credit used in prior years | 155,800 | |
| *Equals*: Allowable credit for current year | $1,575,000 | |
| *Less*, Allowable credit for current year: | | $1,575,000 |
| *Equals*,Gift tax owed for current year: | | $175,000 |

10. **Calculation of Estate Tax with 2012 Date of Death.** Section 2001(b) of the Code provides the formula for calculating federal estate tax. Based on that formula, Allan's estate owes $658,000 in federal estate tax.

The formula aggregates lifetime and death-time transfers for the purpose of applying the progressive rate schedule (which now essentially levels off at a flat 35% for every dollar subject to tax). Specifically, the calculation aggregates the "taxable estate" and "adjusted taxable gifts." IRC § 2001(b). Section 2051 defines "taxable estate" as the gross estate less the deductions allowable against the estate tax. "Adjusted taxable gifts," pursuant to IRC § 2001(b), means the taxable gifts made by decedent after December 31, 1976, other than those gifts includible in the gross estate.

| | | |
|---|---:|---:|
| Amount of taxable estate: | $2,000,000 | |
| *Plus*, Amount of adjusted taxable gifts: | 5,500,000 | |
| *Equals*, Aggregate transfer | $7,500,000 | |
| Tentative tax on aggregate transfers | | $2,605,800 |
| Amount of adjusted taxable gifts | $5,500,000 | |
| *Less*: Tax on adjusted taxable gifts | | $175,000 |
| *Equals*: Tentative estate tax: | | $2,430,800 |
| *Less*: Estate tax applicable credit amount | | 1,772,800 |
| *Equals*: Federal estate tax owed | | $658,000 |

*Explanation of Calculation:* Section 2001(b) of the Code requires a determination of tentative tax based on the aggregate of lifetime and death-time transfers. The tentative tax is based on aggregate transfers in order to be sure that the appropriate progressive rate applies. Subtracted from the tentative tax is the tax that would have been paid on adjusted taxable gifts based on the rate schedule as of the decedent's death applied at the time of the gifts. By subtracting the amount of gift tax paid, the calculation gives the estate credit for gift tax previously paid, but at currently applicable rates. Finally, the applicable credit amount is subtracted. Note that the full applicable credit amount as of the date of decedent's death applies because just as the equation adds back the total amount of adjusted taxable gifts, it must correspondingly add back the full applicable credit amount (including any adjustment for inflation in the year of decedent's death). The cumulative nature of the calculation makes it appear that the credit applies in full at death, but remember that the taxpayer in fact may only use the applicable credit amount once.

*Note on Payment of Estate Tax:* The estate tax return is due the date that is nine months after the date of decedent's death. IRC § 6075(a). Generally, payment is also due at that time. IRC §§ 6075, 6151. A personal representative may bear personal liability for unpaid tax if he or she distributes any assets of the estate before payment of the federal estate tax is due. *See* Treas. Reg. § 20.2002-1. The beneficiaries of the estate may also bear liability for the tax up to the amount of property received. IRC § 6324(a)(2). An extension for filing the estate tax return may be automatically granted for up to six months. IRC § 6081. An extension to pay the tax may be granted under limited circumstances. *See* IRC §§ 6161 (upon showing of reasonable cause), 6163 (tax attributable to remainder or reversionary interests), and 6166 (tax attributable to closely held businesses).

11. **Answer (B) is correct.** IRC § 2033 includes in decedent's gross estate "the value of all property to the extent of the interest therein of the decedent at the time of his death." Thus, for IRC § 2033 to apply, decedent must own an "interest in property." In *Helvering v. Safe Deposit & Trust Co.*, 316 U.S. 56 (1942), the United States Supreme Court distinguished powers of appointment from interests in property, and held that IRC § 2033 did not apply to include in the gross estate an unexercised general power of appointment. (At that time the counterpart to IRC § 2041 did not include in the gross estate, as it does now, unexercised general powers of appointment.) The practical importance of *Safe Deposit & Trust Co.* today is that the court narrowly construed IRC § 2033 to include only "interests in property." It left the issue of whether the gross estate includes a power of appointment to an analysis of IRC § 2041, discussed later.

**Answer (A) is incorrect.** IRC § 2033 includes in the gross estate property owned by decedent. The gross estate includes a decedent's one-half interest in community property regardless of how title is held as between the spouses. The surviving spouse's corresponding community interest in the property is vested in the surviving spouse. As such, the surviving spouse's share is not included in the gross estate of the deceased spouse under IRC § 2033. Whether property amounts to community property is a matter of state law.

**Answer (C) also is incorrect.** Treasury Regulation § 20.2033-1(a) specifically characterizes the estate tax as an excise tax, and indicates that provisions like those exempting interest earned on bonds from income taxation do not extend to the estate tax. Thus, tax-exempt bonds owned by decedent represent interests in property subject to estate taxation. Similarly, in *United States v. Wells Fargo Bank*, 485 U.S. 351 (1988), the Congressional declaration that certain "project notes" issued by municipalities for housing projects were exempt from "all taxation" by the United States did not protect the notes from estate taxation.

**Answer (D) also is incorrect.** IRC § 2033 also includes in the gross estate partial interests in property owned by decedent, such as tenant-in-common interests. The term "interest" in property clarifies that not only does IRC§ 2033 include an entire parcel of land owned by decedent, but also lesser interests in property. It is irrelevant that the property interest is located in Mexico. Regulation § 20.2033-1(a) provides that the value of all real or personal property is included in a decedent's gross estate "wherever situated." That the interest in land was property located outside the United States does not prevent the value of the property from being included in the decedent's gross estate.

*Note on Scope of Gross Estate*: As noted above, IRC § 2033 includes "all property to the extent of the interest therein of the decedent at the time of his death." This section reaches property subject to probate or, in other words, that property owned by decedent prior to death and passing pursuant to decedent's will (or in the absence of a will, pursuant to the intestacy statutes). In addition, IRC § 2033 applies broadly enough to include certain nonprobate transfers; for example, bank accounts of decedent passing by beneficiary designation. To the extent property is not included in the gross estate under IRC § 2033, it may be included under IRC §§ 2034 through 2044. These other sections extend the reach of the estate tax to include most property over which decedent retained an interest in or power over even though ownership and title prior to death was not in the name of the decedent.

12.   **Answer (D) is correct.** As differentiated from the prior problem, all the assets described in this question are intangible interests. Nevertheless, IRC § 2033 requires inclusion of "the value of all property" interests. Regulation § 20.2033-1(a) clarifies that gross estate includes the value of all intangible property held by the decedent at the time of death. As indicated in the previous answer, interest on tax-exempt bonds owned by decedent is included in the definition of property subject to estate taxation. Regulation § 20.2033-1(b) requires that interest which is accrued at the date of a decedent's death is included in the decedent's gross estate. However, interest accrued after the date of decedent's death would not be included in the decedent's gross estate.

   **Answers (A), (B), and (C) are all incorrect** for the reasons described above.

13.   **Answer (C) is correct.** Dividends which are declared payable to a decedent (or her estate) by virtue of the fact that on or before the date of the decedent's death she was a stockholder of record constitute part of her estate. Treas. Reg. § 20.2033-1(b). So long as the dividend is declared payable to shareholders of record as of a date (the "record date") on or prior to the decedent shareholder's death, the dividend must be included in the decedent's gross estate. The "record date" is the date established by the board of directors for the purpose of determining which shareholders are entitled to participate in receiving the dividend. In Answer (C), because the dividend was declared payable to stockholders of record as of June 10, a date after Cindy passes away, the dividend is not included in gross estate under § 2033. Even though in Answer (C) Cindy was a shareholder prior to her death, she passed away prior to the record date of June 10 and, therefore, the dividend would not be considered "property owned by decedent prior to death." *See* IRC § 2033(a).

   **Answers (A) and (B) are incorrect.** In Answer (A), the board of directors of Apple, Inc. resolved to pay a dividend to the shareholders of record on May 15. In Answer (B), the board of directors of Apple, Inc. resolved to pay a dividend to the shareholders of record on June 1. In both (A) and (B) the record date was "on or before" Cindy's death. Thus, the dividend will be included in Cindy's estate. The fact that Cindy's estate received the dividend proceeds on May 30 in Answer (A) and on June 1 in Answer (B) is not relevant to the analysis.

   **Answer (D) is also incorrect.** In Answer (D), the board of directors of Apple, Inc. resolved on June 1st to pay a dividend to the shareholders of record on May 15. Since both the date on which the dividend is declared and the date on which it is payable to shareholders of record are both on or before the date decedent passed away, the dividend proceeds must be included in the decedent's gross estate.

14.   **Answer (C) is correct.** A two-part test applies to determine inclusion under IRC § 2033: (1) decedent must hold a beneficial interest in property immediately prior to death, *see Helvering v. Safe Deposit & Trust Co.*, 316 U.S. 56 (1942) (must own beneficial interest in property); *Connecticut Bank & Trust Co. v. United States*, 465 F.2d 760 (2d Cir. 1972) (interest must arise prior to death), and (2) decedent's interest in property must be capable of transfer at death, *see* Rev. Rul. 75-145, 1975-1 C.B.298 (decedent "must . . . possess rights

that he can transmit to a survivor"). Fred's vested remainder interest meets both parts of this test. Fred's remainder interest amounts to a beneficial interest in property. Keep in mind that the controlling factor in part (2) of the test is not dependent on whether the interest in property is vested, but on whether the beneficial interest is transmissible at death.

**Answers (A) and (B) are incorrect.** These interests terminate as of death. Because Fred could not transmit the interests at death, IRC § 2033 does not apply, and these interests avoid inclusion in Fred's gross estate.

**Answer (D) is also incorrect.** A trustee holds bare legal title, and must administer trust property for the benefit of those with beneficial interests in the trust. Treas. Reg. § 20.2033-1(a). Bare legal title does not confer a property interest capable of taxation. Thus, the gross estate does not include the property of which Fred was trustee under IRC § 2033.

15. **Answer (C) is correct.** Again, analysis under the two-part test outlined in the answer to the immediately preceding question applies. Damages from pain and suffering arise from injuries sustained and suffered during Geri's lifetime. The action for such damages accrues during decedent's life. The answer indicates that Geri's personal representative succeeds to Geri's interest, and brings the action on behalf of the estate. Thus, recovery would pass pursuant to Geri's will or, in the absence of a will, pursuant to state intestacy statutes. The two-part test is met. *See Connecticut Bank & Trust Co. v. United States*, 465 F.2d 760 (2d Cir. 1972).

**Answer (A) is incorrect.** Answer (A) outlines the type of action specifically at issue in *Connecticut Bank & Trust Co. v. United States*, 465 F.2d 760 (2d Cir. 1972). The court distinguished the wrongful death recovery from an action based on pain and suffering on the basis that the right to the wrongful death recovery does not accrue until the moment after the time of death. The court reasoned that what the estate tax "taxes is not the interest to which the legatees and devisees succeeded on death, but the interest which ceased by reason of the death." The court concluded: "Where, as here, there was no property interest in the decedent which passed by virtue of his death, but rather one which arose after his death, such an interest is not property owned at death and not part of the gross estate under § 2033." The court also looked to state law for affirmation that, pursuant to Connecticut statutes, a person has no right to bring an action for damages resulting from the person's death.

*Note on Importance of State Law*: Courts look to state law to determine the property rights accorded to decedent. Based on those property rights and interests, courts apply federal estate tax law to determine whether to subject those rights and interests to tax. The United States Supreme Court in *Comm'r v. Estate of Bosch*, 387 U.S. 456 (1967), addressed whether "a federal court or agency in a federal estate tax controversy is conclusively bound by a state trial court adjudication of property rights or characterization of property interests when the United States is not made a party to such proceeding." In Revenue Ruling 69-285, the Service interpreted the holding of Bosch to mean: "A state court decree is considered to be conclusive in the determination of the Federal tax liability of an estate only to the extent that it determines property rights, and if the issuing court is the highest court in the state." The Service's reading of Bosch limits the controlling effect of lower state court holdings. With regard to the determination of estate tax consequences, only "proper regard" need be given the holdings of lower state tribunals. Where, however, a final and conclusive state court order binding the parties and adjudicating property rights is entered prior to the event causing a tax to be owed, the order does control determination of property rights for purposes of determining estate tax. Rev. Rul. 73-142, 1973-1 C.B. 405.

**Answers (B) and (D) are also incorrect.** Similar reasoning applies to exclude recoveries outlined in Answers (B) and (D) from inclusion as part of the gross estate under § 2033. The Service in Rev. Rul. 54-19, 1954-1 C.B. 179, ruled that recovery under a statute similar to Answer (B), where the survivor may bring the wrongful death recovery, avoids inclusion in the gross estate on the basis that "nothing 'passed' from the decedent to the beneficiaries" because decedent held no right of action as of death. *See also* Rev. Rul. 75-127, 1975-1 C.B. 297 (addresses both Answers (A) and (B)). Similarly, in Rev. Rul. 82-5, 1982-1 C.B. 131, the Service ruled that a survivor's benefit paid under a no-fault insurance policy required by state law in order to maintain a driver's license was not includible in the gross estate of decedent who died from a car accident. In that ruling, the Service indicated: "Since the loss for which the benefits are designed to compensate for did not accrue until after the decedent died, the right of the decedent's spouse to the benefits also did not arise until after the decedent died."

16. **Answer (A) is correct.** Using the now familiar analysis of determining whether decedent held a beneficial interest in property at death that was capable of transfer, the promissory note held by Kathy satisfied both requirements for IRC § 2033 inclusion. Treasury Regulation Section 20.2033-1(b) specifically includes "[n]otes or other claims held by decedent . . . even though they are canceled by the decedent's will."

  **Answers (B) and (D) are incorrect.** Answer (B) sets forth an analysis appropriate to IRC §§ 2036 and 2038. It does not reflect the analysis used to determine inclusion under IRC § 2033. Answer (D) likewise sets forth an analysis irrelevant to application of IRC § 2033, as it does not matter whether Kathy received adequate consideration.

  **Answer (C) is incorrect.** As the correct Answer (A) indicates, forgiveness of the promissory note by will in fact resulted in a transfer of a property interest. If instead, however, the promissory note itself contained a self-canceling feature forgiving repayment on death of Kathy, as did the note in *Estate of Moss v. Comm'r*, 74 T.C. 1239 (1980), it would not result in IRC § 2033 inclusion of the promissory note in the gross estate. The court found that termination of the note prevents a transfer. The holding in *Moss* rested on the fact that the parties stipulated that full and adequate consideration was paid in the form of a premium for the self-canceling feature. The Service carefully scrutinizes self-canceling installment notes between family members. The estate must rebut a presumption that the self-canceling note is a gift. In *Costanza v. Comm'r*, 320 F.3d 595 (6th Cir. 2003), the taxpayer successfully rebutted the presumption by demonstrating the debtor actually made payments on the note, the note was secured by a mortgage, and the father was not expected to die prematurely (although in fact he did). These facts indicated a bona fide transaction. *Compare Estate of Frane v. Comm'r*, 98 T.C. 341 (1992), *aff'd in part and rev'd in part*, 998 F.2d 567 (8th Cir. 1993).

  *Note Regarding Inclusion of Other Payments Due at Death*: Treasury Regulation § 20.2033-1(b) specifically includes income earned but not yet collected at death. It gives as specific examples rent due and owing at death, accrued interest, and dividends declared and payable to the shareholder of record. If these items were not included in decedent's income prior to death, the items become income in respect of a decedent ("IRD"), and taxable to the decedent's estate (or to a beneficiary if passed through) pursuant to IRC § 691. Because items of IRD become subject to both income tax and estate tax following decedent's death, IRC § 691(c) provides an income tax deduction to the extent of estate taxes paid with respect to the IRD. Pursuant to IRC § 1014(c), items of IRD also do not receive a step up in basis at death, thus, preserving the reportable income.

17. The vehicle should be included in the gross estate at its date of death value. IRC § 2031 provides: "The value of the gross estate . . . shall be determined by including . . . the value at the time of death of all property, real or personal, tangible or intangible, wherever situated." Treasury Regulation § 20.2031-1(b) sets "fair market value" as the standard, and defines it as "the price at which the property would change hands between a willing buyer and a willing seller, neither being under any compulsion to buy or to sell and both having reasonable knowledge of relevant facts." The value should reflect the price that a vehicle of approximately the same description, age, and condition could be purchased by the general public, as opposed to a dealer. Fair market value is a question of fact. Typically an appraisal is obtained. For vehicles, publications can provide retail value, for example, Kelley Blue Book value. Value is a key factor in determining the amount of the gross estate.

18. **Answer (B) is correct.** Section 2031(a) of the Code provides that the value is determined by including the value of the asset at the time of the decedent's death. Treasury Regulation § 20.2031-2(b)(1) requires that publicly traded stocks and bonds generally should be valued at the mean of the lowest and highest reported trading price for the date of death. In this example, $75 equals the mean ((50 + 100) / 2). **Thus, Answers (A), (C), and (D) are incorrect.**

*Note on Valuation of Closely Held Business Interests:* Often the stock of a closely held family business has never been sold prior to death. In that event, an appraisal should be obtained from a person qualified to appraise businesses. *See Furman v. Comm'r*, T.C. Memo. 1998-157. Treasury Regulation § 20.2031-3 and Revenue Ruling 59-60, 1959-1 C.B. 237, as it has been modified and amplified, outline factors that should be taken into account in valuing closely held businesses. Arriving at a value depends on the appraisal methodology used by the appraiser. The appraiser may use a method that (1) compares the closely held business to similarly situated businesses, (2) bases the value on a sum of the value of the assets held by the business, or (3) determines value based on the income and cash flows of a business. Typically an appraiser uses a weighted average of all three of these methods. In arriving at value, discounts or premiums may also apply. For example a discount for minority interest or a premium for a controlling interest may apply. Also, a lack of marketability discount may be appropriate to reflect the lack of an actual market for the shares. Business valuation is highly technical and typically requires special expertise.

19. Unlike the facts in Question 18, above, there were no sales of stock on the exchange on the date of death. Whereas publicly traded stocks are valued by calculating the mean between the highest and lowest quoted selling prices on the date of death, if there are no sales on such date, the decedent's estate must use values from alternate dates which are nearest the valuation date. Treasury Regulation § 20.2031-2(b). The fair market value on the date of death under these circumstances is determined by taking "a weighted average of the means between the highest and lowest sales on the nearest date after the valuation date." *Id.* The average must be weighted inversely by the respective numbers of trading days between the

selling date and the valuation date. *Id.* Well, there is the rule but how is it applied? The answer to problem 20, next, will walk you through this but if you want a headstart, you may wish to review the examples given under Regulation § 20.2031-2(b)(3).

20.  **Answer (C) is correct.** As discussed in Answer 19, above, the fair market value on the date of death under these circumstances is determined by taking "a weighted average of the means between the highest and lowest sales on the nearest date after the valuation date." *Id.* The average must be weighted inversely by the respective numbers of trading days between the selling date and the valuation date. Regulation § 20.2031-2(b)(1). Under the circumstances of this problem, the value is calculated as follows:

$$[(2 \times \$46) + (1 \times \$52)] / 3 = 48$$

In arriving at the above equation, you would count 2 trading days (Thursday, March 29 and Friday, March 30) and multiply the 2 by the $46 (mean price of stock trades on Thursday, March 29) and add this product to the product of 1 trading day (Monday, May 2) multiplied by the $52 (mean stock price of trades on Monday, May 2) to arrive at a value of $144. This amount is divided by the total number of trading days (3), to arrive at $48. **Answers (A), (B), and (D) are incorrect** for the reasons described above.

21.  Certain life interests, remainders, and terms of years may be valued pursuant to actuarial tables. Treasury Regulation § 20.2031-7(d)(1) requires these interests to be valued pursuant to the IRC § 7520 regulations. Treasury has promulgated a series of factors for each applicable federal rate, and published them in tables. Treasury Regulation § 20.2031-7(2)(ii) specifies the manner for valuing an ordinary remainder interest. Applying that regulation, determine value by multiplying the present value of the trust property ($100,000) by the actuarial factor corresponding to the applicable federal rate for a life income beneficiary age 60, as indicated on Table S (.21196). Following this formula, the remainder interest is valued at $21,196.

*Note on Use of Actuarial Tables, in General:* Actuarial tables generally apply to value life interests, terms of years, remainders, and reversionary interests. The tables, however, may not be used if the interest being valued is subject to certain limitations or restrictions such as a power to withhold, withdraw, or accumulate income. Treas. Reg. § 20.7520-3(b)(2). If the person, who serves as the measuring life, is terminally ill, the tables also may not be used (with some minor exceptions). Treas. Reg. § 20.7520-3(b)(3). Depending on the circumstances, the Service may issue a special factor, if use of the standard factor is precluded.

22.  In general, the executor of Fiddich's estate would have to value the assets as of the date of his death. IRC § 2031(a). In this case, the value for purposes of gross estate would normally be $1 billion. The problem is that due to a proximate and severe downturn in the economy, Fiddich's assets devalued substantially. If Fiddich's estate were required to pay tax on $1 billion at a 45% estate tax rate (assuming no deductions), there would be relatively little (5%) left for the beneficiaries of his estate. To cure this inequity, § 2032(a) provides for an election to take advantage of the alternate valuation date. Section 2032 of the Code provides an exception to the rule that requires date of death valuation. In order to take advantage of this exception, the executor must make an election to use the alternate valuation method under IRC§ 2032. If the election is properly made, the assets held in the estate may be valued as

of the date six months after the date of the decedent's death. If Fiddich's executor properly makes the election under IRC § 2032(a), the estate may include only $500 million in gross estate (as opposed to $1 billion).

23.    **Answer (B) is correct.** Treasury Regulation § 20.2032-1(a) provides that if an executor makes an alternate value election, the property included in the decedent's gross estate is valued as of several applicable dates. Any property which is sold within six months after the decedent's death is valued as of the date on which it was sold or otherwise disposed of. *See* Treas. Reg. § 20.2032-1(a)(1). Because the executor sold Fiddich's portfolio three months after Fiddich died and later made a valid IRC § 2032 election, the portfolio stocks will be included in his estate at a value of $750,000.

**Answer (A) is incorrect.** Answer (A) represents the value of the portfolio on the date of death. Once the IRC § 2032 election is made, the stock must be valued on one of several alternate dates under the rules.

**Answer (C) is incorrect.** Answer (C) reflects the value that would have been reported if the stocks had been held by the executor through the end of the six-month alternate valuation period. Because the stocks were disposed of, they are included in gross estate at the value on the date of disposal as described above.

**Answer (D) is incorrect.** While it is true that there will likely be gain or loss on the sale of the stock, such income or loss is reflected on the estate's income tax return and has no bearing on the value of the stock that is included for estate tax purposes. As discussed above, value is determined as of the date of sale.

24.    **Answer (C) is correct.** Section 2032(a)(3) of the Code provides that any interest "affected by mere lapse of time" is included in gross estate at its value as of the date of the decedent's death. However, an adjustment must be made for any difference in its value as of the subsequent valuation date not due to mere lapse of time. The regulations specifically identify patents as an example of the type of property interest that is "affected by mere lapse of time." Where a patent is set to expire after a term of years, the passing of time will naturally reduce its value. Here, where the patent had an unexpired term of 10 years and a present value of $480,000, the patent would naturally decline in value over time. Six months after the date of the Fiddich's death, the patent was sold, because of lapse of time and other causes, for $430,000. The Regulations provide an example under which the alternate value would be obtained by dividing $430,000 by 0.95 (the ratio of the remaining life of the patent at the alternate date to the remaining life of the patent at the date of the decedent's death or 9.5 years/10 years), and would, therefore, be $452,632. *See* Treas. Reg. § 20.2036-1(f)(2).

**Answer (A) is incorrect.** Because patents are the type of asset that declines in value due to the lapse or passing of time, they are included in the decedent's gross estate under the alternate valuation method at the patent's value as of the date of the decedent's death but with an adjustment for any difference in value not due to passage of time. Here, $480,000 is the date of death value prior to the adjustment.

**Answers (B) and (D) are incorrect.** The $50,000 represents the value of the post death royalty payment and does not reflect the value of the patent itself. Whereas, $500,000 could conceivably reflect the total of 10 $50,000 payments over 10 years, it does not take into account either the present value of the regulatory method of adjusting the value of the patent for the alternative valuation method.

25. **Answer (B) is correct.** If the election is made to use the alternate valuation date, the alternate valuation method applies to *all* property included in the decedent's gross estate. Treas. Reg. § 20.2032-1(b)(1). Property, which decreases in value will of course operate to reduce overall gross estate and, therefore, reduce the estate tax liability ultimately due. Unfortunately, the decedent's estate may not "cherry pick" by electing the alternate valuation date as to some assets and not others. Stated otherwise, while it would be nice if the election only applied to those assets which decreased in value, the election in fact applies to value all assets as of the alternate date; including those which increased in value.

    **Answers (A), (C), and (D) are all incorrect.** For reasons explained above, the remaining answers are incorrect. However, it is worth noting with respect to Answer (D) that there would not be any gain associated with the real estate in relation to the $25,000,000 increase in value as of the alternate valuation date. In either case, the value of the property for purposes of calculating gross estate will be $100,000,000. Furthermore, the basis will be increased under IRC § 1014(a)(2) up to the $100,000,000 fair market value as of the alternate valuation date.

26. The executor may not make a valid IRC § 2032 election under these circumstances. Treasury Regulation § 20.2032-1(b)(1) provides that the election may be made only if it will decrease both the value of the gross estate and the sum of the estate tax and the generation skipping transfer tax payable by reason of the decedent's death. Thus, where the sum value of all assets increases, the Code does not allow the executor to make an election to use the alternate valuation date. It is important to note that if such an election were allowed, it would open the door to at least one form of abuse. Taxable estates which do not exceed the amount of the exemption equivalent could conceivably make a § 2032 election where the value of gross estate increases within the alternate valuation period. Under these circumstances, the estate would get a "free" step up in basis without incurring any additional taxes.

Estate planners must focus on the estate planning ramifications to all individuals involved in the estate plan. The objective for the estate planner is to minimize federal wealth transfer tax for the donor, and to avoid any adverse consequences to the other parties involved. The following questions assist you in understanding which sections should be used to analyze the estate tax consequences of the various players typically involved in estate planning techniques. Keep in mind that at times more than one section may apply to include property in decedent's gross estate. The following answers, however, have been designed to result in one best answer for purposes of illustration.

27.     **Answer (B) is correct.** When the question presented focuses on the gross estate of the person who transferred the interest in property (the donor), of the choices provided, only IRC §§ 2033, 2036, and 2040 remain viable. In this fact pattern Laura transfers property to a trust and retains rights and interests to the trust property. IRC § 2036 specifically applies to determine whether retained rights to income or use and possession of the property previously transferred by donor cause the inclusion of the underlying trust property in the gross estate. Thus, (B) is the best answer.

**Answer (A) is incorrect.** IRC § 2033 will not apply to include the value of the trust property at death and held by the trustee. (Note that Laura transferred the property prior to death, and may have incurred a federal gift tax liability as a result of the transfer.) Because at death, Laura does not hold a beneficial interest in the entire interest in trust property previously transferred, IRC § 2033 does not apply to include the value of the trust property at death in the gross estate of Laura. Keep in mind, however, that depending on the type of interest retained, IRC § 2033 could apply to include in the gross estate the value of the retained interest in the property transferred, as opposed to the trust property itself. For example, if Laura had retained the remainder interest (or a reversion), IRC § 2033 might apply to include the value of the remainder/reversionary interest at death. Other sections that might apply to include the value of the trust property at Laura's death in Laura's gross estate include IRC §§ 2035, 2037, and 2038.

**Answer (C) is incorrect.** IRC § 2040 applies only to joint tenancy with right-of-survivorship interests or tenancy-by-the-entirety interests. Any time either of those interests is at issue, apply IRC § 2040 to determine inclusion in the gross estate. Neither of these interests is involved in this question.

**Answer (D) is incorrect.** IRC § 2041 applies to determine inclusion of powers of appointment held by persons other than the donor of the power. Treasury Regulation § 20.2041-1(b)(2) specifically indicates: "[T]he term 'power of appointment' does not include powers reserved by the decedent to himself within the concept of sections 2036 to 2038. . . . The power of the owner of a property interest already possessed by him to dispose of his interest, and nothing more, is not a power of appointment, and the interest is includible in his gross estate to the extent it would be includible under section 2033 or some other provision. . . ." Here the question focuses only on the donor.

28.   **Answer (D) is correct.** IRC § 2041 specifically addresses powers held by persons other than the donor of the power. The facts indicate Oscar holds the power to determine who receives trust principal on termination of the trust. This amounts to a power of appointment. Treasury Regulation § 20.2041-1(b) defines power of appointment for purposes of IRC § 2041 as including "all powers which are in substance and effect powers of appointment regardless of the nomenclature used in creating the power and regardless of local property law connotations." For example, the right of a beneficiary to withdraw trust property amounts to a power of appointment. *Id.* Also, for example, the power to alter, amend, or terminate the trust held by a beneficiary, who is not the donor, amounts to a power of appointment. A general power of appointment will be included in the gross estate, and a nongeneral power will not be included under IRC § 2041.

      **Answer (A) is incorrect.** A power of appointment does not amount to an interest in property. The United States Supreme Court in *Helvering v. Safe Deposit & Trust Co.*, 316 U.S. 56 (1942), specifically held that a general testamentary power of appointment over trust property did not amount to an interest in property. Thus, IRC § 2033 does not apply. In order for IRC § 2033 to apply, decedent must have held an interest in property at death.

      **Answers (B) and (C) are also incorrect.** IRC §§ 2036 and 2038 apply only to interests and powers retained by the donor with respect to property transferred by the donor. By their terms, these sections do not apply to powers held by a person other than the donor of the property.

29.   **Answer (D) is correct.** The trustee in this fact pattern is not the donor, and for purposes of analyzing whether the trustee's powers will cause inclusion in the gross estate of the trustee, the analysis is the same as in the immediately preceding question. The trustee Max will be taxed, if at all, under IRC § 2041, and only if the power is a general power of appointment.

      **Answers (A), (B), and (C) are incorrect.** Refer to the analysis in the immediately preceding question for an explanation as to why these answers are incorrect.

30.   **Answer (C) is correct.** The best answer is IRC § 2040 because it specifically addresses joint tenancy interests with right of survivorship. It applies to joint tenancy with right of survivorship as between spouses, and as between others.

      **Answer (A) is incorrect.** Treasury Regulation § 20.2040-1(b) clarifies that IRC § 2040, and not IRC § 2033, applies to determine gross estate inclusion of joint-tenancy-with-right-of-survivorship property. It provides:

      > Section 2040 specifically covers property held jointly by the decedent and any other person (or persons), property held by the decedent and spouse as tenants by the entirety, and a deposit of money, or a bond or other instrument, in the name of the decedent and any other person and payable to either or the survivor. The section applies to all classes of property, whether real or personal, and regardless of when the joint interests were created.

      **Answers (B) and (C) are incorrect.** Answers (B) and (C) are incorrect. Neither IRC § 2034 nor § 2044 address the type of property interest in the question. IRC § 2034 applies to include dower and curtesy interests. This problem does not involve dower or curtesy interests. For that reason, Answer (B) is not the best answer. Dower is an interest held by a widow in her deceased husband's property. Curtesy is an interest held by a widower in his deceased wife's property. These interests protected the surviving spouse from complete disinheritance. The vast majority of states have abolished such interests. Elective share rights, which must be elected by the survivor, have replaced the concepts of dower and curtesy. IRC § 2044 only includes in the gross estate of the surviving spouse that property for which an estate tax marital deduction pursuant to IRC § 2056(b)(7) was taken in the estate of the first spouse to die.

31. **Answer (A) is the correct answer.** Lucy owns a property interest — a life insurance policy. As owner of the life insurance policy, Lucy may transfer ownership of the policy at death. Thus, because Lucy owns a property interest transferable at death, IRC § 2033 applies to include the value of the life insurance policy in Lucy's gross estate.

**Answer (B) is incorrect.** IRC § 2036 addresses interests in income and rights to possession or use of property transferred by a decedent during life. These facts indicate Lucy owned the life insurance policy at death, and had not previously transferred it. Thus, IRC § 2036 does not apply.

**Answer (C) is incorrect.** IRC § 2042 applies only to policies of insurance on decedent's life. It does not apply to ownership of insurance policy on the life of someone other than decedent.

**Answer (D) is incorrect.** IRC § 2044 applies to include in the gross estate of the surviving spouse only that property for which an estate tax marital deduction pursuant to IRC § 2056(b)(7) was taken in the estate of the first spouse to die.

32. **Answer (A) is correct.** The focus of IRC § 2034 is on the property owned by decedent that is subject to a surviving spouse's dower or curtesy interest, or estate in lieu of dower or curtesy. IRC § 2034 specifically includes in the gross estate the "value of all property to the extent of any interest therein of the surviving spouse, existing at the time of the decedent's death as dower or curtesy, or by virtue of a statute creating an estate in lieu of dower or curtesy." Barry's right to an elective share should fall within IRC § 2034. Dower and curtesy provided the surviving widow or widower, respectively, an enforceable interest in the property of the deceased spouse. For example, dower often gave the widow a life estate in one-third of the husband's real property. Most states have statutorily abolished dower and curtesy in favor of a right of election. The inchoate interests of dower and curtesy in common law states generally have been replaced by the concept of an elective share. As indicated by the facts of this problem, an elective share also protects the surviving spouse, and ensures that the surviving spouse obtains a certain amount of a couple's assets.

Whether an elective share right is "in lieu of dower or curtesy" requires an examination of state law. The fact that the right of election differs in character from dower or curtesy interests does not matter. Treas. Reg. § 20.2034-1. *See also Estate of Johnson v. Comm'r*, 718 F.2d 1303 (5th Cir. 1983) (court found Texas homestead interest held by surviving spouse to be an interest in lieu of dower or curtesy). IRC § 2034, thus, ensures that property held by decedent and subject to the right of election does not escape taxation in decedent's estate.

**Answer (B) is incorrect** as it is a red herring. **Answers (C) and (D) are also incorrect.** Congress enacted IRC § 2034 to preclude any argument that the potential ability of the surviving spouse to control disposition of the property or to enforce a claim against the property caused the property to escape inclusion in decedent's gross estate. *See Estate of Johnson v. Comm'r*, 718 F.2d 1303 (5th Cir. 1983); Priv. Ltr. Rul. 8651001. Answer (C) is also incorrect because the answer focuses on Barry's rights, as opposed to Anna's interest in the property. Answer (D) is incorrect for a similar reason.

33. This question addresses the flip side of the issue addressed by IRC § 2034 in the previous question. Rather than focusing, as does IRC § 2034, on the property subject to the elective share, this question focuses on the elective share right itself.

The right to an elective share is not included in Barry's gross estate as surviving spouse. The Service in Revenue Ruling 74-492 directly addressed this issue. It ruled that IRC § 2033 does not apply to cause inclusion because the right of election terminates on Barry's death, and as a result Barry does not own a property interest transferable by Barry on death. It also ruled that IRC § 2041 does not serve to cause inclusion. It reasoned: "Under the Federal estate tax scheme enacted in the Internal Revenue Code for the implementation of widows' right of election laws, an unexercised right during the statutory period does not come within the taxable scope of Section 2041 on the basis that the failure to assert the inchoate right constitutes a complete and effective disclaimer or renunciation of a power of appointment by operation of law." IRC § 2034 has no application because it is Barry's right of election that is at issue here, and not the property held by Anna, the predeceased spouse.

34.  **Answer (B) is correct.** State law creates legal interests and rights. The provisions of the Code designate what interests or rights are taxed. In order to determine whether decedent had an interest in one-half of the community property which would be includable in his estate under Section 2033, it must first be determined what interest Brad had in the property by applying local community property law. Once Brad's property interests are determined under state law, it is then possible to determine whether such interests are includable under Section 2033 in Brad's gross estate at his death. *See, e.g., Comm'r v. Estate of Bosch*, 387 U.S. 456 (1967)(where federal estate tax liability turns upon the character of a property interest held and transferred by the decedent under state law). In general, since during the full length of their marriage, Brad and Deborah lived in a community property state, all the property acquired after their marriage would generally be considered community property. Under most community property systems, the spouse receives outright ownership of one-half of the community property and only the other one-half is included in the decedent's estate. IRC § 2033; *See United States v. Stapf*, 375 U.S. 118 (1963). Thus, $3,000,000 is the most correct answer. Arguably, Answer (C) is also correct and those who selected Answer (C) are not to be criticized. However, the call of the question inquires as to what "amount" of assets would be included and not so much "which" assets are included.

**Answers (A) and (D) are incorrect.** Answer (A) would require inclusion of all of the community assets in Brad's estate. While states that impose a community property system may differ, the focal point of most community property systems is to treat the marital partners as having an equal interest in the marital property. Thus, only a portion of the property, in most community property systems, only half of the communal assets must be included by the first to die. Answer (D) is incorrect for reasons already discussed.

35.  **Answer (C) is the correct answer.** Although this question deals with the basis of property acquired from a decedent and not whether and how much is included in the decedent's gross estate, this is a reasonable place to discuss the basis of assets that are acquired from a decedent. The basis of property in the hands of the person acquiring the property from a decedent is equal to the fair market value of the property at the date of the decedent's death. IRC § 1014(a)(1). In this regard, § 1014 provides for a "step up" in the basis of property "acquired from" or "passed from" the decedent at death. IRC § 1014(b). Property is considered to have been acquired from or passed from the decedent if it is received via a bequest, devise or inheritance. When Brad passed away, he bequeathed all of his assets to his daughter Rennie. Because Rennie received the assets from Brad via a bequest, the assets have passed from Brad as contemplated by IRC § 1014(b) and, therefore, the assets will obtain a step up to fair market value as of the date of death in Rennie's hands. This means that Rennie will acquire the assets with a basis of $3,000,000. It continues to be important to note, as discussed in the answer to problem 34, above, that Brad is attributed ownership of only one-half of the community assets upon his death.

**Answers (A), (B), and (D) are incorrect.** Answer (A) might appear to be correct because it is half of the basis of the assets held by Brad at death. It fails to take the allowed step up in to consideration. Answer (B) represents the basis of all of the community assets held by the community. This answer fails to take into account that Brad only owns half the community assets and that his half of the assets get a step up under IRC § 1014(a). Answer (D) may have relevance in the greater sense but that discussion is left to the next question.

36.  **Answer (C) is correct.** Answer (C) is correct but the answer may not be at all intuitive. Again, IRC § 1014(b) defines property that is acquired by means of bequest, devise or inheritance as having passed from the decedent. However, additionally, IRC § 1014(b)(6) provides that property which represents the surviving spouse's one-half share of community property held by the decedent and the surviving spouse under the community property laws of any state is also considered as having "passed" from the decedent. Provided, however, that this benefit only applies if at least one-half of the whole of the community interests are included in the decedent's gross estate. Upon Brad's death, Deborah's one-half interest in the community property also receives a step up in basis to fair market value as of the date of Brad's death.

**Answers (A), (B), and (D) are incorrect.** Although some not familiar with the nature of community property may have chosen Answer (A) believing that Deborah's one-half share of the community property would retain its historical cost basis because the assets would not have been "passed" by Brad to Deborah, § 1014(b)(6) provides the exception to the rule allowing a step up for both halves of the community property.

37.  If Brad and Deborah had instead resided in a non-community property state, the assets would not be divided in half and attributed equally to the two spouses. Rather, state property law would again determine which spouse owned the property and/or whether some of the property was jointly owned. Regardless, if they resided in a non-community property state, any assets owned by Deborah at the time of Brad's death would not receive a step up in basis under § 1014((b)(6). Rather any such assets would continue to retain the same basis that Deborah had in the assets at the time Brad passed away.

38.  This question focuses on the final issue that often arises regarding estate tax implications of marital rights. Specifically, the issue becomes whether a surviving spouse's claim against a decedent's estate pursuant to a premarital agreement in which the consideration was a waiver of marital rights may be deducted pursuant to IRC § 2053. The requirements of IRC § 2053 are addressed later. This question narrowly addresses whether a waiver of marital rights amounts to "full and adequate consideration" as set forth in IRC § 2043(b). IRC § 2053 generally allows as an estate tax deduction only those claims based on full and adequate consideration.

**Answer (C) is correct.** This fact pattern is based on *Estate of Herrmann v. Comm'r*, 85 F.3d 1032 (2d Cir. 1996). The Second Circuit in *Herrmann* relied upon IRC § 2043(b)(1), which states that "a relinquishment or promised relinquishment of dower or curtesy, or of a statutory estate created in lieu of dower or curtesy, or of other marital rights in the decedent's property or estate shall not be considered to any extent a consideration 'in money or money's worth.'" The court reviewed the purpose underlying this rule: "Section 2043(b)(1) was designed to prevent a husband and wife from entering into agreements that use consideration that is valid under state contract law to transform nondeductible marital rights — such as dower — into deductible contractual claims against the estate thereby depleting the taxable estate." *See also Merrill v. Fahs*, 324 U.S. 308 (1945) (Based on similar facts, finds a release of marital rights does not amount to adequate consideration for gift tax purposes.).

**Answers (A) and (B) are incorrect.** For purposes of federal estate and gift tax, it is irrelevant whether a release of marital rights amounts to adequate consideration, and whether in fact the surviving spouse can enforce a claim under the premarital agreement.

**Answer (D) is incorrect.** There are exceptions to the rule that a release of marital rights does not amount to full and adequate consideration. IRC § 2043(b)(2) indicates that if the requirements of IRC § 2516(1) are met, a release of marital rights will amount to full and adequate consideration if the release is incident to divorce. Specifically, if spouses enter into a written agreement regarding marital and property rights "and divorce occurs within the 3-year period beginning on the date 1 year before such agreement is entered into . . . , any transfers of property or interests in property made pursuant to such agreement . . . shall be deemed to be transfers made for a full and adequate consideration in money or money's worth." The facts of this problem, however, do not fall within this exception because the agreement was not made incident to divorce.

Also note two other exceptions to the general rule. For gift tax purposes, the Supreme Court in *Harris v. Comm'r*, 340 U.S. 106 (1950), held that property transferred in the manner specified in a postnuptial agreement and pursuant to a judicial decree does not need to be supported by consideration for gift tax purposes. This includes agreements that become part of the judicial decree if the court possessed the ability to modify the agreement. Also, if transfers are made in consideration of a release of support rights of a former spouse or for a donor's child, the transfer is deemed made for adequate consideration. Rev. Rul. 68-379, 1968-2 C.B. 414. In order to avoid gift tax consequences, the value of the support rights surrendered must equal the value of the property transferred in exchange. Rev. Rul. 77-314, 1977-2 C.B. 349.

39. **Answer (B) is correct.** One of the purposes of IRC § 2035 is to act as a stop-gap to IRC §§ 2036 through 2038 and 2042. It prevents a donor from retaining an interest in transferred property for the better part of the donor's life and then relinquishing the power or interest within three years of death without tax consequence. To restate this rule in terms of requirements, IRC § 2035 triggers inclusion in the gross estate when —

    a. Decedent transferred property during life and retained a power over or interest in the transferred property that could cause inclusion pursuant to IRC § 2036, 2037, 2038, or 2042;

    b. Decedent then transfers the retained interest or relinquishes the retained power so that decedent no longer possesses the interest or power;

    c. Decedent transfers the retained interest or relinquishes the retained power during the three-year period ending on the date of decedent's death; and

    d. Decedent does not make the transfer subject to a bona fide sale for money or money's worth.

    The amount included in the gross estate is the amount of property that would have been included had decedent not transferred the retained interest or relinquished the power within three years of death.

    In this question, Alice retains a power to determine who is to receive the income from the trust for a period that does not end prior to Alice's death. Thus, if Alice died retaining this power, the trust assets would be included in Alice's gross estate under IRC §§ 2036 and 2038. Alice relinquishes this power when Alice irrevocably resigns as trustee. However, Alice does not relinquish the power during the three-year period ending on the date of her death. Thus, the requirement that the transfer of the retained interest or relinquishment of the power must occur during the three-year period ending on date of death is not met.

    The Service issued Private Letter Ruling 200432016, clarifying application of the three-year time period with respect to the inclusion of gift tax under IRC § 2035. The ruling begins counting on the date of death, and counts backward three years. Thus, in this example the three-year period begins on the date of death or March 6, 2012, includes that date, and counts backwards to March 7, 2009. The transfer in this question was made on March 6, 2009, and thus does not fall within the three-year rule.

    **Answers (A), (C), and (D) are incorrect** for the reasons stated above. Alice initially retained an interest prohibited by IRC §§ 2036 and 2038, thus, **Answer (A) is incorrect**. Also, Alice relinquished the power more than three years prior to her death as required to trigger the statute, thus Answers (C) and (D) are incorrect.

40. **Answer (C) is correct.** Unlike the facts in problem 39, above, IRC § 2035(a) now applies to include the value of the trust property in Alice's gross estate. While Alice relinquished the power to determine who is to receive the income from the trust, Alice did not relinquish the power for at least a three-year period ending on the date of her death. As such, she falls

under the inclusion rule provided by IRC § 2035(a) and the assets contributed by her to the trust must be included in her estate. The requirement that the transfer of the retained interest or relinquishment of the power must occur during the three-year period ending on date of death is now met.

**Answers (A), (B), and (D) are incorrect.** For the reasons stated above, even though Alice relinquished interests prohibited by IRC §§ 2036 and 2038, she did not relinquish the power more than three years prior to her death.

41.  **Answer (D) is correct.** Based on Barney's retained power to revoke the trust, IRC § 2038 causes inclusion of the $900,000 trust property held at decedent's death. Although Barney directed $100,000 of the trust property to be transferred to Barney's child during the three-year period ending before death, IRC § 2035(e) steps in and deems the transfer to be made directly by decedent and not from the revocable trust (that was subject to income taxation in Barney's hands pursuant to IRC § 676). Because, pursuant to IRC § 2035(e), the transfer is deemed to be made directly by decedent, IRC § 2035(a) becomes inapplicable. **Answers (A), (B), and (C) are incorrect** for the reasons stated above.

42.  **Answer (C) is correct.** IRC § 2035 also serves as a stop-gap to IRC § 2042, which includes certain life insurance policies on decedent's life. With respect to life insurance policies, the gross estate includes the value of the insurance proceeds paid at death if:

   a.  Decedent transferred an insurance policy owned by him on his life, or relinquished any incidents of ownership with respect to a policy on his life, and

   b.  Had decedent not made the transfer or relinquished incidents of ownership, the policy would have been included in decedent's gross estate, and

   c.  The transfer or relinquishment occurred during the three-year period ending on the date of decedent's death, and

   d.  Decedent did not transfer the policy subject to a bona fide sale for adequate consideration in money or money's worth.

In this question Collin owned a life insurance policy that would have been included in Collin's gross estate under IRC § 2042 had he not transferred it during the three-year period ending on the date of his death.

**Answers (A), (B), and (D) are incorrect** for the reasons stated above.

The amount included in Collin's gross estate is the amount that would have been included had Collin not transferred the policy or relinquished incidents of ownership within three years of death. This amount would have been the $1 million in policy proceeds, and for that reason Answers (A), (B), and (D) are incorrect.

Note that had Collin instead transferred $20,000 cash to his child, and had the child purchase the policy on Collin's life, neither IRC § 2035 nor § 2042 would have applied to cause inclusion in Collin's gross estate because Collin would never have owned the policy in the first place.

43.  **Answer (A) is correct.** Dorthea did not retain any power over or interest in the property transferred to Dorthea's children. Thus, IRC § 2035(a) does not apply to include any portion of the property in Dorthea's gross estate. IRC § 2035(b) applies to increase the gross estate by the amount of any gift tax paid by decedent on transfers made by decedent or decedent's spouse during the three-year period ending on decedent's date of death. Because the

amounts transferred by Dorthea fell within the annual gift tax exclusion amount, no gift tax was payable with respect to the transfers, and for that reason IRC § 2035(b) also would not apply. **Answers (B), (C), and (D) are incorrect** for the reasons stated above.

44. **Answer (A) is correct.** As discussed above, IRC § 2035(a) generally does not apply to include outright transfers. This is because an outright transfer of property would never have caused the transferred property to be included in decedent's gross estate under IRC §§ 2036 through 2038. Thus, the amount of the cash gift is not included in Elise's gross estate. Because the cash gift was made more than three years prior to decedent's date of death, IRC § 2035(b) does not apply to gross up the estate by the amount of gift tax paid. Only if the gift was made within the three-year period ending on the date of decedent's death does IRC § 2035(b) kick in to include in the gross estate the amount of any gift tax paid by decedent on a gift made by decedent or decedent's spouse. **Answers (B), (C), and (D) are incorrect** for the reasons stated above.

45. **Answer (B) is correct.** Again, IRC § 2035(a) generally does not apply to include outright transfers. Thus, the amount of the cash gift of $200,000 is not included in Bono's gross estate. Because the cash gift was made less than three years prior to decedent's date of death, IRC § 2035(b) does apply to gross up the estate by the amount of gift tax paid. Here, the $90,000 of gift tax paid in 2010 would be included in Bono's gross estate in relation to the gift that he made in 2009 (less than three years prior to Bono's death).

**Answers (A), (C), and (D) are incorrect** for the reasons stated above. Note that the $90,000 gift tax paid by Bono is included in Bono's gross estate pursuant to IRC § 2035(b). This result prevents the taxpayer from taking advantage of the tax-exclusive nature of the gift tax by making what is essentially a death-bed transfer. Gift tax is not paid on the amount of property used to pay gift tax owed, but estate tax is paid with respect to property used to pay the estate tax. Thus, the gift tax is tax-exclusive, and the estate tax is tax-inclusive. Absent application of IRC § 2035(b), a donor/decedent would pay less tax by transferring all property during life and paying a gift tax. IRC § 2035(b) precludes this result for transfers made during the three-year period ending on the date of decedent's death by grossing up the estate by the amount of gift tax paid during that time.

46. In an effort to prevent "death-bed" manipulation of assets for purposes of qualifying for special-use valuation under IRC § 2032A, in determining the applicability of that section, IRC § 2035(c) includes in the gross estate all taxable transfers by decedent (other than transfers of an insurance policy and other than those for which a gift tax marital deduction is allowed) made within the three-year period ending on decedent's date of death. Thus, Fred's transfer would be deemed to be included in the gross estate for the sole purpose of determining whether the estate may make the special-use valuation election.

A similar rule applies for determining applicability of the special election for redemption of stock to pay death taxes, the special election to defer payment of estate tax related to certain closely held businesses, and the application of certain liens for taxes.

*Congress enacted IRC § 2036, and its sister sections IRC §§ 2035, 2037, and 2038, to protect the integrity of the estate tax. Absent these sections, a taxpayer could transfer title to property, and yet retain all the important attributes of ownership without triggering estate tax. IRC §§ 2036 through 2037 step in and require inclusion in decedent's gross estate of any property transferred where decedent retains an important attribute of property ownership as specified in those sections. IRC § 2035 provides a safety net where within three years of decedent's death, decedent relinquishes a prohibited retained right or interest in property under those sections. IRC § 2035 thus protects against death-bed manipulation of IRC §§ 2036 through 2038.*

47.　**Answer (C) is correct.** In order for IRC § 2036 to include property in the gross estate, the following requirements must be met: (1) decedent must have transferred an interest in property, (2) decedent must have retained either the right to income, possession, or enjoyment of the property, or the right to designate who receives the income, possession, or enjoyment of the property, and (3) the property interest must be retained for decedent's life, a period not ascertainable without reference to decedent's death, or a period that does not in fact end before decedent's death. IRC § 2036, thus, focuses on the important property rights or income and possession and enjoyment of property.

While Alyssa meets two of the IRC § 2036 requirements (she transferred an interest in her home and retained the right to possess and enjoy her home), she did not retain the interest for the requisite period of time. IRC § 2036 applies only when decedent retained the right to possess the property for "life or for any period not ascertainable without reference to his death or for any period which does not in fact end before his death." If decedent survives the period during which decedent retained the right to possess the property, as did Alyssa, none of the transferred property is included in the gross estate.

This leads to an important planning strategy — the qualified personal residence trust, where taxpayer may transfer a residence pursuant to the requirements of IRC § 2702 at a reduced federal gift tax cost, and avoid estate tax if taxpayer survives the term of the trust.

**Answers (A) and (B) are incorrect.** IRC § 2036 does not focus on when the donor's retention of the interest begins, but only whether the interest was retained for life, for any period not ascertainable without reference to decedent's death, or for a period that does not end before decedent's death.

**Answer (D) is also incorrect.** The requisite time period for application of IRC § 2038 differs from that of IRC § 2036. IRC § 2038 focuses on whether decedent retained a power to alter, amend, or revoke an interest "where the enjoyment thereof was subject at the date of his death to any change through the exercise of a power ." The answer in (D) incorrectly focuses on a time period not ascertainable without reference to decedent's death.

48.　The answer to the prior Question 47 would change. Alyssa's gross estate would include the value of the trust property at her death because under these facts she has retained the right to possess the home transferred to trust for a period that does not in fact end before her death, and as discussed in Question 47 the other two factors are met.

49.   **Answer (A) is correct.** Barry's gross estate will include the trust property pursuant to IRC § 2036 because Barry retained the right to income from the trust property that Barry transferred to the trust, and Barry retained the interest for life. As noted above, retention of a "life interest" falls within the requisite time period for application of IRC § 2036. Barry thus met all three requirements of IRC § 2036 for inclusion in the gross estate. (Note that the answer would not change if instead what Barry retained was a life estate interest with remainder to Barry's child.)

     **Answers (B) and (C) are incorrect.** IRC § 2038 applies in those instances where decedent transfers an interest, and holds at death the "power" to "alter, amend, revoke or terminate" the interest. In this fact pattern, Barry does not retain any "power" over the property transferred, and for that reason IRC § 2038 would not apply. IRC § 2037 applies under certain circumstances where decedent retains a reversionary interest in property transferred. Barry has not retained such an interest. Also, Treasury Regulation § 20.2039-1(e) indicates that in this situation IRC § 2036 is the appropriate section for inclusion in the gross estate, and not IRC § 2039.

     **Answer (D) is incorrect.** Answer (D) is incorrect for the reason that IRC § 2036 does include the property in Barry's gross estate. The focus of these sections is on the retained rights and powers of Barry with respect to transferred property, and not the rights of others.

50.   Barry's gross estate will also include the trust property despite the changed fact. IRC § 2036(a)(2) includes the trust property in the gross estate, whereas in this problem, decedent retained "the right, either alone or in conjunction with any person, to designate the persons who shall possess or enjoy the property or the income therefrom." Your answer also would not change even if Barry shared this power with Cassie. Alternatively, IRC § 2038, as discussed in Topic 7 would cause inclusion.

51.   **Answer (B) is correct.** IRC § 2036 applies to include trust assets in the transferor's gross estate where transferor has retained an interest in trust assets "for his life or for any period not ascertainable without reference to his death or for any period which does not in fact end before his death." If Hannah retains an interest for a term of years, which she outlives, then she has not retained an interest in the trust which satisfies the requirements of the statute. The term of 15 years is not for her life and is not a time period that requires reference to her death. Further, because Ally lives long past her normal life expectancy, the 15-year term does in fact end before her death. Students may wish to make note that a grantor retained annuity trust ("GRAT"), where the retained interest is in the form of an annuity interest (specific periodic amount), and a unitrust interest, (specified percentage) ("GRUT") are premised upon this analysis. Similarly, qualified personal residence trusts ("QPRT") are premised on a term of years. In each of these instruments, the grantor contributes an asset to the trust and retains an interest for a term of years. So long as the grantor outlives the term of years chosen for the GRAT, GRUT or QPRT, the assets are not required to be included in grantor's estate under IRC § 2036.

     **Answers (A) and (C) are incorrect.** On the other hand, an annuity for life or annuity for life combined with a right to principal fall into the proscribed language under IRC § 2036. With respect to a grantor retaining an income interest for life, at least a portion of the assets must be included in grantor's gross estate. Note that a life interest is only a partial interest in the whole. Partial interests are discussed in questions that follow. However, students should make note that Regulation § 20.2036-1(c) specifies how to determine the amounts included in a grantor's gross estate under such circumstances.

**Answer (D) is incorrect.** Because Answer (B) does not result in inclusion under IRC § 2036, Answer (D) is incorrect.

52.     **Answer (A) is correct.** Although Daisy does not retain the right to income or to possess or enjoy the trust property pursuant to the trust terms, it can be inferred that the child and Daisy in reality agreed Daisy would retain such possession based on the objective fact that Daisy continued to live in the home rent-free, and that a portion of the trust income was used to pay Daisy's personal living expenses.

If an implied agreement can be shown that taxpayer intended to retain a proscribed interest for life, as here, courts generally apply IRC § 2036 to include the trust property in taxpayer's gross estate. *See Estate of Linderme v. Comm'r*, 52 T.C. 305 (1969); Rev. Rul. 78-409, 1978-2 C.B. 234. Note, however, that the Service does not argue implied agreement where the transfer of a home (as opposed to home and other income-producing assets) is between spouses, and the transferor spouse continues to co-occupy the home with the transferee spouse, as indicated in Rev. Rul. 70-155, 1970-1 C.B. 189. The implied agreement argument may be avoided if fair rental value is paid for the home, but not if after taking into account the entire transaction a fair rent is not in fact paid. *See Estate of Maxwell v. Comm'r*, 3 F.3d 591 (2d Cir. 1993). Similarly, use of trust income for the benefit of the donor, although not technically allowed, requires inclusion of the income-producing property in the gross estate. *See Estate of Paxon v. Comm'r*, 86 T.C. 785 (1986); *Estate of Hendry v. Comm'r*, 62 T.C. 861 (1974); *Estate of McCabe v. United States*, 475 F.2d 1142 (Ct. Cl. 1973); *Estate of McNichol v. Comm'r*, 265 F.2d 667 (3d Cir. 1959).

**Answers (C) and (D) are incorrect** for the reasons stated above. An implied agreement to retain a proscribed interest in transferred property for life will cause inclusion in decedent's gross estate regardless of the legally enforceable terms of the trust or retention of rights as a trustee.

**Answer (B) also is incorrect.** Answer (B) is incorrect because there generally is no duty of support owed to an adult child.

53.     **Answer (B) is correct.** Eva retained a proscribed interest in property because trustee was required to satisfy Eva's legal obligation of support to her child. Thus, Eva retained a right to income and to enjoy the trust property. Had the trustee failed to provide for child's support, Eva would have had to spend her own money to do so. Treas. Reg. § 20.2036-1(b)(2). Eva also retained the interest for a period that in fact did not end before her death, thus meeting the requisite time requirement. **Answers (A), (C), and (D) are incorrect.** For the same reason that Answer (B) is correct, the other answers are incorrect.

54.     **Answer (D) is correct.** IRC § 2036 requires inclusion in gross estate where: (1) decedent transferred an interest in property, (2) decedent retained either the right to income, possession, or enjoyment of the property, or the right to designate who receives the income, possession, or enjoyment of the property, and (3) the property interest is retained for

decedent's life, a period not ascertainable without reference to decedent's death, or a period that does not in fact end before decedent's death. Again, IRC § 2036, focuses on possession and enjoyment of property. Here Turner meets the requirements of IRC § 2036 which results in inclusion of the LLC assets in his estate. Turner transferred his interest in the apartment building and impliedly retained the right to possess a portion of the building by using it rent free. A similar outcome resulted in *Guynn v. United States*, 437 F.2d 1148 (4th Cir. 1971), wherein real property was held to be includible in a decedent mother's gross estate under IRC § 2036 notwithstanding that title to the property was transferred to the decedent's daughter. The decedent remained in possession, paid taxes, made improvements and paid no rent for use of the property until her death.

**Answers (A), (B) are incorrect.** Answers (A) and (B) both contemplate a sale for adequate consideration. IRC § 2036(a) does not apply where the transfer is a bona fide sale for adequate consideration in money or money's worth. Because under scenarios (A) and (B), Turner sells the LLC interests to his child for fair value, he is not considered to have retained an interest under IRC § 2036(a). As such, the section does not operate to include the assets in his estate.

**Answer (C) is incorrect.** While Turner did not receive adequate consideration (or any consideration for that matter) in relation to the gift of the LLC units to his son, he did pay rent. By paying rent, Turner effectively paid adequate consideration for his use of the property. *See, e.g., Estate of Barlow v. Comm'r*, 55 T.C. 666 (1971) (held no interest under IRC § 2036 where decedent gifted farm to children and contemporaneously leased back the farm from the children).

55.      Here, the provisions of the LLC operating agreement result in a retention of an interest on the part of Turner. IRC § 2036(a)(2) operates to include in gross estate the value of property over which the decedent retains the right to either alone or in conjunction with any person, who designate the persons who shall possess or enjoy the property or the income therefrom. It should be noted that during life, a decedent may become subject to the inclusion requirement of IRC § 2036 via, among other things, the provisions of a partnership agreement. The facts of this question are similar to the facts in *Estate of Turner v. Comm'r*, T.C. Memo 2011-209. In *Turner*, the Tax Court found that because the decedent had absolute discretion to amend the partnership agreement and make pro-rata distributions without consent of the other partners, that IRC § 2036(a)(2) required inclusion of the value of the assets contributed to the limited partnership in decedent's estate. By retaining the right to amend the agreement, Turner made it possible to rescind the agreement altogether thereby retaining a modicum of control over the assets sufficient to cause him to retain an interest under IRC § 2036(a)(2).

56.      **Answer (B) is correct.** Called the anti-*Byrum* provision, IRC § 2036(b) was passed in an effort to overrule *United States v. Byrum*, 408 U.S. 125 (1972), where the Court held retention of the right to vote transferred stock did not trigger application of IRC § 2036. Now, Section 2036(b)(1) deems the retention of the right to vote, directly or indirectly, transferred stock of a controlled corporation as retention of the enjoyment of the transferred stock. Thus, Julius retained a power prohibited by IRC § 2036. Not only must Julius retain the right to vote the stock that was transferred, but the corporation also must be a controlled corporation. IRC § 2036(b)(2) defines a controlled corporation as one where at any time after the transfer and during the three years immediately prior to decedent's

death, decedent owned or had the right to vote, alone or with another, at least 20 percent of the total combined voting power of all classes of the corporation stock. Immediately prior to his death, Julius owned or had the right to vote 25 percent of the stock, which exceeds 20 percent. Thus, both requirements of IRC § 2036(b) are met, and Julius's gross estate includes the stock transferred to his son.

To answer this question it is not necessary to apply the IRC § 318 ownership attribution rules to determine whether the definition of "controlled corporation" is met because Julius directly owns or has the right to vote more than 20 percent of the stock. If the 20 percent requirement had not been met, it would have been necessary to apply the IRC § 318 ownership attribution rules to definitively determine whether the definition had been met.

**Answer (A) is incorrect.** Answer (A) incorrectly focuses on the percentage of the stock transferred, as opposed to the focus of IRC § 2036(b)(2), which is on the percentage of stock the donor owned or had the right to vote after the transfer and within three years of transferor's death.

**Answers (C) and (D) also are incorrect.** IRC § 2036(b)(2) does not focus only on ownership to determine control, but also includes stock that transferor had the right to vote. It also is not limited to transfers in trust.

57.  In Revenue Ruling 81-15, 1981-1 C.B. 457, the Service ruled that transfer of nonvoting stock with concurrent retention of voting stock in a controlled corporation did not trigger inclusion of the transferred stock in the gross estate under IRC § 2036(b). This ruling provides an easy strategy for a donor to avoid application of IRC § 2036(b) and still retain the same right to vote as before the transfer. It should be noted that it is unclear whether the Service would issue the same ruling under the facts of Revenue Ruling 81-15 in light of recent cases in the area of family limited partnerships. Recent cases have held that retention of a general partner interest in a family entity after transfer of limited partnership interests triggers inclusion under IRC § 2036(a). *See Estate of Strangi v. Comm'r*, T.C. Memo. 2003-145, *aff'd*, 417 F.3d 468 (5th Cir. 2005); *see also Estate of Turner v. Comm'r*, T.C. Memo. 2011-209.

58.  **Answer (A) is correct.** At first glance it appears that Lacey's gross estate should not include any trust assets because Lacey did not retain any benefits with respect to assets Lacey transferred to trust. Before IRC § 2036 can apply to include assets in a decedent's gross estate, the decedent must retain a benefit from the property transferred. Courts, however, look to the substance of the transaction to determine who transferred the property. The Court in *United States v. Grace*, 395 U.S. 316 (1969), held "that application of the reciprocal trust doctrine requires only that the trusts be interrelated, and that the arrangement, to the extent of mutual value, leaves the settlors in approximately the same economic position as they would have been in had they created trusts naming themselves as life beneficiaries." Applying the reciprocal trust doctrine, the Court uncrossed the trusts, and deemed the decedent to be the transferor of the trust held for decedent's benefit. The Court included in decedent's gross estate the value of the trust held for the benefit of decedent. The facts of this problem are similar to that of *Grace*, and should lead to application of the reciprocal trust doctrine.

**Answers (B), (C), and (D) are incorrect.** These answers are incorrect because they fail to uncross the trusts and deem Lacey to be the transferor of the trust for Lacey's benefit.

59.  **Answer (B) is correct.** One-half the value of the trust assets is includible in Nels' gross

estate. Treasury Regulation § 20.2036-1(a) indicates that if decedent retained an interest to only a portion of the property, then only a corresponding portion is included in decedent's gross estate. Nels retained an interest in one-half the income of the trust, so one-half is included. Nels meets the other requirements of IRC § 2036 — Nels transferred the property to the trust, and Nels retained a right to the income of the trust for life. **Answers (A) and (D) are incorrect for the same reasons.**

**Answer (C) also is incorrect.** If decedent retains an interest in trust for life, the entire proportionate value of the trust property is included in the gross estate, and not just the value of decedent's life estate. Were this not the result, taxpayer could avoid estate tax on the value of the remainder simply by transferring property to trust and retaining all the attributes for life.

60.    **Answer (D) is correct.** In general, this question brings up the use of intentionally defective grantor trusts ("IDGTs"). While many estate planners are comfortable that such trusts operate to avoid inclusion of the assets in the grantor's gross estate, the courts have yet to rule on the validity of such trusts. The Service has acknowledged that these powers will not cause inclusion in the gross estate under very specific circumstances as enunciated in Revenue Ruling 2008-22. It is useful for the student of estate and gift taxes to be exposed to the analysis. IDGTs are used by estate planners to create trusts the object of which is to exclude the value of the trust assets from gross estate upon the grantor's death. An IDGT is an irrevocable trust in which the grantor retains certain limited interests in trust assets. As indicated, a main goal of an IDGT is to avoid inclusion of the value of the trust asset in grantor's gross estate upon his or her death. Additionally, the grantor will remain liable for income tax owed on trust income. Answers (A), (B), and (C) each contain a provision that arguably does not amount to a retention of an interest under IRC § 2036. Answer (A) grants the power to borrow money from the trust. In general, such a power should not affect beneficial enjoyment of the trust assets and also would not amount to a power to alter or amend the trust terms. Answer (B) gives Ricky the power to substitute trust assets of equal value. In general, a power to substitute assets should not result in the value of the trust assets being included in gross estate because such a right has no impact and does not alter the beneficiary's various interests in the trust and does not reduce in any way the value of the trust assets. Finally, the provision in Answer (C) gives an unrelated party the power to add a charitable beneficiary. While such a power would appear to affect the parties who may enjoy the trust assets, so long as an unrelated disinterested party is given this power, however, since grantor has no power to alter or amend the trust no portion of the trust should be includable in the grantor's gross estate. Based upon this analysis, estate planners have used one or more of the above provisions to create trusts which do not result in the grantor retaining an interest under IRC § 2036. **Answers (A), (B) and (C) are all incorrect.** Note that for reasons explained above under current estate planning practice, the trust provisions in these remaining answers do not result in an interest that is described in IRC § 2036. Therefore, none of the provisions would result in inclusion of the trust assets in Ricky's gross estate.

61.    **Answer (A) is correct.** IRC § 2038 includes in the gross estate the value of any interest in property transferred by decedent which, as of the date of decedent's death, is subject to a power to "alter, amend, revoke, or terminate." It also includes property interests that were subject to such a power that was relinquished within the three-year period ending on decedent's date of death. In this fact pattern, Andy meets all three requirements of IRC § 2038 — Andy transferred the property to the trust, Andy held the power to revoke the entire trust, and the property was subject to the power as of Andy's date of death. Note that the relevant time period focuses only on whether decedent held the power as of date of death. Because the power of revocation extended to all trust property, IRC § 2038 includes the entire value. Also, there are no facts indicating that the property was transferred subject to a bona fide sale for full and adequate consideration, so that exception does not apply.

> *Note:* Revocable trusts similar to this one are often used as the primary vehicle to pass property at death. These trusts serve several non-tax purposes including the ability to avoid probate with regard to assets owned by trustee. While the power to alter or revoke the trust allows the transferor to change the dispositive terms of the trust in much the same way that a will may be changed, revocable trusts do not necessarily provide any estate tax savings.

       **Answer (B) is incorrect.** The entire value of the trust will be subject to tax under IRC § 2038, and not just the value of the remainder interest, because in this fact pattern both the income and principal are subject to the power to revoke. Pursuant to IRC § 2038 the gross estate includes the value of any interest subject to the power to alter, amend, revoke, or terminate. This causes IRC § 2038 to overlap with the reach of IRC § 2036(a)(2). While IRC § 2036(a)(2) includes property subject to retained powers over income interests, IRC § 2038 applies to include property subject to powers over both income and principal. Property, however, is only included once, and under the section that includes the greatest value.

       **Answer (C) also is incorrect.** It is sufficient that decedent held a power to alter, amend, revoke, or terminate as of the date of decedent's death. No requirement exists regarding exercise of the power.

       **Answer (D) also is incorrect.** IRC § 2038(b) specifically prohibits easy avoidance by providing that a power will be deemed to exist as of date of death even though it is "subject to a precedent giving of notice" or even if it "takes effect only on the expiration of a stated period after exercise." Thus, the fact that the revocation cannot occur until after 60 days' notice does not serve to avoid application of the statute based on the time requirement.

62.    The answer would not change. Again, IRC § 2038 includes in the gross estate the value of any interest in property transferred by decedent which, as of the date of decedent's death, is subject to a power to "alter, amend, revoke, or terminate." It also includes property interests

that were subject to such a power that was relinquished within the three-year period ending on decedent's date of death. Of course, if Andy had relinquished all of his power to amend, revoke or terminate the trust more than three years before he passed away, IRC § 2038 would no longer apply to include the value of the assets in his estate.

63.    **Answer (B) is correct.** While Char holds a power that allows her to revoke trust, she cannot revoke all interests in the trust. Only the value of an interest in property subject to a power to which IRC § 2038 applies is included in the decedent's gross estate. Treas. Reg. § 20.2038-1(a). Under similar facts in *Blackman v. United States*, the decedent had the right together with other family members to revoke a trust that the decedent was both the trustee and a beneficiary. *Blackman v. United States*, 98 Ct. Cl. 413, 426 (1943). Upon revocation, decedent would have been entitled to receive one-half of the corpus. Upon his death, the decedent's rights in one-half of the corpus of the trust ended and that part of the corpus passed to members of his family. *Id.* The Court of Claims agreed with the Commissioner that only the value of the decedent's one-half interest in the trust must be included in his gross estate for estate tax purposes.

     **Answer (A) is incorrect.** Char's estate would only include the value of property over which she retained the right to alter, amend or revoke the right of another to enjoy. Here, Char only retained the right to revoke as to half of the property. Thus, the value of all the property would not be included.

     **Answers (C) and (D) are incorrect.** For reasons explained above, Char's estate will not completely avoid inclusion. With respect to Answer (C), it's not the actual election to revoke that causes inclusion, it is Char's retention of the right to revoke until her death that causes inclusion of a portion of the property in the trust.

64.    **Answer (A) is correct.** Becca holds the power to "alter" the timing of when the beneficiary receives income and principal. The Supreme Court in *Lober v. United States*, 346 U.S. 335 (1953), held the power to impact timing of income sufficient to cause inclusion under IRC § 2038. **Answers (B) and (C) are incorrect.** For the same reasons that (A) is correct, (B) and (C) are incorrect.

     **Answer (D) is incorrect.** IRC § 2038 includes powers to alter, amend, revoke, and terminate held at decedent's death regardless of whether the power is held "by decedent alone or in conjunction with any other person." It does not matter whether the person has an adverse interest. It also does not matter in what capacity decedent may exercise the power, and even though decedent is a co-trustee, IRC § 2038 may apply to trustee powers held by Becca. Thus, Answer (D) is incorrect.

65.    **Answer (D) is correct.** IRC § 2038 does not include in the gross estate powers subject to a determinable external standard. Generally, determinable external standards are those that allow distribution in terms of maintenance, education, support, and health. (A determinable external standard is similar to, but a bit broader than, an ascertainable standard.) The court in *Jennings v. Smith*, 161 F.2d 74 (2d Cir. 1947), determined that such powers become "a duty enforceable in a court of equity." Powers subject to determinable external standards compel a trustee to distribute pursuant to the standard, and eliminate discretion. Generally, standards that base distribution on a beneficiary's happiness or comfort, without more, fail to meet the definition of determinable external standard because of the broad discretion remaining with trustee.

**Answers (A), (B), and (C) are incorrect.** Just as with IRC § 2036, under IRC § 2038, if a transferor has the power to remove and replace a trustee with herself, the transferor will be deemed to hold the powers of the trustee. Here, however, the powers of the trustee are insufficient to cause inclusion in the gross estate in light of the determinable external standard, and for that reason Answer (A) is incorrect. IRC § 2038 applies to powers, and not the retention of income or the possession and enjoyment of property as indicated in Answer (B). In addition, Cindy generally will not owe a duty of support to her adult child. However, IRC § 2038 does apply to powers over both income and principal, and for that reason Answer (C) is incorrect.

66. Yes, the answer would change. As discussed above, IRC § 2038 does not include in the gross estate powers subject to an ascertainable or determinable external standard. Generally, such standards are those that allow distribution in terms of maintenance, education, support, and health. Because Cindy now has the ability to replace the trustee and distribute assets to her child for comfort and enjoyment, the powers of the trustee are likely to be sufficient to cause inclusion in the gross estate.

*Note:* State law is determinative of property rights. However, distributions for a beneficiary's "happiness," "welfare," "comfort," or "enjoyment" are not ascertainable standards as contemplated by IRC § 2041(b)(1)(A). Although state law generally determines the nature of any powers held by a decedent, drafters are advised not to deviate from the standards listed in the code and regulations thereunder. *See* Rev. Rul. 77-60, providing that "[a] power to use property to enable the donee to continue an accustomed mode of living, without further limitation, although predictable and measurable on the basis of past expenditures, does not come within the ascertainable standard prescribed in IRC section 2041(b)(1)(A) since the standard of living may include customary travel, entertainment luxury items, or other expenditures not required for meeting the donee's 'needs for health, education or support.' Nor does the requirement of a good faith exercise of a power create an ascertainable standard. Good faith exercise of a power is not determinative of its breadth." Rev. Rul. 77-60 also provides a list of examples of powers which are limited by an ascertainable standard including: "support in reasonable comfort," "maintenance in health and reasonable comfort," "support in his accustomed manner of living," "education, including college and professional education," "health," and "medical, dental, hospital and nursing expenses and expenses of invalidism." Use of these standardsbetter ensures compliance with the statutes and regulations avoiding any dispute by the service.

67. No, the answer would not change from that in Question 65. In *Estate of Wall*, the decedent had created a trust for the benefit of others and designated an independent corporation as trustee. 101 T.C. 300 (1993). The corporate trustee was given broad discretionary powers of distribution. The decedent reserved the right to remove and replace the corporate trustee with another independent corporate trustee. However, she could not herself serve as trustee. The court concluded that the decedent's retained power was not equivalent to a power to affect the beneficial enjoyment of the trust property as contemplated by IRC Sections 2036 and 2038. The Service agreed with this outcome in Rev. Rul. 95-58, wherein the Service ruled that a grantor's reservation of a power to remove a trustee and to appoint an individual or corporate successor trustee that is not related or subordinate to the decedent, is not considered a reservation of the trustee's discretionary powers of distribution over the property transferred. Accordingly, the trust corpus is not included in Cindy's gross estate under § 2036 or § 2038. *See also* Priv. Ltr. Rul. 201134017.

68.     IRC §§ 2038 and 2036(a)(2) overlap to a certain extent. Both include powers that impact the possession and enjoyment of income from property transferred by decedent, as is the case here. Just as with IRC § 2038, under IRC § 2036(a)(2), courts hold that decedent has not retained sufficient power to cause inclusion when the power is subject to a determinable external standard. Also, just as with IRC § 2038, when decedent can replace and remove trustee with himself or herself, decedent is deemed to hold the powers of trustee. The only difference between the answers is that IRC § 2036 applies only to income interests, as opposed to interests in or powers over corpus.

69.     **Answer (A) is correct.** While both IRC §§ 2036 and 2038 cause inclusion in the gross estate because Demetra held a power to alter enjoyment of the trust income as of her death, only IRC § 2036 includes the value of "all" trust property in Demetra's gross estate. IRC § 2038 includes in the gross estate only the value of the trust property subject to the power, and here that would equal the value of the income interest for Demetra's life. Demetra retains no power over the remainder interest.

        **Answers (B), (C), and (D) are incorrect** for the reasons stated above.

70.     **Answer (D) is correct.** In order for IRC § 2036 to trigger inclusion in Hanson's gross estate, Hanson would have to retain an interest in the income of the property transferred or a power over the income from the property transferred. In order for IRC § 2038 to trigger inclusion, Hanson would have to hold a power at death to alter, modify, revoke, or terminate the trust. In this problem, Hanson does not retain any interest in or hold any power over the trust property. Thus, the trust property is not includible in Hanson's gross estate under either IRC § 2036 or § 2038. **Answers (A), (B), and (C) are incorrect** for the reasons stated above.

71.     **Answer (A) is correct.** This problem mirrors the facts of *Estate of Farrel v. United States*, 77-1 U.S. Tax Cas. (CCH) ¶ 13,185 (Ct. Cl. 1977). Under both IRC §§ 2036 and 2038, a transferor is deemed to hold the powers held by the trustee if the transferor may replace the trustee with a trustee of transferor's choosing. This result is avoided only where transferor's discretion is limited to naming a trustee who is not related or subordinate to transferor. Rev. Rul. 95-58, 1995-2 C.B. 191. However, IRC § 2038 applies only to those powers decedent holds as of date of death. Decedent did not hold any power to replace a trustee as of date of death. IRC § 2036(a)(2) leads to a different result because it includes property to the extent that transferor retains a power over enjoyment of income "for . . . life or for any period not ascertainable without reference to his death or for any period which does not in fact end before his death." Here Jaime retained a power to replace trustee for life, and, because of the replacement power, is deemed to hold trustee's discretionary power over income.

        **Answers (B), (C), and (D) are incorrect** for the reasons stated above.

72.    **Answer (B) is correct.** IRC § 2037 includes an amount of trust assets in Anderson's gross estate because Anderson's interest in the trust meets all the requirements of IRC § 2037. Specifically, IRC § 2037 requires:

    **a.**   decedent transfer property,

    **b.**   possession or enjoyment of the transferred property by someone other than decedent could only be obtained by surviving decedent (the "survivorship" requirement),

    **c.**   decedent retained a possibility that the property (and not just the income interest in the property) would return to decedent or would be subject to a power of disposition by decedent (called a "reversionary interest"),

    **d.**   the value of the reversionary interest immediately before decedent's death was greater than 5 percent of the entire value of the transferred property (the "5 percent test"), and

    **e.**   decedent did not transfer the property subject to a bona fide sale for adequate consideration in money or money's worth.

Treas. Reg. § 20.2037-1(a). Applying these requirements to the facts of the problem, (1) Anderson transferred property, (2) Anderson's child could obtain possession of the property only by surviving Anderson, (3) Anderson retained the possibility the property would return to Anderson if he survived his spouse, or in the words of the statute, Anderson retained a reversionary interest, and (4) these questions assume the reversionary interest meets the 5 percent test. Treas. Reg. § 20.2037-1(e), example 3. In order to determine whether the reversionary interest exceeds 5 percent of the value of the transferred property, the valuation tables promulgated by Treasury apply. Treas. Reg. § 20.2037-1(c)(3). Also, there are no facts to indicate that the exception for a bona fide sale for adequate consideration in money or money's worth should apply.

**Answer (A) is incorrect.** Any interest Anderson retained with respect to trust property terminates upon Anderson's death. For that reason, IRC § 2033 does not apply. In order for IRC § 2033 to apply there must be a property interest capable of transfer by decedent as of decedent's death. **Answers (C) and (D) are also incorrect** for the reasons discussed above.

73.    **Answer (A) is correct.** Under these circumstances, the child does not have to survive the decedent in order to possess or enjoy the transferred property. Since the child may possess or enjoy the property without surviving the decedent, none of the property is included in decedent's estate under IRC § 2037. Note, however, that Anderson does have a possibility of reversion that will be included in his estate. Unlikely though it may be, if Anderson outlives both his wife and his child, the remainder of his spouse's assets will go to him. While IRC § 2037 will not cause inclusion of the value of this reversionary interest in Anderson's estate, IRC § 2033 will indeed cause inclusion of the value of the remainder in Anderson's estate.

**Answer (B) is incorrect.** IRC § 2037 does not apply to include Anderson's interest in gross estate because the retained interest does not meet the "survivorship" requirement. Thus,

Anderson's child may enjoy the property without having to survive Anderson.

**Answers (C) and (D) are incorrect.** For reasons explained above, neither (C) nor (D) is correct.

74.   IRC § 2033 includes in the gross estate the value of the transferred property to the extent of the reversionary interest in Andersen. Anderson's gross estate thus includes the value of the property transferred less the value of Anderson's spouse's outstanding life estate and the contingent remainder in Andersen's child.

75.   **Answer (D) is correct.** IRC § 2033 does not apply because Cynthia gave away all interest and control over the property transferred on the date of the gift, even though the property does not actually pass outright to Cynthia's descendants until Cynthia's death. Cynthia did not retain any interest that could be transferred by Cynthia at death. IRC § 2037 does not apply because Cynthia did not retain any reversionary interest. *See* Treas. Reg. § 20.2037-1(e), example 2. **Answers (A), (B), and (C) are incorrect** for the reasons stated above.

76.   **Answer (A) is correct** and states the requirements of IRC § 2037 in the most accurate manner. Retention of the possibility that the trust property will be subject to a power over both income and principal, retained by Ellen, falls within the definition of "reversionary interest." Treas. Reg. § 20.2037-1(c)(2). Thus, Ellen retained a reversionary interest, as required by IRC § 2037. Ellen's niece could possess the property only by surviving Ellen, thus meeting the survivorship requirement of IRC § 2037. Finally, the problem assumes that the value of the reversionary interest immediately before Ellen's death exceeded 5 percent of the value of the trust property.

   **Answers (B), (C), and (D) are incorrect** for the reasons stated above. Answer (B) does not clearly state the test for IRC § 2037. Answer (C) is wrong because Ellen has retained a reversionary interest as defined by the statute. Answer (D) does not properly focus on whether Ellen retained any interest in the transferred property.

77.   **Answer (C) is correct.** IRC § 2037(b) specifies that decedent's gross estate will not include transferred interests in property "if possession or enjoyment of the property could have been obtained by any beneficiary during the decedent's life through the exercise of a general power of appointment . . . which in fact was exercisable immediately before the decedent's death." The question poses the fact pattern addressed by this statement. *See* Treas. Reg. § 20.2037-1(e), example 6. This fact pattern fails the survivorship requirement because on exercise of the power of appointment the appointee may enjoy the property without surviving Frances.

   **Answers (A), (B), and (D) are incorrect** for the reasons stated above. Generally, powers of appointment are not attributed as between spouses. In addition, the exception does not require exercise of the power, only that it be held immediately before decedent's death.

78.   IRC § 2037 includes in the gross estate only reversionary interests retained by a decedent that exceed 5 percent of the trust property immediately before decedent's death. Here Greg's reversionary interest will be compared to the value of the trust property without any deduction for the value of niece's outstanding life estate. Actuarial tables will apply to determine the value of the reversion. The value is determined without regard to the fact of

decedent's death, and without regard to whether the estate elects alternate valuation. Treas. Reg. § 20.2037-1(c)(3), (4).

79. **Answer (C) is correct.** Congress enacted IRC § 2039 specifically to deal with the survivor annuity under an employer-funded retirement plan. Litigation had raised an issue as to whether a decedent's gross estate included the value of a survivor annuity where decedent did not contribute to the fund. IRC § 2039 clarifies Congress' intent to include these types of plans. Thus, Answer (C) is correct. Prior to enactment of IRC § 2039, the Service successfully litigated some cases on the basis of IRC § 2033, and some on the basis of IRC §§ 2036 through 2038.

Answer (A) is incorrect. Answer (A) is incorrect because IRC § 2039 specifically does not apply to benefits payable under a life insurance contract. It states: "The gross estate shall include the value of an annuity or other payment receivable by any beneficiary by reason of surviving the decedent under any form of contract or agreement . . . (other than as insurance under policies on the life of the decedent)." IRC § 2039(a). Whether a contract amounts to a life insurance contract has been litigated. In those cases, courts ask whether underwriting for the contract shifts or spreads risk of premature death. The life insurance contract, thus, takes into account more than just "investment risk." *See All v. McCobb*, 321 F.2d 633 (2d Cir. 1963). Courts may apply the integrated transactions doctrine to determine whether the contract is one of life insurance where a series of contracts are involved. *See Montgomery v. Comm'r*, 56 T.C. 489 (1971),*aff'd*, 458 F.2d 616 (5th Cir. 1972).

Answer (B) is incorrect. The Service has issued regulations indicating it will not apply IRC § 2039 to include assets held in a grantor-retained annuity trust in the estate of decedent. Treas. Reg. § 20.2039-1(e)(1). Rather, the Treasury Regulations specify the amount to be included in the gross estate under IRC § 2036, and generally include that amount of trust assets necessary to generate the annuity payment received by decedent under that section.

Answer (D) also is incorrect. Generally, IRC§ 2039 does not apply to government benefits on the basis that a federal act does not constitute a "contract or agreement" as required by IRC § 2039. Rev. Rul. 60-70, 1960-1 C.B. 372, *as modified*, Rev. Rul. 73-316, 1973-2 C.B. 318. *See also* Rev. Rul. 2002-39, 2002-2 C.B. 33 (indicating inapplicability of IRC § 2039 with regard to annuities payable to New York City firefighters and police who die from injuries sustained while performing duties). The Service, however, indicates that such benefits may be includible in the gross estate pursuant to IRC § 2033 if decedent may designate the beneficiary.

80. **Answer (D) is correct.** A decedent's gross estate includes the value of an annuity *"or other payment receivable by any beneficiary"* by reason of surviving the decedent to the extent that such payment is attributable to contributions made by the decedent. IRC § 2039(a). Note that the lump sum payment to Robert is still a payment which is received under the annuity contract. Further, because the lump sum payment to Robert was receivable upon Richard's death, the amount of the lump sum payment to Robert is includable in Richard's gross estate. *See* IRC § 2039(a).

**Answer (B) and (C) are incorrect.** Note that if the lump sum payment were received by Robert during his life, there is no guaranty that it would be in his estate upon his death. Answer (B) is therefore incorrect. Conversely, with respect to Answer (C), if Robert held onto the lump sum payment, it would be included in Robert's estate.

**Answer (A) is incorrect.** Because the lump sum payment will be included in Richard's gross estate for reasons explained above, Answer (A) is incorrect.

81.  **Answer (A) is correct.** IRC § 2039 applies broadly to include more than just employer-sponsored annuities. It includes commercial annuities, private annuities, and other annuities payable under agreements or plans if the following requirements are met:

   a.   A beneficiary receives an annuity or other payment by reason of surviving decedent,

   b.   The annuity or other payment is made under a contract or agreement other than a life insurance policy on decedent's life,

   c.   An annuity or other payment was also payable to decedent or decedent possessed the right to receive such payment, either alone or with another, under the terms of such contract or agreement, and

   d.   Decedent received the annuity or other payment or possessed the right to do so for decedent's life, for a period not ascertainable without reference to decedent's death or for a period that does not in fact end before decedent's death.

The amount included in the gross estate equals the value of the annuity or amount of other payment that is proportionate to the total amount of the purchase price contributed by decedent.

In this question, pursuant to the terms of the agreement with the lottery agency, Alice was in fact receiving an annuity for a period that did not end before her life, and Alice's descendants were entitled to receive the annuity upon surviving Alice. Because Alice paid 100 percent of the price of the lottery ticket, Alice's gross estate must include 100 percent of the value of the annuity as of Alice's death.

**Answer (B) is incorrect.** The estate in *Estate of Shackleford v. United States*, 1998 U.S. Dist. LEXIS 12442 (E.D. Cal. 1998), *aff'd*, 262 F.3d 1028 (9th Cir. 2001), argued that only a minute portion of the value of the annuity should be included in decedent's gross estate because decedent was only one of millions of people who bought lottery tickets to provide the winner the annuity benefits. The Court easily dispensed of this argument, and included the full value of the annuity as of decedent's death in his estate. Decedent's purchase of $1 resulted in receipt of the winnings in the form of an annuity.

**Answers (C) and (D) are also incorrect.** Answer (C) is incorrect because it does not matter whether or not the decedent could direct who is to receive the annuity payments following decedent's death. *See* Treas. Reg. § 20.2039-1(b)(2), example 2. Although the annuity was for a term of years, decedent was receiving the annuity at the time of death. Thus, decedent was paid the annuity for a period that did not in fact end before his death. IRC § 2039(a).

82.  **Answer (A) is correct.** The question here is whether the form of "separate" plans should be respected so that IRC § 2039 does not apply to either plan. Based on these facts, Treas. Reg. § 20.2039-1(b)(2), example 6, takes the position that "[t]he scope of section 2039(a) and (b) cannot be limited by indirection." It indicates that IRC § 2039 does include the value of the annuity payable by reason of Clarice's death to Clarice's spouse in the gross estate. The regulation focuses on the substance and interconnectedness of the agreements. To find

otherwise would create a simple way in which to avoid application of IRC § 2039 in every situation. When considered together, these two plans meet all the requirements of IRC § 2039 for inclusion in the gross estate.

In contrast, note that if the facts were changed so that Plan 1 did not pay decedent an annuity, but instead, for example, paid decedent a salary for consulting services or provided a disability plan, then even were the contracts to be construed together, the requirement that decedent be paid an annuity or other payment would not necessarily be met if the payment to the employee was not of the same type as the payment to the beneficiary. *See Estate of Schelberg v. Comm'r*, 612 F.2d 25 (2d Cir. 1979); *Kramer v. United States*, 406 F.2d 1363 (Ct. Cl. 1969).

**Answer (D) is incorrect.** For the reasons stated above, Answer (D) is incorrect. **Answers (B) and (C) are incorrect.** Answer (B) is incorrect because the fact that the beneficiary could forfeit the payments does not preclude inclusion. It would, however, impact the value to be included in Clarice's gross estate. Treas. Reg. § 20.2039-1(b)(2), example 2. Answer (C) is incorrect because Clarice was in pay status and in fact received annuity payments prior to death so that the condition of forfeiture based on Clarice reaching a specific age no longer applied.

83. **Answer (A) is correct.** The full value of the annuity as of Dani's date of death is included in Dani's gross estate because payments by Dani's employer are treated as being made by Dani. IRC § 2039(b) states: "any contribution by the decedent's employer or former employer to the purchase price of such contract . . . shall be considered to be contributed by the decedent if made by reason of his employment." *See also* Treas. Reg. § 20.2039-1(c), example 2. Because of the attribution of the employer's payments to Dani, the entire value of the annuity is included in Dani's gross estate.

**Answer (B) is incorrect for the reason stated above.** Note, however, that if the facts were changed so that Dani's spouse (and not Dani's employer) had contributed one-half of the payments for the joint and survivor annuity, only one-half of the annuity would be included in Dani's gross estate per Treas. Reg. § 20.2039-1(c).

**Answers (C) and (D) are incorrect.** Answer (C) is incorrect because it does not matter if Dani was in pay status because Dani had "the right" to receive payments had Dani lived. Answer (D) is incorrect because IRC § 2039 includes the annuity if decedent had the right to receive the annuity "either alone or in conjunction with another for his life." The facts indicate that Dani had the right to an annuity for her life. Dani's spouse also had the requisite right to receive payments "by reason of surviving the decedent." IRC § 2039(b).

84. The issue here is whether payments made by the decedent's spouse are treated as being made by the decedent such that the whole annuity is required to be included in Dani's gross estate. The purpose of the ratio created by IRC § 2039(b) is illustrated by Treas. Reg. § 20.2039-1(c), Example (1). Under the example, the amount includible in the gross estate was one-half of the value of the survivor's annuity where the decedent and his wife had each contributed equal amounts towards the purchase of a joint and survivor annuity. In enacting IRC § 2039(b) Congress indicated that the value of an annuity attributable to contributions by the surviving beneficiary should not be included in gross estate of the decedent. *See Neely v. United States*, 613 F.2d 802, 808 (Ct. Cl. 1980). The value of such contributions does not represent assets of the decedent which should be subject to estate tax. *Id.* at 808.

**85.**     **Answer (D) is correct.** IRC § 2040 specifically indicates that it applies to property held as joint tenants with right of survivorship and that held as tenants by the entirety. IRC § 2040. Treasury Regulation § 20.2040-1(b) clarifies that IRC § 2040 applies to all classes of property, including real property, bank accounts, and bonds. Property owned as joint tenants with right of survivorship allows either joint tenant to enjoy the entire property subject to the interest of the other joint tenant. The characteristic that sets joint tenancy with right of survivorship apart from other types of tenancies is that on the death of a joint tenant, the interest of the predeceased joint tenant in the property passes by operation of law to the surviving joint tenant or joint tenants. Tenancy by the entirety property is property held only between a husband and wife, and similarly, on the death of a spouse, the entire interest in the tenancy by the entirety property passes to the surviving spouse. The primary differences between tenancy by the entirety property and joint tenancy with right of survivorship property are that the former (1) is held only between spouses, and (2) both spouses must consent to a termination of the tenancy by the entirety. In contrast, a joint tenant may unilaterally terminate the joint tenancy with right of survivorship by conveyance or by a request for partition.

    **Answers (A), (B), and (C) are incorrect.** As indicated above, IRC § 2040 specifies the extent of its application. It does not apply to tenancies in common or community property. Neither of those tenancies carries with it a survivorship interest. A tenant in common may pass the tenancy-in-common interest by will. Likewise, a spouse can pass his or her community property interest by will.

**86.**     **Answer (C) is correct.** An exception to the general rule applies for qualified joint interests. When the only two joint tenants are spouses, and the spouses hold title as joint tenants with right of survivorship, or when the spouses hold property as tenants by the entirety, the jointly held property meets the definitional requirements of a "qualified joint interest." IRC § 2040(b) includes in the gross estate one-half the value of the qualified joint interest regardless of the amount contributed by each joint tenant. Congress enacted this straightforward 50 percent inclusion rule to avoid the need to trace contributions by spouses.

    **Answers (A), (B), and (D) are incorrect** due to the 50 percent inclusion rule applicable to qualified joint interests.

**87.**     **Answer (B) is correct.** An exception to the general rule applies for joint tenants with right of survivorship property received by decedent and the other joint tenants by gift, inheritance, devise, or bequest. IRC § 2040(a); Treas. Reg. § 20.2040-1(a)(1). In the event that decedent and the other joint tenants received the joint tenancy with right of survivorship interests by gift, inheritance, devise, or bequest, decedent's gross estate includes a fractional share of the jointly held property. Here, Ellie owned the land with Carl and David, so Ellie's fractional share is one-third. As a consequence, Ellie's gross estate includes one-third the fair market value of the land. *See* Treas. Reg. § 20.2040-1(c)(8).

**Answers (A), (C), and (D) are incorrect.** Where property is received by the joint tenants as a result of a gift, inheritance, devise, or bequest, tracing rules do not apply to determine gross estate inclusion. Instead, a simple rule requiring inclusion of a fractional share equal to decedent's fractional interest in the property applies.

88.     **Answer (D) is correct.** For the reasons stated below, because neither the qualified joint interest exception nor the exception for property received by gift, inheritance, devise, or bequest applies, the general rule of IRC § 2040(a) applies to avoid inclusion in Gavin's gross estate. The general rule of IRC § 2040 includes the entire value of the jointly held property in a decedent's gross estate, unless the estate can demonstrate that a portion of the consideration for the property was supplied by the other joint tenants. In the event the other joint tenants provided a portion of the consideration, the gross estate includes the value of the jointly held property less the portion attributable to consideration supplied by the other joint tenants. Treas. Reg. § 20.2040-1(a)(2). Here, the other joint tenant Fred supplied all of the consideration. Thus, Gavin's gross estate does not include any of the jointly held property. Treas. Reg. § 20.2040-1(c)(3). Note that if instead Fred had died before Gavin, Fred's estate would include the entire value of the jointly held property because he provided all of the consideration. Treas. Reg. § 20.2040-1(c)(1).

**Answers (A) and (C) are incorrect.** Neither Gavin's ability to access the account during life nor the amount of income received by Gavin during life impact the amount included in the gross estate under IRC § 2040. Gross estate inclusion under that section focuses only on the consideration, if any, provided by the deceased joint tenant.

**Answer (B) is incorrect.** The exception applicable to property received by joint tenants by gift, inheritance, devise, or bequest applies only where all joint tenants so received the property. Where one of the joint tenants provided consideration for the property, the general rule of IRC § 2040(a) applies instead.

89.     **Answer (A) is correct.** Because all consideration contributed toward the purchase of the land and home held as joint tenants with right of survivorship originated from Heidi, her gross estate includes the entire date-of-death value of the land and home. It does not matter that the land appreciated in value from the time of the gift to Heidi's daughter until the time the land and home were placed in joint tenancy. Treas. Reg. § 20.2040-2(c)(4).

**Answers (B), (C), and (D) are incorrect** for the reasons noted above.

90.     **Answer (D) is correct.** IRC § 2040(a) applies to the extent that the property was acquired jointly with the decedent. Here, Dolph is the sole owner of account #1 and it is not held as joint tenants with rights of survivorship with Charles. The fact that Dolph later sold the apartment building and put the gains in bank account #1 is of no consequence to Charles or his estate. None of the $1,000,000 is included in Charles' gross estate under IRC § 2040. Finally, note that this is primarily an irrevocable gift of the apartment building and income earned from the property is not property over which the decedent had any control or interest.

**Answers (A), (B), and (C) are incorrect.** Answers (A) through (C) each contemplate that some portion of the value of the bank account is included in Charles' gross estate. For reasons explained above, none of the value of bank account #1 is included in Charles' gross estate.

**91.** **Answer (D) is correct.** Again, apartment building #1 was given outright to Charles. Charles does not jointly own the property with Dolph. Rather, Dolph is the sole owner of the property and, as such, IRC § 2040 does not apply to these facts.

**Answers (A), (B), and (C) are incorrect.** For reasons explained above and explained in the answer to question 90, above, each of these answers is incorrect.

**92.** **Answer (B) is correct.** IRC § 2040 specifically applies to a deposit of money in the name of the decedent and another person. It makes no difference that the survivor takes the entire interest or that the decedent's interest in the property is not included in his probate estate. Charles and Dolph hold bank account #2 as joint tenants with rights of survivorship. Before acquiring apartment building #2, Charles transferred apartment building #1 (income producing property) to Dolph for no consideration and Dolph subsequently sold and realized $1 million gain on the apartment building #1, which became Dolph's contribution to building #2. Thus, the value of apartment building #2 (the jointly held property) minus the portion of the value attributable to the income furnished by Dolph to purchase apartment #2 is included in Charles' gross estate. Specifically, since Dolph furnished half of the consideration to purchase apartment #2, half of the value of apartment #2, or $2,000,000 is included in Charles' gross estate. *See* Treas. Reg. § 20.2040-1(c)(example 5). This outcome is also supported by the holding in *Estate of Goldsborough v. Comm'r*, 70 T.C. 1077 (1978).

**Answer (A) is incorrect.** Because Dolph first sold apartment #1, realized the gain and then used such gain to purchase an interest in apartment #2, IRC § 2040 does not operate to include the full value of apartment #2 in his estate. *See also Estate of Kelley v. Comm'r*, 22 B.T.A. 421 (1931); *Harvey v. United States*, 185 F.2d 463 (7th Cir. 1950). Note, however, that if instead Dolph had exchanged apartment building #1 originally received from Charles for apartment building #2, the entire value would be included in Charles' gross estate. The key factual difference was the realization of income by Dolph in the sale of apartment #1. Here, formality appears to control to a certain extent over the substance of such a transaction. Clients will be well served by knowing the distinction in the tax treatment of the different forms that the transaction may take.

**Answers (C) and (D) are incorrect.** For reasons described above, Answers (C) and (D) are incorrect.

**93.** **Answer (B) is correct.** If the decedent furnished a part of the purchase price, only a corresponding portion of the value is included. Reg. § 20.2040-1(c)(example 2). Thus, the amount excluded from Charles' gross estate is calculated as follows:

| Amount Excluded | = | × | Date-of-Death Value (survivor's consideration) |
|---|---|---|---|
| | | | (entire consideration paid) |
| or, | | | |
| Amount Excluded | = | | $4,000,000 |
| | | × | ($1,000,000/$2,000,000) |
| | = | | $2,000,000 |

Thus, Charles' gross estate includes $2,000,000 or the date-of-death value of apartment building #2 less $2,000,000 excluded as attributable to consideration provided by Dolph, as discussed in the prior answers.

**Answers (A), (C), and (D) are incorrect.** Each of these answers is incorrect for reasons already explained above.

94.    **Answer (B) is correct.** The Service in Revenue Ruling 76-303, 1976-2 C.B. 266, takes the position that, on the simultaneous deaths of joint tenants where property owned by right of survivorship passes one-half to each of their gross estates, the gross estate of the contributing joint tenant, here Ingrid, includes the entire value of the property, and the gross estate of the noncontributing joint tenant, here Joan, includes one-half the value. Essentially the Service applies the general rule of IRC § 2040(a) to the one-half of the property passing by survivorship from the contributing joint tenant to the noncontributing joint tenant; and applies IRC § 2033 to the one-half of the property passing by state law under the contributing joint tenant's estate. Based on this reasoning the entire value of the apartment building is included in Ingrid's gross estate. The noncontributing joint tenant's estate includes one-half the value of the jointly held property passing pursuant to the noncontributing joint tenant's estate under IRC § 2033.

    **Answers (A), (C), and (D) are incorrect** for the reasons stated above.

95. **Answer (A) is correct.** A general power of appointment includes any power exercisable at the time of his death in favor of the decedent, his estate, creditors or creditors of his estate. Here, Cooper can appoint trust property to anyone without limitation. Treas. Reg. § 20.2041-1(c)(1). A power exercisable during life is often referred to as an inter vivos or lifetime power of appointment, and Cooper's ability to appoint to anyone including his creditors falls within this category. He holds both an inter vivos and a testamentary power of appointment. Thus, he holds a general power over the property that is held in trust at the time of his death. Since all of the cash in the trust was appointed away during life, it is not included in Cooper's gross estate upon his death under IRC § 2041. On the other hand, since marketable securities remain in the trust, the amount of property in trust subject to his power is included in Cooper's gross estate.

    **Answers (B), (C), and (D) are incorrect.** For reasons explained above, the remaining answers are all incorrect.

96. **Answer (A) is correct.** IRC § 2041(b)(1) defines a general power of appointment as a power "exercisable in favor of the decedent, his estate, his creditors, or the creditors of his estate." This type of general power of appointment, if held at death, is subject to federal estate taxation. Because Cooper can appoint trust property during life or by will to his creditors (or the creditors of his estate), he holds a general power of appointment. Although Cooper does not own the property subject to the power, Cooper may exercise control over the property in the same manner as if he owned it, due to the fact that he can transfer it to creditors or creditors of his estate. Regardless of whether he actually exercises the power during life or at death, all of the value of the trust property in the trust at death will be included.

    **Answers (B), (C) and (D) are incorrect** for reasons explained above.

97. **Answer (D) is correct.** Under these circumstances, Cooper does not hold a general power of appointment. Treas. Reg. § 20.2041-1(c)(1). The power only allows Cooper to distribute to his sister. As such, the power prohibits appointment to himself, his estate, his creditors, or the creditors of his estate. The distribution provision avoids estate tax in Cooper's estate as the power holder, but allows Cooper to distribute to his sister for any reason. (Note that if the power was drafted to include one of these four categories of appointees, the answer would change because then property could be appointed for the power holder's benefit.) Thus, none of the assets held in trust upon Cooper's death is included in his gross estate.

    **Answers (A), (B), and (C) are incorrect.** For reasons explained above, the remaining answers are all incorrect.

98. **Answer (D) is correct.** The Code excepts from the definition of general power of appointment "[a] power to consume, invade, or appropriate property for the benefit of the decedent which is limited by an ascertainable standard relating to the health, education

support or maintenance of the decedent . . ." IRC § 2041(b)(1)(A). This is sometimes referred to as a MESH [Maintenance-Education-Support-Health] standard. The regulations clarify: "A power is limited by such a standard if the extent of the holder's duty to exercise and not to exercise the power is reasonably measurable in terms of his needs for health, education, or support (or for any combination of them)." Inclusion of an ascertainable standard effectively prevents Cooper in this case from simply appointing the property to himself or his creditors during life or upon death. Drafters generally should try to use one of the ascertainable standards prescribed in the regulations if the client's goal is to avoid classification as a "general power of appointment" and the client prefers to avoid the need to obtain a court order addressing the ability of the state court to enforce or ascertain the standard. None of the property held in trust upon Cooper's death is included in his estate.

**Answers (A), (B), and (C) are incorrect.** For reasons explained above, the remaining answers are all incorrect.

99. **Answer (C) is correct.** If a power of appointment exists as to only a portion of a group of assets or only over a limited interest in property, IRC § 2041 applies only to such part or interest. IRC § 20.2041-1(b)(3). The facts of this questions closely parallel those in the case of *Fish v. United States*, 432 F.2d 1278 (9th Cir. 1970), wherein the terms of a trust gave decedent taxpayer the power to freely appoint trust income annually to anyone including herself. The trust terms further provided that any corpus and unpaid income were to be distributed to grandchildren on decedent taxpayer's death. Notwithstanding that decedent failed to appoint any income to herself, the Court of Appeals held that decedent had a power of appointment over such income. Further, that a lapse of that power, under § 2041(b)(2), was a release of the income causing inclusion in decedent's gross estate. The court also held that because decedent had no power to appoint any of the corpus of the trust, the value of these assets would not similarly be included in the decedent's gross estate.

**Answers (A), (B), and (D) are incorrect.** For reasons explained above, the remaining answers are all incorrect.

100. The answer would not change. Incompetence of the holder of the power does not prevent the holder from being required to include the value of the assets over which the holder has a general power of appointment. The court in *Fish v. United States*, 432 F.2d 1278 (9th Cir. 1970), found that inaction or failure to exercise a power due to incompetence was irrelevant. The court held that a lapse of the power held by the decedent, under § 2041(b)(2), constitutes a release of the income to the gross estate, regardless of how the lapse occurred. Consistent with this conclusion, the court in *Estate of Alperstein v. Comm'r*, 613 F.2d 1213 (2d Cir. 1979), also held that the incapacity of a power holder was irrelevant to the determination of whether the power holder held the general power at death. The *Alperstein* court relied on legislative history and prior case law in arriving at its conclusion that IRC § 2041(a)(2) intended to reach all powers granted a decedent. It also cited the prior Supreme Court case, *Comm'r v. Noel*, 380 U.S. 678 (1965), stating: "It would stretch the imagination to think that Congress intended to measure estate tax liability by an individual's fluctuating, day-to-day, hour-by-hour capacity to dispose of property." Likewise, a child's minority does not impact application of IRC § 2041(a)(2) to general powers held by a minor.

101. **Answer (B) is correct.** Nancy's gross estate includes only the property subject to the general power of appointment held as of the date of her death. On the date of her death, Nancy held the power to appoint to herself up to $5,000. Thus, her gross estate includes

$5,000. Although IRC § 2041(a)(2) includes in the gross estate property "with respect to which the decedent has at any time exercised or released [a general] power of appointment by a disposition which is of such nature that if it were a transfer of property owned by the decedent, such property would be includible in the decedent's gross estate under section 2035 to 2038 inclusive," this inclusionary rule does not apply to Nancy. The "5 and 5" exception precludes application of the general rule. IRC § 2041(b)(2) treats the lapse of a power as a release, but only if the lapse "exceeded in value, at the time of such lapse, the greater of" $5,000 or 5 percent of the assets subject to the power at the time of the lapse. Because the trust instrument limited the annual general power of appointment to $5,000, the lapse of Nancy's power during years 1 and 2 fall within the "5 and 5" exception. Thus, Nancy's gross estate does not include any portion of the property over which she could have exercised a power of appointment prior to its lapse. Treas. Reg. § 20.2041-3(d)(3). **Answers (A), (C), and (D) are incorrect** for the reasons stated above.

102. **Answer (C) is correct.** The gross estate includes property subject to a general power of appointment held by decedent at death. IRC § 2041(a)(2). At death, Oscar held a general power of appointment over $10,000 of trust assets because he could pay that sum to himself. Thus, at least $10,000 is includible in Oscar's gross estate. The gross estate also includes property with respect to which decedent (1) exercised or released a power of appointment and (2) following the exercise or release of the power decedent retains an interest in the property such that, had decedent instead owned and transferred the property, it would have been included in decedent's gross estate under IRC §§ 2035 through 2038. IRC § 2041(a)(2); Treas. Reg. § 20.2041-3(d)(1). A lapse of a power is deemed a release to the extent the lapse exceeds the greater of $5,000 or 5 percent of the property subject to the power as of the date of the lapse. IRC § 2041(b)(2). Thus, Oscar is deemed to release the power of appointment to the extent of $5,000 (i.e., $10,000 withdrawal power less $5,000). [Note that $5,000 is greater than 5 percent of $60,000 or $3,000.] Under the terms of the trust, Oscar continues to receive all income from the $5,000 of property over which Oscar previously released a general power of appointment for each of years 1 through 3. Treasury Regulations direct that the portion of trust assets deemed to be retained each year following the release should be aggregated to determine the fraction of trust assets at death subject to inclusion in the gross estate under IRC § 2041(a)(2). Oscar retained $5,000/$60,000 or one-twelfth of the assets each year. Thus, an additional three-twelfths of $60,000, or $15,000, is included in Oscar's gross estate. Treas. Reg. § 20.2041-3(d)(4). The total amount included in Oscar's gross estate equals $25,000 or the $10,000 of assets subject to his general power of appointment at death, plus the aggregate of the proportions of trust property over which Oscar was deemed to release a power but retain a prohibited interest.

**Answers (A), (B), and (D) are incorrect** for the reasons stated above. Oscar held at death at least a $10,000 general power of appointment so at least some of the trust assets are included in his gross estate. Thus, Answer (A) is incorrect. In addition, the amount of assets deemed released each year for three years is $5,000, and not $7,000 (or the excess of 5 percent) as assumed by Answer (D).

103. The answer to Question 102 would change because, under the new facts, Oscar did not retain an interest that would have been includible under IRC §§ 2035 through 2038 had he owned and transferred the property. Thus, the release of the power of appointment in excess of $5,000 would not cause inclusion in Oscar's gross estate under IRC § 2041(a)(2). Under the changed facts, only $10,000 of trust assets subject to the withdrawal right held at death

would be included in Oscar's gross estate. IRC § 2041(a)(2).

104. The answer to Question 103 would change because, under the additional facts, Oscar did not retain any general power of appointment at death, and did not retain any prohibited interest on release of the general power of appointment. Treasury Regulation § 20.2041-3(b) indicates that if decedent may exercise the power only in the event of a contingency that has not occurred at death, such as attaining a certain age, the decedent does not possess the power at death. Here the contingency is that exercise may only occur in November. Thus, no assets would be includible under Oscar's gross estate under the facts in Question 103. Treas. Reg. § 20.2041-3(d)(3).

105. **Answer (A) is correct.** Powers that must be exercised jointly can cause a power that would otherwise be a general power of appointment, to avoid inclusion under IRC § 2041. Treasury Regulation § 20.2041-3(c)(1) provides that a power exercisable only with the consent of the creator of the power is not a general power of appointment, and, thus, is not includible under IRC § 2041. **Answers (B), (C), and (D) are incorrect for this reason.**

106. **Answer (A) is correct.** A power does not amount to a general power of appointment if the holder may only exercise it with the consent of a person with a substantial adverse interest. IRC § 2041(b)(1)(C)(ii); Treas. Reg. § 20.2041-3(c)(2). The question becomes when a co-holder has an adverse interest. In this question, any one particular child would not have necessarily been in a better economic position after the decedent's death by refusing to exercise the power in favor of the decedent during the decedent's lifetime. The fact that such child might survive the decedent and receive an interest in the property, if the decedent failed to exercise the testamentary power in favor of other persons, does not elevate such child's interest as a consenting party of the lifetime power to a substantial adverse interest. Under the terms of the trust here, Bob only needed the consent of one of his children to distribute trust property. As such, the interest held by any one child does not amount to a substantial interest in the property subject to the power, that is adverse to exercise of the power in favor of the decedent, for purposes of IRC § 2041(b)(1)(c)(ii). Consequently, the decedent's power falls within the definition of a "general power of appointment" because no child had a substantial interest in the property that was adverse to the exercise of the power in favor of the decedent.

**Answers (B), (C), and (D) are incorrect** for the reasons stated above.

107. **Answer (D) is correct.** Here, Jim is the decedent's only child. Jim would have had a vested interest in the trust remainder that would have been substantially adverse to the exercise of the decedent's lifetime power of appointment. Treas. Reg. § 20.2041-3(c)(2) specifies that a taker in default of appointment has an interest adverse to the power holder. Jim would take the property absent an exercise of the power. *See* Rev. Rul. 79-63, 1979-1 C.B. 302. As such, Bob is not treated as having a power of appointment.

**Answers (A), (B), and (C) are incorrect** for the reasons stated above.

**108.** **Answer (D) is correct.** IRC § 2042(1) supplies two rules of inclusion with respect to life insurance proceeds on a decedent's life. The full amount of the insurance proceeds are includible in Alena's gross estate under IRC § 2042(1), which includes proceeds receivable "by the executor." Treasury Regulation § 20.2042-1(a) interprets the Code to include proceeds receivable "by or for the benefit of the estate." **For this same reason, Answer (A) is incorrect** — "estate" falls within the meaning of "executor."

**Answers (B) and (C) are also incorrect.** It does not matter what, if any, consideration decedent paid for the policy. IRC § 2042 does not take consideration into account. Notably, IRC § 2043 also does not take consideration into account with respect to inclusion of life insurance proceeds under IRC § 2042. The full amount of the proceeds payable to or for the benefit of the estate are includible under IRC § 2042(1). Treas. Reg. § 20.2042-1(a)(3).

**109.** The gross estate would still include the full amount of the insurance proceeds in Alena's estate, but would do so under IRC § 2042(2). IRC § 2042(2) provides the second rule of inclusion under IRC § 2042. It includes in the gross estate of decedent proceeds of life insurance on decedent's life paid to persons other than the estate or for its benefit over which decedent held "incidents of ownership" as of his or her death. An owner of a policy, such as Alena, generally holds incidents of ownership of the policy. The theory underlying IRC § 2042(2) is that if decedent holds incidents of ownership, decedent holds sufficient indicia of ownership up until death to require inclusion in the gross estate of the monies passing under the policy.

**110.** **Answer (A) would be the correct answer.** IRC § 2042(1) does not apply because trustee was not obligated to pay the estate taxes owed by Alena's estate. Payment of such taxes was entirely within the trustee's discretion, and trustee was not under any legally binding obligation to pay such taxes. If the facts were changed so that the trust required the trustee to pay such taxes, then the answer would change and the "proceeds required for the payment in full (to the extent of the beneficiary's obligation)" would be includible in Alena's gross estate under Treas. Reg. § 20.2042-1(b)(1). In addition, IRC § 2042(2) does not apply because the trustee as owner of the policy held all incidents of ownership from its inception. **Thus, Answer (D) is incorrect.** As before, **Answers (B) and (C) are incorrect** because IRC § 2042 does not focus on the amount of premiums paid to determine inclusion.

**111.** **Answer (A) is correct.** IRC § 2042 applies only to life insurance on decedent's life. It does not apply to life insurance owned by decedent on the life of another. For that reason, Bob's gross estate does not include any portion of the value of the policy under IRC § 2042. It may, however, include the value of the life insurance policy under a different Code section. Treas. Reg. § 20.2042-1(a)(2). In this problem, IRC § 2033 will apply to include the fair market value of the policy at the date of death as determined under the IRC § 2031 Treasury Regulations. Generally that amount is the terminal interpolated reserve value with some exceptions.

**Answers (B), (C), and (D) are incorrect** for the reasons stated above. Neither the amount paid for premiums nor the face amount of the policy give an accurate measure of the value of life insurance on the life of another. Terminal interpolated reserve value, however, is sometimes used to determine inclusion under IRC § 2033. Terminal interpolated reserve value is calculated by the life insurance company using Form 712 and provided by the company to the taxpayer on request.

112. **Answer (C) is the best answer.** In a situation similar to the facts in this question the Service has ruled that the insurance proceeds avoid inclusion in the decedent insured's gross estate where decedent held incidents of ownership over a policy on his life transferred to the trust by someone other than decedent. Rev. Rul. 84-179, 1984-2 C.B. 195. The Service followed the holding of the court in *Estate of Skifter v. Comm'r*, 468 F.2d 699 (2d Cir. 1972), and declined to follow the contrary holding in *Terriberry v. United States*, 517 F.2d 286 (5th Cir. 1975). The ruling, however, is limited to its narrow facts. If decedent purchases a policy and transfers it to a trust of which decedent is trustee, decedent will be deemed to hold incidents of ownership. The key issue is how decedent became a fiduciary. Under the Service's ruling, Hayden's gross estate avoids inclusion of the life insurance proceeds on Hayden's death. **For these same reasons, Answers (A) and (B) are incorrect. Answer (D) is incorrect** and clearly makes no sense under these facts, as no beneficial interest in the trust is sufficient to qualify for the marital deduction that passes to Hayden.

113. Ingrid's gross estate includes the value of the policy proceeds because she retains an incident of ownership. Treasury Regulation § 20.2042-1(c)(2) indicates:

> the term 'incidents of ownership' is not limited in its meaning to ownership of the policy in the technical legal sense. Generally speaking, the term has reference to the right of the insured or his estate to the economic benefits of the policy. Thus, it includes the power to change the beneficiary, to surrender or cancel the policy, to assign the policy, to revoke an assignment, to pledge the policy for a loan, or to obtain from the insurer a loan against the surrender value of the policy.

Here, Ingrid retained the power to cancel the policy. Retention of any incident of ownership is sufficient to cause inclusion.

114. The fact that Ingrid reserved the right to cancel the policy only with her child's consent does not change the fact that Ingrid has retained an incident of ownership. IRC § 2042(2) specifically states that it does not matter whether the incident of ownership must be exercised "alone or in conjunction with any other person." Thus, jointly held incidents of ownership still cause inclusion in the gross estate of the decedent insured under IRC § 2042(2).

115. **Answer (D) is correct.** If Jamie had not transferred the life insurance policy, IRC § 2042(2) would have included the policy in her gross estate. Jamie, however, transferred the life insurance policy within three years of her death. Thus, both elements of IRC § 2035(a) are met. As a result, the entire amount of the policy proceeds is included in Jamie's gross estate. **Answers (B) and (C) are incorrect** for the reasons indicated. Note, however, that if someone other than Jamie had paid the premiums, arguably based on *Estate of Silverman v. Comm'r*, 521 F.2d 574 (2d Cir. 1975), only the portion of the policy proceeds attributable to the premiums paid by the decedent insured would be includible in the gross estate. **Answer (A) is incorrect** because a decedent insured must survive for three years from the date of

the transfer of a life insurance policy owned by decedent in order to achieve any estate-planning benefit from the transfer. This planning strategy, thus, only works if decedent lives for more than three years from the date of transfer of the policy. Otherwise, IRC § 2035 steps in to include the policy proceeds in the decedent insured's estate.

**116.** **Answer (A) is correct.** IRC § 2042 does not apply because the policy proceeds are not payable to or for the benefit of her estate, and because Mary never held any incidents of ownership with respect to the policy. For the same reason, IRC § 2035 will not apply to include the policy in Mary's gross estate. It applies only if decedent insured initially owned the policy and transferred it within three years of her death. **Answer (D) is incorrect for this reason.**

**Answers (B) and (C) are incorrect.** In 1981, Congress amended IRC § 2035 to eliminate any argument that payment of policy premiums by the decedent insured within three years of death would cause inclusion of a portion of the policy proceeds in decedent's gross estate where, as here, the decedent insured never owned the policy. Prior to the 1981 amendment of IRC § 2035, the Fifth Circuit in *Bel v. United States*, 452 F.2d 683 (5th Cir. 1971), held that payment of premiums by decedent constituted a constructive transfer of the policy.

This question demonstrates that the best way to achieve estate tax savings is to structure the purchase of the life insurance policy so that decedent insured never owns the policy. It is important that the application for insurance indicate the life insurance trust or, if no life insurance trust, someone other than the insured as owner. Note, however, that state law requires the owner to have an insurable interest in the policy.

**117.** **Answer (B) is correct.** Generally, community property is deemed owned one-half by each spouse. Treasury Regulation § 20.2042-1(c)(5) provides that incidents of ownership are possessed by decedent insured as "agent" for decedent's spouse. Under the regulation, decedent insured is deemed to hold incidents of ownership to only one-half of the policy. Thus, one-half the proceeds of the life insurance policy are included in Luke's gross estate. Note that the same answer would result if Luke instead had named his estate as beneficiary of the policy under Treas. Reg. § 20.2042-1(b)(2). **Answers (A) and (D) are incorrect** for the reasons stated. **Answer (C) is also incorrect** as it is a red herring.

**118.** **Answer (D) is correct.** IRC § 2044 includes in the gross estate of the surviving spouse the value of property in which decedent had a qualifying income interest and for which a 2056(b)(7) QTIP election was made. (Note: IRC § 2044 also includes property for which a 2523(f) QTIP election was made for property passing from one spouse to another by gift.) The facts indicate Henry had a qualifying income interest, and also indicate a QTIP election was made. Treasury Regulation § 20.2044-1(d)(1) includes "the value of the entire interest in which the decedent had a qualifying income interest for life, *determined as of the date of the decedent's death.*" (Emphasis added.) Thus, Henry's gross estate includes $1 million date-of-death value. **For this reason, Answer (C) is incorrect.** This makes sense because the purpose of the QTIP election is to treat the couple as one unit for tax purposes to ensure that the survivor may benefit from the assets of both spouses during the survivor's life. Thus, the marital deduction allows only a postponement of estate tax until the survivor's death. Although Wilma's gross estate included the assets of the QTIP trust, her estate also received a 100 percent marital deduction, so in effect it paid no estate tax on the QTIP trust assets. Congress ensured that tax would be paid in the survivor's estate by enacting IRC § 2044. Thus, **Answer (A) is incorrect.** In order to ensure taxation of the assets for which a deduction was allowed in Wilma's gross estate, the full value and not the life income interest must be subject to tax in Henry's estate. **For this reason, Answer (B) is incorrect.**

**119.** **Answer (D) is correct.** IRC § 2207A grants to Henry's estate a right of recovery for the incremental amount of estate tax incurred by his estate due to the inclusion of the QTIP assets. The difference as to whether the right of recovery is based on the incremental additional estate tax caused or the proportionate amount of estate tax caused makes a difference when the estate faces a progressive estate tax rate for the amount subject to tax after application of the unified credit. Technically, however, the correct answer requires recovery based on the incremental increase in tax caused by inclusion of the QTIP assets. **For this reason, Answers (A) and (C) are incorrect.** The right of recovery is against the persons receiving the property from the QTIP trust. Treasury Regulation § 20.2207A-1(d), defines "persons receiving the property" as the trustee of the QTIP trust if property is still held in trust, or any person who has received a trust distribution if property has already been distributed. **Thus, Answer (B) is incorrect.** Note, that to the extent the estate does not exercise its right of recovery, the waiver may be deemed a gift and/or a below-market loan. *See* Treas. Reg. § 2207A-1(b).

**120.** **Answer (C) is the best answer.** The Tax Court in *Estate of Letts v. Comm'r*, 109 T.C. 290 (1997), imposed a duty of consistency. It held that, if a QTIP marital deduction has been taken in the estate of the first spouse to die, the estate of the survivor must include the QTIP trust assets under IRC § 2044 even though a technical reading of the trust indicated a QTIP election should not have been made. **For this reason, Answer (A) is incorrect.**

**Answer (B) is also incorrect.** A QTIP election may be deemed null and void upon request under Revenue Procedure 2001-38, 2001-2 C.B. 124. The Service will declare a QTIP election null and void when the election in the estate of the first spouse to die was not necessary to avoid an estate tax on the death of that spouse. This, however, was not the case under these facts. **Answer (D) is incorrect** as it is a red herring.

121.   The applicable exclusion amount available to decedents dying in 2011 equals the basic exclusion amount plus any available deceased spousal unused exclusion amount. Because Alfred was never married, his estate would not be entitled to any deceased spousal unused exclusion amount. The basic exclusion amount for 2011 equals $5 million. With zero taxable gifts and a taxable estate of no more than $5 million, Alfred's estate falls within the applicable exclusion amount and will not owe any estate tax.

*Historical Note*: Beginning in 2011 (and continuing until sunset of the 2010 Tax Act provisions) the applicable exclusion amount is comprised of two amounts: (1) the basic exclusion amount of $5 million, which is adjusted for inflation beginning 2012, and (2) the deceased spousal unused exclusion amount. The 2012 inflation adjusted applicable exclusion amount is $5,120,000. Prior to 2011, the applicable exclusion amount was a specifically stated dollar amount as follows:

| Year | Applicable Exclusion Amount |
|---|---|
| 2010 | $5 million |
| 2009 | $3.5 million |
| 2006–2008 | $2 million |
| 2004 and 2005 | $1.5 million |
| 2002 and 2003 | $1 million |
| 2000 and 2001 | $675,000 |
| 1999 | $650,000 |
| 1998 | $625,000 |

Prior to 1998, the Code did not speak in terms of an applicable exclusion amount. Rather the unified credit would be translated in terms of an exemption equivalent amount that a taxpayer could transfer tax free.

122.   **Answer (C) is correct.** Because Alfred's applicable exclusion amount is $5 million, IRC § 2010 provides an estate tax credit equal to $1,730,800 based on a high marginal tax rate of 35%. The credit is calculated by determining the estate tax that would be charged with respect to the applicable exclusion amount. A tentative estate tax of $1,730,800 would be charged on an amount of $5,000,000 (i.e., {[($5,000,000 − $500,000) × .35)] + $155,800}; thus, an applicable credit amount of $1,730,800 will shelter assets of $5 million. *See* IRC § 2001(c). Essentially, the unified credit shelters from tax assets equal in value to the applicable exclusion amount, which in Alfred's case is $5 million. Note that for estates of decedents dying in 2011 and thereafter (provided Congress acts to extend the amendments of the 2010 Tax Act beyond 2012), the applicable exclusion amount is the aggregate amount of wealth a person may transfer during life and at death free of estate tax. In addition, the question asks for the answer to be stated in terms of a credit amount, and not the applicable exclusion amount, and for that reason, **Answers (A) and (B) are incorrect.** Indexing of the basic

exclusion amount does not begin until 2012, and it is the basic exclusion amount only that is subject to indexing, and not the unified credit amount, thus, **Answer (D) is incorrect.**

123. **Answer (B) is correct.** The applicable exclusion amount available to Bob's estate under IRC § 2010 is equal to the basic applicable exclusion plus the deceased spousal unused exclusion amount. In 2012, the basic exclusion available to Bob's estate is $5,120,000. Because Bob has not remarried, the deceased spousal applicable exclusion amount or DSUE amount available to Bob's estate equals the basic applicable exclusion amount in Betsy's estate or the applicable exclusion amount less the amount on which tentative tax was determined in Betsy's estate. Temp. Treas. Reg. § 20.2010-1T(d)(4). The basic exclusion (and the applicable exclusion amount) available to Betsy's estate in 2011 was $5 million and the amount subject to tentative tax was zero because Betsy's estate took the full marital deduction and she did not make any taxable gifts. Thus, the DSUE amount available to Bob's estate is $5 million [i.e., $5 million less 0]. As a consequence, the applicable exclusion amount in Bob's estate is equal to $10,120,000, or the $5,120,000 basic exclusion amount for 2012 plus the $5 million DSUE amount courtesy of the election in Betsy's estate. Note that the DSUE amount does not depend on the assets owned by the predeceased spouse, but instead depends on the amount of the predeceased spouse's applicable exclusion amount that went unused. **Answers (A), (C), and (D) are, thus, incorrect.**

124. **Answer (C) is correct.** The applicable exclusion amount available to Emily's estate under IRC § 2010 equals the sum of the basic exclusion amount in 2012 of $5,120,000 and the deceased spousal unused exclusion amount or DSUE amount available to Emily's estate from an election made by Fred's estate, if any. The DSUE amount is calculated by taking the lesser of (i) the basic exclusion amount available on Fred's death in 2011 ($5 million), and (ii) the applicable exclusion less the amount on which tentative tax was determined in Fred's estate ($5 million – $4.5 million). Treas. Reg. §§ 20.2010-1T(d)(4) and -2T(c)(1)(ii). As a result, the DSUE amount is $500,000. Emily's applicable exclusion amount is, thus, $5,620,000 or the 2012 basic exclusion of $5,120,000 plus the DSUE amount elected in Fred's estate of $500,000. **Answer (A) is incorrect** because the question asks for the applicable exclusion available to Emily's estate, and not the DSUE amount available to her estate. **Answers (B) and (D) are incorrect** because the DSUE amount is the lesser of the basic exclusion and the amount as calculated, plus the basic exclusion of the survivor.

125. **Answer (C) is correct.** The analysis remains the same as in Question 124, thus, **Answers (A), (B), and (D) are incorrect.** The only time remarriage impacts the deceased spousal unused exclusion amount or DSUE amount available in a surviving spouse's estate is if upon remarriage the "new" or "second" spouse also predeceases. Because George survives Emily, the answer does not change from that in Question 124. [If the facts, however, were changed to indicate instead that George predeceased Emily, Emily's estate would in that event be unable to use the DSUE amount from the estate of her first spouse Fred unless she made lifetime gifts of up to that amount. Temp. Treas. Reg. § 20.2010-3T(b)(1). Her estate would be limited to the DSUE amount, if any, elected by George's estate in the event the facts were changed.]

126. Delores' executor should not reduce the IRC § 2010 unified credit amount. In order to determine federal estate tax owed, the tax is computed based on the aggregate of (i) those assets included in Delores' gross estate, and (ii) the taxable gifts made by Delores after December 31, 1976. IRC § 2001(b)(1). Thus, because taxable gifts are added back into the

equation, the full amount of allowable IRC § 2010 unified credit of $1,730,800 in 2012 may be taken as a credit by Delores' executor. Note that Delores' estate may also subtract any gift taxes payable, based on the current rate schedule, so that her estate receives full credit for gift taxes previously paid. IRC § 2001(b)(2). The estate tax is calculated in this manner to ensure that all estates pay tax based on the progressive rate schedule. This was important when taxable estates faced a progressive rate schedule after application of the unified credit amount. Currently taxable estates pay tax at a 35 percent rate from the first dollar of estate tax actually payable. With the decrease in the top rate to 35 percent, the Service requires gift tax payable be recalculated and only the recalculated amount subtracted in determining federal estate tax owed.

127. **Answer (B) is correct.** Callie's gross estate is entitled to a deduction for state estate, inheritance, and succession taxes actually paid when a deduction is claimed within the specified time limits of IRC § 2058. The state estate tax attributable to Callie's estate need not be paid prior to filing the federal estate tax return so long as it is paid within four years of filing the return, or, if later, within certain other specified time limits. Because Callie's estate paid state estate taxes in the amount of $400,000, she may take a deduction for the full amount. For that reason, **Answer (C) is incorrect** because it calculates a lesser deduction. The amount of the state death tax deduction should equal the amount of state death taxes paid within the specified time limits. **Answer (D) is also incorrect** since Callie's estate can deduct state estate taxes paid even though they were paid after the time for filing the federal return. **Answer (A)** is incorrect because it refers to a state death tax credit. (Note that if Callie had died prior to 2005, her estate would instead have been allowed a state death tax credit, limited in amount by IRC § 2011. If the provisions of the 2001 Act sunset, decedents may once again claim a state death tax credit, as opposed to a deduction.)

*On a historical note*, prior to the repeal of IRC § 2011, many states tied the amount of state estate tax to the amount allowed by the federal government as a state death tax credit against the federal estate tax. These types of state taxes were known as "pick-up" or "soak-up" taxes designed to share federal estate tax revenue with the federal government to the maximum amount allowable, and at the same time avoid any additional tax burden to the estate. Following repeal of IRC § 2011 many states have now enacted state succession and inheritance taxes that result in an additional burden to the estates of their citizens because at the federal level estates are allowed only a deduction and not a credit.

128. **The correct answer is (B).** The IRC § 2013 tax on prior transfers credit applies to alleviate the heavy tax burden on property passing between two persons who die within a relatively short time of each other. The estate receives a 100 percent credit if the two decedents die within two years of each other. If the initial transferor predeceases the decedent by three to four years, the estate may take 80 percent of the credit; if the transferor predeceases the decedent by five to six years, the estate may take 60 percent of the credit; if by seven to eight years, 40 percent of the credit; and if by nine to 10 years, 20 percent of the credit. If the transferor predeceases decedent by more than 10 years, the estate may not claim an IRC § 2013 credit. Thus, because Dirk died three years prior to Ed, Ed's estate receives a credit equal to 80 percent of the smaller of two limitations: (i) the amount of estate tax paid by Dirk's estate attributable to the property passed to Ed, and (ii) the amount of estate tax paid by Ed's estate attributable to the property received from Dirk. (It should be noted that to arrive at the estate tax attributable to the property passing from transferor to decedent, the Code and Treasury Regulations require certain adjustments for certain deductions

taken by the estate and an adjustment for any state death taxes paid. IRC § 2013(c) and (d); Treas. Reg. §§ 20.2013-2, -3, and -4.) Based on these two limitations, the smaller is $400,000, and 80 percent of $400,000 equals $320,000. For these same reasons, **Answers (C) and (D) are incorrect. Answer (A) is incorrect** because it does not matter whether or not the decedent retains or sells the property transferred. The fact that Ed sold and reinvested the stock does not matter. It should also be noted that the term "property" for purposes of IRC § 2013 should be broadly construed and can include an interest in trust and an interest subject to a general power of appointment. IRC § 2013(e); Treas. Reg. § 20.2013-5.

129.   **The correct answer is (D).** In order for an estate to take an IRC § 2013 credit, case law clarifies that both Clara's and Edna's estate must pay tax. *Estate of LeCaer v. Comm'r*, 135 T.C. No. 14 (2010). As noted above, the credit allowable is equal to the smaller of the estate tax paid in the transferor's estate and the transferee's estate. Since Clara's estate paid zero estate tax, that is the lesser amount, and a credit is therefore not allowed on Edna's estate tax return. **Answers (A) and (B) are incorrect** for that same reason. **Answer (C) is incorrect** because the time limit for taking the credit is not 18 months, but is instead 10 years as noted in Answer 128, above.

130.   Fred's estate will not receive an IRC § 2012 gift tax credit because the gift by Fred was made after 1976. The IRC § 2012 credit applies only to gifts made in 1976 or prior years. After 1976, Congress unified the estate tax and in doing so accounted for gift tax paid in the calculation of estate tax due under IRC § 2001. (If Fred had made the gift prior to 1976, because the gift was included in his gross estate, his estate would have received a credit for gift tax paid limited to the lesser of the amount of gift tax paid, or the proportion of estate tax attributable to the gift as adjusted for certain credits and deductions.) Because the gift was made in 2009, IRC § 2001 subtracts from tentative federal estate tax the amount of gift tax (which would have been payable if calculated based on current rates) paid on prior taxable gifts made after 1976. IRC § 2001(b)(2). The IRC § 2012 credit is taken so rarely that, beginning in 2008, the Service deleted any reference to it on the Form 706.

131.   Gary's estate may receive a credit equal to the lesser of estate tax paid to the foreign country and the proportionate amount of U.S. estate tax paid with respect to the foreign property based on the ratio of the foreign property to the gross estate. IRC § 2014. The credit may be taken only to the extent the property is situated in a foreign country, subjected to tax in that foreign country, and included in the gross estate for federal estate tax purposes. A careful practitioner would begin the analysis by first determining if a treaty between the United States and the foreign country applies. If for any reason the estate recovers the foreign tax, the executor is under a duty to report the recovery to the Service, so that the Service may redetermine estate tax owed the United States. IRC § 2016.

132.    **Answer (D) is correct.** The gift tax is imposed for each calendar year on the transfer of any property by gift during such year by any individual who is either a citizen or a resident of the United States. *See* Treas. Reg. § 25.2501-1(a)(1). The gift tax also applies to the transfer of real and tangible personal property located in the United States at the time of the transfer. IRC § 2511(a); Treas. Reg. § 25.2511-1(a)(1). The citizenship and residency of the donee has no bearing on whether the gift tax applies. Thus, Adam, who is neither a citizen nor a resident of the United States, may gift an item of tangible personal property in his possession located in England to Bernice without U.S. gift tax implications.

*Note:* It should be noted that Treas. Reg. § 25.0-1(a)(1) provides that some of the provisions of the regulations may be affected by the provisions of an applicable gift tax convention between the United States and other foreign countries. A gift tax convention between the United States and another country may exempt certain transfers by means of a gift from gifts otherwise subject to the gift tax under the Internal Revenue Code. An estate and gift tax convention is in force between the United States and the United Kingdom. Article 6, section (1), of the U.S.-U.K. convention addresses real property and provides real property may only be taxed in the country in which such property is situated. Thus, for example, where the real property is situated in the United States, only the United States may impose gift tax. Convention for the Avoidance of Double Taxation with Respect to Taxes on Estates of Deceased Persons and on Gifts, Oct. 19, 1978, U.S.-U.K, T.I.A.S. No. 9580 at Article 6, section (1). The convention also generally provides that except as to real property and certain types of business property, if the decedent or transferor was domiciled in either the U.S. or the U.K. at the time of the death or transfer, property held by the decedent shall not be taxable in the other State. *See* Article 5, section 1(a). Thus, with respect to tangible personal property, the outcome under the treaty is the same as the outcome under the gift tax code in that a gem held by Adam who is a citizen and resident of the U.K. will not be subject to the U.S. gift tax.

**Answer (B) is incorrect.** IRC § 2511(a) of the Code provides that, in the case of a nonresident who is not a citizen of the United States, the gift tax shall apply to a transfer only if the property is situated within the United States. A nonresident who is also not a citizen of the United States is generally subject to the gift tax if the property that is the subject of the gift is real estate or tangible personal property and is located in the United States at the time of the gift. IRC § 2511(b); *see also* Rev. Rul. 56-438, 1956-2 C.B. 604; Priv. Ltr. Rul. 8342106. Because the real property here is situated in the state of Wyoming within the United States, it will be subject to U.S. gift tax. As described in the above note regarding international estate and gift tax treaties, real property located in the United States may be taxed only in the country in which such property is situated. Thus, the transfer of the real property here is subject to the U.S. gift tax.

**Answers (A) and (C) also are incorrect.** Gift tax is imposed for each calendar year on the transfer of property by gift during such year by any individual residing in the United States.

*See* IRC § 2501(a)(1). In Answers (A) and (C), the grantor of the gift is a U.S. citizen and therefore, the gift is subject to tax. Again, it is of no consequence that the gift is made to either a resident or, as is the case in Answer (A), to a nonresident. The rule focuses on the residency of the individual giving the gift and not the residency of the individual receiving the gift.

133.    **Answer (A) is correct.** For purposes of applying the gift tax, transfers for less than adequate and full consideration in money or money's worth become subject to gift tax to the extent such consideration is not received by the transferor. IRC § 2512(b). The facts of this problem bear similarity to those in *Comm'r v. Wemyss*, 324 U.S. 303 (1945), where the promise to marry did not qualify as "adequate and full" consideration reducible to "money or money's worth." Treasury Regulation § 25.2512-8 further states: "A consideration not reducible to a value in money or money's worth, as love and affection, promise of marriage, etc., is to be wholly disregarded." The fact that a promise to marry under state law would suffice as consideration to support a contract is not relevant to determining the amount of any gift for purposes of the federal gift tax, and as a consequence, **Answer (C) is incorrect.** *Wemyss* also makes clear that the consideration in money or money's worth must pass from the transferee to the transferor in order to negate any implication of gift. Here, Harry did not receive anything of value in terms of "money or money's worth" as a result of Alicia forgoing the stream of monthly support payments. Treasury Regulation § 25.2511-1(g)(1) further clarifies "donative intent is not an essential element in the application of the gift tax to the transfer" and for that reason **Answer (D) is incorrect.** The three-year rule referenced in **Answer (B)** is a red herring and reminiscent of the requirements to avoid gifts with regard to transfers incident to divorce. Also, to obtain favorable gift tax treatment, transfers under IRC § 2516 must be between the spouses who are divorcing.

*Note:* It is important to distinguish among the definition of a "gift" for gift tax purposes, federal income tax purposes, and a "gift" that results in a non-probate transfer during life for state property law purposes. Whereas a promise to marry is not consideration for gift tax purposes in *Comm'r v. Wemyss*, a promise to marry was determined to be consideration where a suitor offered, among other things, stock in a corporation. *See, e.g., Farid-es-Sultaneh v. Comm'r*, 160 F.2d 812 (2d Cir. 1947). Although the release of marital rights is not treated as consideration in money or money's worth in administering the estate and gift tax laws, the income tax laws are not construed the same way. *Id.* Further, while donor intent is not a required element for a transfer to qualify as a gift for gift tax purposes, it generally is required in order for a transfer to qualify as a valid inter vivos gift under state property law. For example, in the state of New York, in order to have a valid inter vivos gift, donor intent must exist to make a gift. *See, e.g., Gruen v. Gruen*, 496 N.E.2d 869 (N.Y. 1986).

134.    **Answer (D) is correct.** A gift is not complete until such time as the donor relinquishes "dominion and control" over the transferred property. Treas. Reg. § 25.2511-2(a). A relinquishment of dominion and control means that the donor no longer retains any power to change the disposition of the transferred property. Treas. Reg. § 25.2511-2(b). If the donor of the property transferred (in trust or otherwise) reserves any power over the disposition of the property, the gift may be either wholly or partially incomplete. *Id.* A gift is wholly incomplete in every instance in which the donor reserves the power to revest beneficial title to the property in herself. Treas. Reg. § 25.2511-2(c). Under the terms of the bank account contract Teresa retains the ability to withdraw all moneys. It is only when Seth withdraws $40,000 that Teresa no longer has dominion and control over the amount withdrawn. Thus,

**Answer (A)** is incorrect because Teresa does make a gift at such time as Seth withdraws funds from the bank account.

**Answers (B) and (C) are incorrect** because at the time the account is opened Teresa retains dominion and control over the $500,000 since she can pull the funds out at any time and thereby deprive Seth of the funds. The gift is, thus, not complete until Seth withdraws the funds. Treasury Regulation § 25.2511-1(h)(4) specifically speaks to the timing of any gift upon creation of a joint bank account.

135. **Answer (C) is correct.** Geri makes a gift at the time she relinquishes dominion and control of the transferred property. The only power Geri retains over the $1 million transferred to the trust is to determine when Shawn receives the income. Geri does not retain any power to change who it is that receives the property after making the initial transfer to the irrevocable trust. The ability to affect only the timing of income from the trust does not amount to a retention of dominion and control. Treas. Reg. § 25.2511-2(d). The gift becomes complete at such time as the donor no longer retains dominion and control, thus, Geri made a gift on the transfer of $1 million to the irrevocable trust.

**Answers (A), (B), and (D) are incorrect.** The annual transfers of income to Shawn do not constitute a gift from Geri because she did not retain any right to control who received the income following the initial gift to the trust.

136. **Answer (B) is correct.** A gift occurs when a transfer is made for less than full and adequate consideration in money or money's worth. Thus, a gift arises to the extent the value of the property transferred by the donor exceeds the value of money or other property given as consideration by the donee. Treas. Reg. § 25.2512-8. Here, Mom transferred the apartment building, valued at $500,000, to daughter for $400,000. The difference results in a taxable gift of $100,000 from Mom to daughter.

**Answers (A) and (C) are incorrect.** Answers (A) and (C) are incorrect because partial consideration of $400,000 was paid by daughter to Mom. The regulations clearly allow for a transfer that qualifies as part gift and part sale. Thus, the donee's gift is reduced by the amount of consideration given. In each Answers (A) and (C), Mom is improperly determined to have made a $500,000 taxable gift. **Answer (D) is also incorrect.** For reasons explained above, the transaction cannot be treated strictly as a sale. It is important to note, however, that an exception exists in the regulations for transactions between unrelated parties. The regulations provide that the gift tax does not apply to ordinary business transactions. Treas. Reg. §§ 25.2511-1(g)(1), 25.2512-8.

137. Yes, if the parties were unrelated, the answer provided in Question 136, above, would change. A sale or exchange of property in the ordinary course of business is considered under the regulations to be made for adequate consideration. Treas. Reg. § 25.2512-8. Where the parties are truly unrelated, the transaction will be treated as arm's length and free from any donative intent. *See id.* It is in this fashion that the regulations address the bad business deal. Notwithstanding that the seller was asking $500,000, the seller accepted a counter-offer of $400,000 from the buyer. Seller may well have transferred an asset to buyer that was worth more than the offer he or she accepted. Nevertheless, the seller had no donative intent in consummating the transaction. Therefore, notwithstanding that it may have been a bad business deal, there is no gift in this transaction.

138.    **Answer (B) is correct.** The issue being explored here is whether the use of property rent-free qualifies as "property" such that the value of Junior's use of the Manhattan flat qualifies as a taxable gift. IRC § 2501(a)(1) generally provides that the gift tax is imposed for each calendar year on the "transfer of property." In *Dickman v. Comm'r*, 465 U.S. 330 (1984), the Supreme Court addressed the issue of whether the gratuitous transfer of the right to use money is a "transfer of property" within the meaning of § 2501(a)(1). In holding that the right to use money interest-free is a cognizable interest in property and is a "transfer of property" for purposes of imposing the gift tax, the court noted that "a parent who grants to a child the rent-free, indefinite use of commercial property having a reasonable rental value of $8,000 a month has clearly transferred a valuable property right." *Dickman v. Comm'r*, 465 U.S. 330, 336 (1984). Here, Mom has rented her flat out in the past for $10,000 per month ($120,000 per year). As such, the flat is akin to a commercial property and, consistent with the reasoning in *Dickman*, the annual rent-free use of the property by the son should be treated as a gift equal to the $120,000 of the forgone rent. **Answer (D) is incorrect.** Answer (D) takes the position that the rent-free use of Mom's flat is not a gift at all. In *Dickman*, the taxpayers argued that such intra-family gifts should not be treated as taxable gifts as a matter of policy. The Court acknowledged that parents are required to provide their minor offspring with the necessities and conveniences of life. However, the Court cautioned that tax issues arise when parents provide more than the necessities in significant quantities. The Court reasoned that while it is common that parents provide their adult children with such things as the use of cars and vacation cottages, the Court assumed that the focus of the IRS is not on such traditional family matters and declined to address such issues. *Dickman*, *supra* at 341. While in theory one could argue that Junior's use of the Manhattan rental property is similar to the temporary use of a vacation condominium, it is unlikely that the Court would agree. Rather, it is more likely that the Court would treat the rent-free use of a Manhattan rental property by Junior, Mom's adult son, as a significant gift of more than the necessities and not a mere familial gift.

        **Answers (A) and (C) are also incorrect.** Answers (A) and (C) are incorrect because Mom has not made a gift of the Manhattan flat itself. Thus, the $2,000,000 value of the flat would not, where the flat is being leased or rented to Junior, be considered a gift.

139.    As alluded to in the answer to Question 138 above, the Supreme Court has specifically held that an interest-free demand loan results in a taxable gift of the reasonable value of the use of the money lent. *Dickman*, supra at 344. Thus, Gary's $100,000 demand loan to Martin will be treated as a gift equal to the reasonable value of the use of the $100,000. Since the Court's opinion in *Dickman*, Congress enacted IRC § 7872, which applies in calculating the amount of the interest treated as a gift. Generally, in the case of any below-market loan that is either a gift or demand loan, the forgone interest must be treated as transferred from lender to borrower and retransferred from borrower to lender as interest. IRC § 7872(a)(1). The deemed transfer of interest is treated as having occurred on the last day of the calendar year. IRC § 7872(a)(2). A "below-market loan" is defined as any loan if, in the case of a demand loan, interest is payable at a rate less than the applicable federal rate (the "AFR") in effect under IRC § 1274(d) for the period compounded semiannually. IRC § 7872(e)(1)(A), 7872(f)(2)(A). Under these rules, because the demand loan from Gary to Martin has stated interest at 9 percent, which is less than the 10.45 percent AFR, it will be classified as a below-market loan. The amount of the forgone interest that will be treated as a taxable gift from Gary to Martin is equal to the excess of (i) the interest due at 10.45 percent (the AFR

blended annually), over (ii) the sum of all amounts payable as interest on the loan. IRC § 7872(e)(2); Prop. Reg. § 1.7872-13(a)(1). Thus, the amount of the forgone interest is $1,450, computed as follows:

$$\$10,450 = \$100,000 \times 10.45\%$$

This calculation represents annual interest calculated on the loan at the AFR.

$$\$1,450 = \$10,450 - \$9,000$$

This calculation represents the difference between annual interest of $10,450 as calculated above and the $9,000 (2 × $4,500) interest paid by Martin at 9% percent.

The forgone interest of $1,450 is treated under the holding in *Dickman* and the requirement under IRC § 7872(a)(1)(A) as transferred from Gary to Martin as a taxable gift. *See* Prop. Reg. § 1.7872-13(a)(2) (Example).

**140.**   **Answer (D) is the correct answer.** Among other things, Topic 15 analyzed whether a gift was actually made. In general, the gift tax applies to any transfer of "property" wherein the donor has parted with dominion and control. Treas. Reg. § 25.2511-2(b). Abby makes a gift only at such time as she relinquishes dominion and control over the property transferred. Treasury Regulation § 25.2511-2(c) specifically provides: "A gift is incomplete in every instance in which a donor reserves the power to revest beneficial title to the property in himself. A gift is also incomplete if and to the extent that a reserved power gives the donor the power to name new beneficiaries or to change the interests of the beneficiaries as between themselves unless the power is a fiduciary power limited by a fixed or ascertainable standard." At the time of the transfer, Abby retains the right to direct which, if any, of her descendants receive principal. Thus, she retains dominion and control over who is to receive the income and the principal for when she exercises her power to direct payment of principal to one particular descendant, the exercise of the power impacts the ability of other descendants to receive both income and principal. For this reason, **Answers (A) and (B) are incorrect. Answer (C) is incorrect** because Abby may make a gift even though the property transferred is also included in Abby's gross estate. The Supreme Court in *Estate of Sanford v. Commissioner*, 308 U.S. 39 (1939), specifically acknowledges a donor may make a completed gift even though the property transferred will also be included in transferor's gross estate. In fact, the formula for determining federal estate tax pursuant to IRC § 2001, specifically contemplates inclusion of prior gifts in the gross estate as evidenced by its definition of adjusted taxable gifts as being those gifts not otherwise included in the gross estate.

**141.**   **Answer (B) is correct.** Madeline makes a gift in trust at such time as she relinquishes dominion and control over the trust property as specified in Treas. Reg. § 25.2511-2(b). Prior to that time she may revoke the trust and regain title to the property previously transferred to trustee. **Answer (A) is incorrect** because at the time of the initial transfer Madeline has not relinquished dominion and control. **Answer (C) is incorrect,** because while a transfer of income or principal to a niece or nephew would constitute a gift by Madeline at the time of the transfer, the value of the gift would be limited to the amount transferred to the niece or nephew as indicated in Treas. Reg. §.25.2511-2(f). Answer (C) states that the gift would equal the entire value of trust assets, which is incorrect. **Answer (D) is incorrect** because a gift cannot occur at death. It must occur, if at all, during the lifetime of the donor.

**142.**   **Answer (A) is correct.** Answer (A) is correct because Chloe retains an enforceable right to income and principal subject to an ascertainable standard. Treasury Regulation § 25.2511-2(b) specifically indicates: "[I]f the exercise of the trustee's power in favor of the grantor is limited by a fixed or ascertainable standard . . . enforceable by or on behalf of the grantor, then the gift is incomplete to the extent of the ascertainable value of any rights thus retained by the grantor." Thus, the gift is not complete to the extent of the interest retained. It is complete, however, with respect to the remainder interest that will pass to the niece on Chloe's death, and a gift has been made to the extent of the value of the remainder interest. For the same reason, **Answer (B) is incorrect.** While it is true as indicated in Answer (C) that the full value of the trust assets will be includible in Chloe's gross estate pursuant to IRC § 2036, **Answer (C) is incorrect** as noted, the mere fact that trust assets are included in the gross estate of donor, does not preclude a finding that a gift of the assets occurred during the life of the donor. As discussed in the prior question, a gift cannot occur at death, but must occur during the lifetime of the donor. **Answer (D) is incorrect** because a gift cannot occur at death.

143.   **Answer (B) is correct.** Olivia makes a gift of the entire value of the property transferred in trust as of the time of the transfer because she does not retain any interest or power over the property transferred. She has given up all dominion and control over the trust property as of the transfer. Treasury Regulation § 25.2511-2(b) provides: "[I]f a donor transfers property in trust to pay the income to the donor or accumulate it in the discretion of the trustee [and retains no powers over the trust] the entire transfer would be a completed gift." **Answer (A) is incorrect** because Olivia has relinquished dominion and control as to all property and not just the remainder interest. **Answer (C) is incorrect.** It is a red herring that makes no sense. **Answer (D) is incorrect** because it is not the best answer. Her interest, although incapable of valuation is subject to gift tax at the time of transfer because she has relinquished dominion and control. The inability to value an asset may cause an otherwise retained interest to be subject to tax as was the case in *Smith v. Shaughnessy*, 318 U.S. 176 (1943). In this problem, however, Olivia does not retain any interest.

144.   **Answer (B) is the best answer.** Alan does not retain any ascertainable interest in or enforceable power over the trust because his power must be exercised, if at all, with his brother who has a substantial adverse interest in the trust. If his brother chooses not to agree to distribute the trust property, Alan's brother (or his estate) will receive all property in the trust as of Alan's death. The law presumes that Alan's brother will provide consent only if it is in his economic best interest to do so. In this case because Alan's brother or his estate receives all property of the trust simply by waiting until Alan's death, it will be in his economic best interest to not consent to any distribution. Alan's brother, thus, has a substantial adverse interest to Alan, and Alan will be deemed to make a gift as of the date of the transfer. This problem employs the first rule set forth by the First Circuit in *Camp v. Comm'r*, 195 F.2d 999 (1st Cir. 1952), which states:

> If the trust instrument gives a designated beneficiary any interest in the corpus of the trust property or of the income therefrom, which is capable of monetary valuation, and the donor reserves no power to withdraw that interest, in whole or in part, except with the consent of such designated beneficiary, then the gift of that particular interest will be deemed to be complete. Because Alan's brother is both the income and principal beneficiary, the gift is of the entire transfer to the trust. **Answer (A) is not**

**the best answer** because Alan's joint power is enforceable, and in order to determine whether Alan in fact made a gift on the initial transfer to the trust, an analysis of whether Alan's brother holds a substantial adverse interest is necessary. For the reasons already stated, **Answer (C) is incorrect.** In order for a partial gift to the trust to occur Alan must retain an enforceable interest or power in a proportionate part of the trust property. **Answer (D) is incorrect** because Alan gives up dominion and control immediately upon the transfer to the trust. Distributions thereafter are not subject to gift tax.

**145.**   **Answer (A) is the correct answer.** Among other things, Topic 14 analyzed whether a gift was actually made. In general, the gift tax applies to any transfer of "property" wherein the donor has parted with dominion and control. Treas. Reg. § 25.2511-2(b). There are, however, instances in which an individual does not hold legal title to property but nevertheless may control property to such an extent that gift taxes are imposed when the individual exercises control over the property.

For example, the exercise of a general power of appointment is "deemed a transfer of property" by the individual possessing such power. IRC § 2514(a). A general power of appointment is any power that is exercisable in favor of the individual possessing the power. IRC § 2514(c). A general power of appointment will also exist in favor of the possessor if the power of appointment is exercisable in favor of the possessor's estate, his or her creditors, or the creditors of his or her estate.

Ally has the right to appoint any portion or the entire corpus of a trust created by her father Jim to anyone other than Betty. Except for the restriction with respect to Betty, Ally is free to appoint to anyone. Ally may appoint the trust corpus to herself, her creditors, or her estate. This results in Ally having a general power of appointment over the trust corpus. It is important to note that while Ally has a power that is exercisable, she has not in fact exercised her right. A gift will occur when Ally actually exercises her right to control the trust corpus by directing it to another person. IRC § 2514(c).

**Answers (C) and (D) are incorrect.** Answer (C) does not result in a general power of appointment. IRC § 2514(c)(3) contains several exceptions that apply to powers of appointment created after October 21, 1942. IRC § 2514(c)(3)(A) provides that if a power is exercisable only in conjunction with the creator of the power, then it is not considered a general power. Note that this makes sense because the creator to an extent continues to retain the right to control the disposition of the property. *See* IRC §§ 2036, 2038.

In Answer (C), Ally can exercise her power only with Jim's consent, and Jim was the creator of the trust. By retaining the power to cancel or reject any exercise of Ally's power over the trust corpus, Jim has retained a degree of control over the trust property. Further, by requiring that Ally first obtain Jim's consent, Jim has not granted Ally a general power of appointment.

The circumstances of Answer (D) also do not result in Ally possessing general power. Under IRC § 2514(c)(3)(B), if Ally's power is exercisable only in conjunction with a person having an adverse interest in the property, the power is not general. In order for this exception to apply in these circumstances, George must have an interest substantially adverse to the exercise of the power in favor of Ally. George's interest is substantially adverse to Ally's interest because George alone has the power to appoint the trust corpus to anyone, including himself, after Ally's death. *Id.* Here, after Ally's death George has the right to appoint the trust corpus to himself, and he would likely do so. Thus, George's interest is deemed to be substantially adverse to Ally's, and Ally does not hold a general power of appointment over the trust corpus for gift tax purposes.

It is important to note that the Tax Court has indicated a substantial adverse interest does necessarily result where a person is both a coholder of power of appointment and permissible appointee under the power. *See Estate of Towle v. Comm'r*, 54 T.C. 368 (1970); Rev. Rul. 79-63. In order for the interest of a coholder to be substantially adverse, the coholder must become the holder upon a failure to exercise the power. *See Estate of Towle v. Comm'r, supra*, at 372.

**Answer (B) is also incorrect.** To a certain extent, Answer (B) does result in Ally having a general power of appointment over a portion of the trust corpus. However, under these circumstances Ally does not have a general power over "all" of the trust property. IRC § 2514(c)(3)(C) contains a final exception that applies to powers of appointment created after October 21, 1942. If such circumstances exist, then the possessor will be deemed to have a general power of appointment only over an allocable share of the property determined with reference to the number of joint power holders. *See* Treas. Reg.§ 20.2041-3(c)(3).

In Answer (B), Ally and Cindy jointly have the power to appoint. Ally's power to appoint is not exercisable without the consent of Cindy, who also has the power to appoint the assets to herself, her estate, or her creditors. Under IRC § 2514(c)(3)(C), Ally is deemed to possess a general power of appointment over an allocable share of the property as between her and Cindy. Because Ally and Cindy are the only two joint holders of the power, Ally has a general power of appointment only in respect to one-half of the trust assets.

146.    In general, the answer would not change. With respect to a power of appointment created on or before October 21, 1942, the power was not considered a general power of appointment if it was exercisable only in conjunction with another person. IRC § 2514(c)(2). No distinctions were made as to the specific kind of rights or powers held by the coholder of the power. As discussed in Question 145, above, after October 21, 1942, property is not treated as subject to a general power of appointment if the power was exercisable only in conjunction with another person and one of the three exceptions under IRC § 2514(c)(3) were met. Because Answers (B) through (D) each meet one of the exceptions under IRC § 2514(c)(3) and because all include scenarios wherein Ally may only exercise her power in conjunction with another person, no general power of appointment would exist either before or after October 21, 1942.

The question should now arise as to what scenario would result in a difference in pre-versus post-October 21, 1942 rules. A power of appointment created today that restricts the holder's power by requiring that any appointment made by the holder be made in conjunction with another person does not automatically destroy the general nature of the power. Such restrictions are more likely to fall under classification as a general power because the additional limitations under IRC § 2514(c)(3) result in a narrower application of the rules, resulting in fewer instances where classification as a general power can be avoided.

For example, assume that Ally and Lorri are trustees of a trust under which income is to be paid to Lorri for life. Assume further that, as trustees, Ally and Lorri may designate whether corpus of the trust is to be distributed to Ally or to Ally's brother Tyler after Lorri's death. Under these circumstances, Lorri will receive trust income for life, but Lorri is not designated to receive the corpus. Thus, Lorri has no interest in the trust corpus and, therefore, no interest that is adverse to Ally's interest in the corpus. Post-October 21, 1942, because Lorri's interest is not adverse to the exercise of the power in favor of Ally, Ally continues to have a general power of appointment over the trust corpus. *See* Treas. Reg. 25.2514-(3)(b) (example (3)). However, if the trust had been created on or before October 21, 1942, solely because Ally must obtain Lorri's consent prior to making a distribution of corpus, Ally's power over the trust corpus is not treated as a general power of appointment.

147. **Answer (D) is the correct answer.** The issue explored in this problem is the difference in treatment between the exercise or release of a power of appointment during life versus a power of appointment that is possessed at death. Generally, property subject to a post-1942 general power is included in the holder's estate upon his or her death. IRC § 2041(a)(2). Because Martine can cause the trust assets to be distributed to her estate, her creditors, or the creditors of her estate, she possesses a general power of appointment. IRC §§ 2041(b)(1), 2514(c).

With respect to a general power of appointment created after October 21, 1942, a release of such power is equivalent to the exercise of the power. IRC § 2514 treats a complete release of a post-1942 general power as a transfer of property for gift tax purposes. Treas. Reg. § 25.2514-1(a). Dimitri created the general power in favor of Martine in 2010, long after 1942. When Martine irrevocably gave up her interest in the trust in July of 2012, she completely released the power that she had over the trust assets. As a result of her release of the power, she will be treated as having gifted all of the trust assets to the three children.

**Answer (A) is incorrect.** Although Martine never exercised her power of appointment during her lifetime, she continued to possess the power until her death. For purposes of IRC § 2041(a)(2), so long as Martine possessed the power of appointment upon her death, the trust property subject to her general power is included in Martine's estate. Treas. Reg. § 20.2041-3(a). It is irrelevant that she never exercised it. *See* Treas. Reg. § 20.2041-3(b)

**Answers (B) and (C) are also incorrect.** While a lifetime release of a general power of appointment is equivalent to an actual exercise of the power, if the power is released by means of a testamentary disposition, it is included in the holder's estate as opposed to being treated as a gift. The question of whether the release of the power is gift or testamentary disposition depends on the manner in which the holder released the power of appointment. Property subject to a post-1942 general power of appointment is includible in the estate of the decedent holder of the power if the property would have been includible in the decedent holder's estate under IRC §§ 2035, 2036, 2037, or 2038. *See* Treas. Reg. § 20.2041-3(d).

In Answer (B) Martine amended the trust to provide that her sister Cindy would receive all remaining trust property upon Martine's death. However, Martine retained the right to alter, amend, or revoke the trust. IRC § 2038(a)(1) applies to revocable transfers after June 22, 1936, and generally requires a decedent's gross estate to include the value of all property that the decedent had at any time made a transfer where the enjoyment of the property was subject at the date of the decedent's death to a change via the exercise of a power to amend or revoke the transfer. Martine did transfer the remainder interest in the trust property to her sister Cindy. However, Martine retained the right, as contemplated by IRC § 2038(a)(1), to revoke Cindy's right to enjoy the property. Martine's revocable transfer does not result in a gift. Rather, it is more in the nature of a testamentary transfer whereby the trust property is required to be included in Martine's estate upon her death.

In a similar fashion, IRC § 2036 transfers with retained life estates apply to the facts presented in Answer (C). A decedent must include the value of all property to the extent that he or she transferred the property but retained for life the right to possess or enjoy the income from the property. IRC § 2036(a)(1). Here, Martine did irrevocably amend the trust to provide that her sister Cindy would receive all remaining trust property upon Martine's death. However, because Martine retained the right to receive trust income for the duration of her life, the transfer is testamentary in nature and is not treated as a gift of the entire interest.

148.  **Answer (C) is the correct answer.** The lapse or failure to exercise a general power of appointment or the intentional release of such a power is treated for gift tax purposes as a transfer of property by the individual possessing the power of appointment. IRC § 2514(b). Because Lisa has the power to cause the trust to distribute the accumulated income to her, she has a general power of appointment over the trust income in favor of herself. By choosing not to exercise her power or by failing to exercise her power, Lisa has allowed the power to lapse. By allowing the power to lapse, Lisa is deemed to have transferred her interest in the property, and a gift has occurred. Even though Lisa did not actually direct where the accrued trust income will go, Lisa's failure to exercise the power effectively resulted in a transfer to Randall. The deemed transfer is treated as a gift from Lisa to Randall for gift tax purposes. *See* Treas. Reg. § 25.2514-3(c)(4), 25.2514-3(e) (example 2). Treating the lapse as a gift for gift tax purposes makes sense in that Lisa effectively was in a better economic position prior to the release as compared to after the release.

**Answer (D) is incorrect.** A power to consume, invade, or appropriate income or corpus, or both, for the benefit of the possessor that is limited by an ascertainable standard relating to health, education, maintenance, or support is a non-general power of appointment. IRC § 2514(c)(1). The exercise or release of a non-general power of appointment generally is not treated as a taxable gift. *See* Treas. Reg. § 25.2514-3(e) (example 2). Here, Lisa has a non-general power of appointment because her ability to request a distribution is limited to an ascertainable standard. The fact that she allows the 10 years to expire without requesting a distribution does not result in a gift. The distinction between Answer (C), the correct answer, and Answer (D) is that in Answer (C) Lisa had a general power of appointment that allowed her to take for herself without any limitation. In Answer (D), Lisa is limited in her ability to control the trust property. By limiting her ability to request a distribution, the trust property here passes in full to Randall without any action or control on the part of Lisa.

It is important to note, however, that while under these circumstances the release of a non-general power of appointment is not treated as a taxable gift, there are some instances in which a special power of appointment may be exercised or released and treated as a gift for gift tax purposes. *See* Treas. Reg. § 25.2514-3(e) (example 4).

**Answers (A) and (B) are incorrect.** Answer (A) does not result in a gift from Lisa to Randall, as Lisa retains all of her rights in the income. Answer (B) also does not result in a gift. By failing to exercise his right to appoint trust principal to Lisa, Randall has merely allowed Lisa to retain her annual income interest in the trust. Randall's power here is only a right to dispose of his remainder interest, a right that he will continue to possess regardless of the expiration of the 10-year period. *See* Treas. Reg. § 25.2514-3(e) (example 4).

149.  The facts in this problem are similar to the facts in *Estate of Regester v. Comm'r*, 83 T.C. 1 (1984), wherein the Court held that the exercise of a non-general or special power of appointment in relation to the corpus of a trust resulted in a taxable gift of the power

holder's lifetime income interest in the trust. As previously discussed, IRC § 2514 governs the imposition of the gift tax on the exercise, release, or lapse of powers of appointment. In general, a power that can be exercised for the benefit of the holder of the power is a general power of appointment. However, if an individual cannot exercise a power of appointment in his or her favor, it is a non-general power or "special" power of appointment.

Under circumstances such as those presented in this problem, an indirect gift may arise where a special power of appointment is exercised. For example, if a person has the right to trust income for life and the ability to transfer the right to the income to any other person, such a transfer results in a taxable gift. If Lisa had transferred her right to trust income during her life to another, there would have been a taxable gift. The issue arises in the context of this problem in that while Lisa does not directly transfer her income interest in the trust, her exercise of the special power over the corpus of the trust results in Taylor receiving all future income. As stated by the Court in *Regester*, "because the income from the corpus follows the corpus, the method used to transfer the income interest was to 'piggyback' it onto the property that was transferred under the [special] power of appointment." *Estate of Regester v. Comm'r*, 83 T.C. 1, 16 (1984). Thus, when Lisa exercises her power to specially appoint the corpus of the trust to Taylor, Lisa's right to the income interest in the corpus is also "piggybacked" or transferred to Taylor. It is the transfer of the value of the income interest by Lisa that results in a taxable gift to Taylor.

150. **Answer (B) is correct.** The right to withdraw an amount of property from a trust created by another amounts to a general power of appointment pursuant to IRC § 2514(c). It is the exercise or release of a power during the life of the power holder that results in a taxable gift. IRC § 2514(b). A lapse of a power of appointment does not constitute a transfer for gift tax purposes except to the extent the lapse exceeds the greater of (1) $5,000 and (2) 5% of the aggregate value of trust assets from which the exercise of the lapsed power may be paid. Since in our fact pattern $5,000 is the greater of the two amounts, the amount of property considered to be transferred by each of Jack and Jill is the amount of the transfer less $5,000, or in our case $8,000. IRC § 2514(e). **Answer (A) is incorrect** because the transfer for gift tax purposes is limited in amount to the excess of the greater of the two amounts. **Answers (C) and (D) are incorrect.** Answer (C) is incorrect because it is not necessary to exercise or release a power in order to make a taxable gift; it is sufficient to allow a withdrawal power to lapse. Answer (D) is incorrect because it is the fact that someone other than the withdrawal holder is a potential beneficiary that in fact causes a taxable gift to potentially occur.

**151.**   **Answer (D) is the correct answer.** The issue being explored here is whether a transfer was effectuated and, if so, whether the transfer was complete enough to incur gift tax. At the heart of these issues is the question of whether a trust was created for the benefit of Barry. If so, a taxable gift was effectuated. The gift tax is not applicable to a mere transfer of bare legal title. Treas. Reg. § 25.2511-1(g).

Thus, for example, the gift tax does not apply to a transfer of bare legal title in property to a trustee. *Id.* In order for a gift to occur, there must be a transfer of a beneficial interest in the property. *Id.* A trustee who holds legal title to property but who has no beneficial interest in the same will not incur gift tax upon distribution of the property from the trust. Instead, the grantor of the trust will be liable for gift tax when he or she has parted with dominion and control of the property. Generally, the grantor will have parted with dominion and control either when the assets are irrevocably contributed to the trust or, if the trust is revocable, when a distribution of assets takes place.

The creation of certain types of bank accounts may result in the formation of a trust if the creator of the account intends that a trust be formed. For example, a "totten" trust can be created when a settlor deposits money in a bank account for the benefit of another. *See, e.g., Green v. Green*, 559 A.2d 1047 (R.I. 1989). However, a gift requires a transfer of property to the recipient. The validity of a trust does not require actual delivery of property to the beneficiary. In the bank account setting, the property is money that is delivered or deposited into a bank account. As discussed above, a simple deposit or transfer of the money does not amount to a gift unless there is also intent to create a trust for the benefit of another individual. The settlor's intent to transfer a beneficial interest in the money is paramount to the creation of a trust in the form of a bank account or otherwise. *Id.* at 1050. Intent to create a trust must be shown by an act or declaration made during the settlor's lifetime. *Id.*

Here, Dad creates a joint bank account for himself and names Barry as a cosignatory of the account. Upon deposit of funds into the account, there has been no delivery of a beneficial interest in the property (here money) to Barry and, therefore, no gift at the time of the deposit. If Dad retains the right to withdraw amounts from the account without Barry's consent, then Dad can regain control of all the account funds without Barry's consent. *See* Treas. Reg. § 25.2511-2(c). However, in Answer (D), Dad indicates that if Barry gets into financial trouble he is welcome to withdraw some of the money for himself. Dad's assertion here indicates clear intent to transfer the funds for the benefit of Barry. The gift occurs when Barry actually withdraws some money and pays off his sports car. When Barry draws upon the account for his own benefit, delivery has taken place. With both intent to transfer a beneficial interest and delivery, Dad has completed a gift to Barry at the time of and to the extent Barry withdraws amounts without any obligation to account for the proceeds to Dad. *See* Treas. Reg. § 25.2511-1(h) (example 4).

*Note:* Determination of the donee's rights under local law is important to the determination of gift tax consequences associated with the transfer. As discussed above, where a donor retains the ability to revoke, amend, or modify the rights of the donee, generally there is no completion of the gift and no gift tax is incurred.

**Answers (A), (B), and (C) are all incorrect.** In each of the remaining answers, unlike Answer (D), Barry is either not authorized to take any of the money for himself or is authorized to take some of the money but does not actually take any. In Answer (C), Dad has indicated intent to transfer a beneficial interest by authorizing Barry to withdraw funds. However, no delivery has occurred because Barry never actually withdraws. He simply continues to pay his father's medical bills.

In Answer (B), Dad has delivered the money, but he has only delivered bare legal title. By indicating that from that point in time forward, he wanted Barry to use the money only to pay his medical bills, the requisite intent to make a gift is lacking on Dad's part. The fact that Barry thereafter takes the money and purchases a new boat does not reflect a gift. Rather, Barry has taken the money without authorization.

Finally, in Answer (A), Dad stuffed some money into his bed mattress and authorized Barry to use the money if necessary to pay Dad's medical bills. By taking some of the money to pay one of Dad's hospital bills, Barry has not received any amounts. Under these circumstances, delivery does not exist, and no gift has been made from Dad to Barry. However, Dad's remark to Barry indicating that whatever money is left when I die is yours would indicate intent to give some as yet undetermined amount. However, in order for a gift to exist, the donor must depart with dominion and control. Dad continues to reserve the right to use of the funds in his mattress while he continues to live. Again, no gift would result under these facts.

152.     **Answer (C) is the correct answer.** A gift does not occur so long as Mom, as donor, retains dominion and control over the property transferred. Because Mom may unilaterally withdraw the entire $500,000 balance of the joint account at any time, Mom does not make a taxable gift on January 30, 2011, the date she named her Daughter as joint tenant on the checking account. For this reason, **Answers (A) and (B) are incorrect.** Treasury Regulation § 25.2511-1(h)(4) indicates the taxable gift occurs when Daughter withdraws $100,000 because that is the time that Mom no longer has dominion and control over the withdrawn amount. **Answer (D) is incorrect** for this same reason. It is notable, however, that to the extent property remains in the joint account on Mom's death, IRC § 2040 includes the amount remaining in the account in Mom's gross estate.

153.     **Answer (B) is the correct answer.** Given the fact that under local law the son has the right to unilaterally sever the joint interest in the home, Father does not retain any dominion and control over the one-half interest in the home that is transferred to Son. This problem mirrors the facts and the conclusion of Treasury Regulation § 25.2511-1(h). In answering this question it is important to determine whether or not state law would allow the joint tenant to unilaterally sever the property. **Answer (A) is incorrect** because the father can also unilaterally sever the joint tenancy and obtain his one-half tenant in common interest in the property, thus, the amount of the taxable gift to Son is only one-half the value of the home or $500,000. **Answer (D) is also incorrect.** Because Son has the immediate right to sever his interest on being named joint tenant, the gift is made at that time as Father no longer has any dominion and control over the Son's one-half interest. The right to sever is enough; the Son does not in fact actually sever the interest to trigger the taxable gift. **Answer (C) is**

**incorrect** for the reasons stated, but if the home remained in joint tenancy with right of survivorship on Father's death, IRC § 2040 would include the full value of the home in Father's gross estate.

154. **Answer (D) is the correct answer.** These facts draw on the same analysis as in the immediately prior question. Where the joint tenants contribute an equal amount to the purchase of joint tenancy with right of survivorship real property that is unilaterally severable, neither has made a gift to the other because the contribution made in consideration of the receipt of the joint interest is equal to full and adequate consideration in money or money's worth. Likewise, on termination of the joint tenancy, each receives a one-half tenant in common interest. Because the interest is unilaterally severable, each takes the share they are entitled to receive on severance of the survivorship interest, and for that reason there is no need to actuarially value the interests received and/or transferred to determine the gift. **Thus, Answers (A), (B), and (C) are incorrect.** If the interest was not unilaterally severable then it would be necessary to actuarially value the transfers to determine the gift tax consequences as indicated in now withdrawn regulation § 25.2515-2.

155. **Answer (C) is the correct answer.** This problem begins with the analysis as indicated in the prior question. Each tenant contributed equally to the down payment, and for that reason no taxable gift results because of the initial purchase. Each tenant has provided full and adequate consideration for their respective interests. Pursuant to local law, each tenant could unilaterally sever the interest and retain a one-half interest in the home. The Service addresses similar facts in Revenue Ruling 78-362, which addresses a unilaterally severable joint interest where on making of the mortgage payment by one joint tenant, the payment is made without expectation of reimbursement by the other co-tenant. The ruling finds that the joint tenant making the mortgage payment made a gift of one-half the mortgage payment to the other joint tenant. Applying Revenue Ruling 78-362 to our facts, Michelle will be deemed to make a gift of $12,000 to Amelia when she makes the mortgage payment in 2012. **Answers (A) and (B) are incorrect** because both joint tenants contribute equally to the purchase and are equally liable for the mortgage. **Answer (D) is incorrect** because the transfer is deemed made at the time the mortgage payment is made without expectation of reimbursement. If, however, the home remained in joint tenancy on Michelle's death, at least a portion of the home would be included in Michelle's estate under IRC § 2040, and the exact amount would depend on the relative contributions of each tenant to the purchase of the home.

156.    **Answer (B) is the correct answer.** In order to make a qualified disclaimer pursuant to IRC § 2518, the disclaimant must make the disclaimer "not later than the date which is 9 months after the later of — (A) the date on which the transfer creating the interest in such person is made, or (B) the day on which such person attains age 21." The question, thus, becomes "when" did the transfer creating the interest occur? Treasury Regulations § 25.2518-2(c)(3) states that "a transfer creating an interest occurs when there is a completed gift for Federal gift tax purposes. . . ." They further state: "With respect to transfers made by a decedent at death or transfers that become irrevocable at death, the transfer creating the interest occurs on the date of the decedent's death. . . ." Because the transfer from Frank was made to a revocable trust, no gift occurred on the initial January 1, 2011 transfer because Frank continued to retain dominion and control over the transferred property. Thus, Benson may disclaim within nine months from the date of Frank's death, June 30, 2012, because that is the time the transfer becomes irrevocable. The facts of this problem are similar to Treas. Reg. § 25.2518-2(c)(5) Example 6. For this same reason **Answer (A) is incorrect.**

The exception to the general rule that the disclaimer must be made within nine months of the earlier of the time the gift becomes complete, or, if the transfer becomes irrevocable on death, within nine months of death is when the disclaimant is under 21 years of age at that time. If a disclaimant is under 21 years of age at the time the disclaimer must otherwise be made, the disclaimant may disclaim the interest up until the date that is nine months after she turns age 21. Although Cathy is under age 21, she is not the disclaimant. Benson is the disclaimant and he must make the disclaimer within the requisite time period. Thus, **Answer (C) is incorrect.**

**Answer (D) is incorrect** as it does not state the correct time frame for disclaiming an interest. The time for disclaimer does not begin to run at the time the estate tax return is filed, but instead runs for a period after death that will cause the disclaimer to occur within the time for filing the return.

157.    **Answer (A) is correct.** As noted in the preceding answer, in order to make a qualified disclaimer pursuant to IRC. § 2518, the disclaimant must make the disclaimer "not later than the date which is nine months after the later of — (A) the date on which the transfer creating the interest in such person is made, or (B) the day on which such person attains age 21." The question, thus, becomes "when" did the transfer creating the interest occur? Treasury Regulations § 25.2518-2(c)(3) states that "a transfer creating an interest occurs when there is a completed gift for Federal gift tax purposes." They further state: "With respect to transfers made by a decedent at death or transfers that become irrevocable at death, the transfer creating the interest occurs on the date of the decedent's death." A transfer of a joint tenancy with right of survivorship interest that is unilaterally severable results in a completed gift of the one-half joint tenancy interest on the date of transfer. The survivorship interest, however, does not become irrevocable until the first death of a joint

tenant. Thus, Tamera must disclaim her one-half joint tenancy interest, if at all, within nine months of January 1, 2011, the date her mother names her as joint tenant. Tamera may then disclaim the one-half survivorship interest within nine months of her mother's death on September 1, 2012. For this same reason **Answers (B) and (C) are incorrect.** In response to the court's holdings in *Estate of Dancy v. Comm'r*, 872 F.2d 84 (4th Cir. 1989) and *McDonald v. Comm'r*, 853 F.2d 1494 (8th Cir. 1988), Treasury added examples 7, 8, 9 and 10 of Treas. Reg. § 25.2518-2(c)(5) to the regulations. The time period indicated in Answer (D) bears no relation to time in which the transfer becomes complete for transfer tax purposes, and for that reason **Answer (D) is incorrect.**

158.    **Answer (D) is correct.** In addition to the requirement that the disclaimer be made within the requisite nine month time period, a qualified disclaimer under IRC § 2518 requires: (1) the disclaimant not accept any interest or benefits in the disclaimed interest, (2) as a result of the disclaimer, the interest must pass "without direction on the part of the" disclaimant (3) either to the spouse of the decedent or to a person other than the person making the disclaimer. Because Demetra holds a special power of appointment over the disclaimed property she holds the power to direct how the interest will pass. Treasury Regulation § 25.2518-2(e)(1)(i) indicates that if the "disclaimant, either alone or in conjunction with another . . . has the power to direct the redistribution or transfer of the property or interest in property to another person unless such power is limited by an ascertainable standard." the disclaimer fails to meet the requirement that property pass without direction of the disclaimant. **Answer (A) is incorrect** because it is not enough that Demetra refrain from directing who receives the disclaimed interest, she also may not retain a power to do so. **Answer (B) is incorrect** because it does not make any difference whether the power to direct is general or special, either power will cause the disclaimer to violate the 'passage without direction' requirement. **Answer (C) is incorrect** because there is no limitation in the requirements of IRC § 2518 as to who can receive the disclaimed interest.

159.    **The best answer is Answer (A).** In order to make a qualified disclaimer, the general rule is that the disclaimed property must pass to a person other than the person making the disclaimer, unless that disclaimant is the surviving spouse of the decedent. IRC § 2518(b)(4). Thus, Patricia as the surviving spouse may disclaim property to a trust of which she is the beneficiary. **Answer (B) while true is not the best answer** because it simply does not matter whether or not the interest the surviving spouse takes after the disclaimer is subject to an ascertainable standard. For similar reasons **Answer (D) is also incorrect. Answer (C) is incorrect** because it is overbroad.

**160.**   **Answer (B) is correct.** The annual exclusion under IRC § 2503(b) allows a taxpayer to make certain gifts without gift tax consequences. In general, "taxable gifts" include the total amount of gifts made during the calendar year less any deductions. IRC § 2503(a). However, the first $10,000 (as that amount is adjusted for inflation after 1998) of present-interest gifts made by a donor to a donee during any calendar year are excluded from taxable gifts. IRC § 2503(b)(1), (2). The annual gift tax exclusion applies on a per donee, per year basis. There is no limit to the number of persons that may receive an excludible gift in one calendar year from a particular donor. There is also no limit on the relationship of the donee to the donor. Thus, John can make 26 annual exclusion gifts per year to his 26 children and grandchildren. **Answer (A) is incorrect** because annual exclusion gifts can be made to children and grandchildren. **Answer (C) is incorrect** because annual exclusion gifts can be made each year.

       **Answer (D) is incorrect.** The annual exclusion is determined on a per person basis. In Answer (D) the donor attempts to circumvent the per person dollar limit by passing property to the intended donee's parent to increase the amount per year that would pass free of tax. The Service, however, will ignore the transfer to the child's spouse, and will deem John to have made the transfer, and not the child's parent. In a similar case, *Sather v. Comm'r*, 251 F.3d 1168 (8th Cir. 2001), taxpayers, three brothers and their spouses, each made 10,000 gifts to children and to their nieces and nephews. The court applied the reciprocal trust doctrine and uncrossed the gifts, deeming each parent to make all the transfers received by that parent's child. Planning strategies should be assessed under a substance over form analysis, and in doing so an eye should be kept on the trail of money and assets.

**161.**   **Answer (C) is correct.** The annual exclusion from gross gifts provided by IRC § 2503(b) applies only to present-interest gifts. IRC § 2503(b)(1). A transfer (or portion thereof) that constitutes a future interest may not be excluded in determining the total amount of taxable gifts made during a calendar period. A "future interest" includes, for example, reversions, remainders, and other interests that may be used, possessed, or enjoyed only by the recipient at some future point in time. Treas. Reg. § 25.2503-3(a). The United States Supreme Court in *Fondren v. Comm'r*, 324 U.S. 18 (1945), discusses the meaning of "present interest":

> [H]e must have the right presently to use, possess or enjoy the property. These terms are not words of art . . . but connote the right to substantial present economic benefit. The question is of time, not when title vests but when enjoyment begins. Whatever puts the barrier of a substantial period between the will of the beneficiary or donee now to enjoy what has been given him and that enjoyment makes the gift one of a future interest. . . .

Present interest includes the right to a steady flow of income. *Id.* A gift of property that is unproductive and that the donee is unable to convert to productive property will not qualify for the annual exclusion. For example, in *Maryland National Bank v. United States*, 609 F.2d 1078 (4th Cir. 1979), donor transferred farm and waterfront property with a history of net losses to an all income trust. Because the property was unproductive, and beneficiaries of the trust could not require the trustee to convert the unproductive property to income producing property, the court denied an annual exclusion for transfers to the trust. Similarly, in *Hackl v. Comm'r*, 118 T.C. 279 (2002), transfers of limited liability company interests where parent controlled distributions to members, and where any right to sell the LLC interests was subject to the consent of parent manager, the Tax Court denied the annual exclusion. In order to ensure a transfer qualifies as a present interest, the donee should have the ability to convert the transferred property to productive property. **Answer (C) is correct** because the donee of the tenant in common interest not only has the right to receive rent payments, but can also sell the tenant in common interest. For that reason, the donee of the tenant in common interest possesses a right to the "present economic benefit" of the transferred property. **Answer (A) is incorrect** because the limited partnership interests described in Answer (A) are similar to the LLC interests in *Hackl*. The general partner controls distributions, and there is no ability to sell the limited partnership interests without complying with the restrictions on sale. **Answer (B) is incorrect** because none of the beneficiaries has a right to all income of the trust. Rather distributions of income are entirely within the discretion of the trustee. **Answer (D) is incorrect** because the co-owners of the life insurance policy do not receive a present economic interest. The life insurance proceeds do not pay out until such time as the insured dies, and none of the co-owners of a life insurance policy can convert the policy without the consent of the other co-owners. *See Skouras v. Comm'r*, 14 T.C. 523 (1950).

162.  An unrestricted right to immediate use, possession or enjoyment of property or income from the property is treated as a present interest to which the annual exclusion applies. Treas. Reg. § 25.2503-3(b). For example, the value of an all income interest in property for a term certain or for life qualifies as an excludible present interest. Because Sam immediately benefits from mandatory distributions of income, the value of Sam's income interest is an excludible present interest. An annual exclusion is allowable, but the amount of the exclusion is limited to the value of Sam's life interest of $9,000. Even though Alice transferred $50,000 to the trust only $9,000 of that amount is eligible for the annual exclusion. The exclusion is allowed only to the extent of the value of the present interest.

163.  **Answer (A) is the correct answer.** The question asks which of the alternative answers will best effectuate Trevor's tandem goals of maximizing the annual exclusion while at the same time limiting or preventing the children from accessing trust income and principal prior to reaching the age of 40. By its terms, the trust provisions in Answer (A) limit access of the beneficiaries in accordance with Trevor's wishes by requiring trustee to make distributions of net income and principal under a restrictive ascertainable standard (e.g., maintenance, education, support, or health). Consistent with Trevor's wishes, the trustee may distribute the remaining income and principal only when the beneficiary attains the age of 40. However, it must be acknowledged that the children under Answer (A) each have the ability to withdraw amounts contributed within the 15-day notice period. It is unlikely, however, that such withdrawals will occur as discussed below.

An important issue in this problem is whether the full amount of the contribution to the trust qualifies as a present interest gift for purposes of the annual exclusion as allowed under IRC § 2503(b). In *Crummey v. Comm'r*, T.C. Memo. 1966-144, *aff'd in part and rev'd in part*, 397 F.2d 82 (9th Cir. 1968), the court allowed an annual exclusion for transfers in trust where a minor beneficiary was allowed a demand right. In *Crummey*, the Ninth Circuit Court of Appeals focused on the legal right of the minor beneficiaries to demand payment from the trustee. The Ninth Circuit indicated that the only requirement to find a present interest is that the trustee could not legally have resisted the minor beneficiary's demand for payment from the trustee. The Court rejected a test based upon the likelihood that an actual demand would be made. Thus, the ability of an individual to demand an amount equal to the annual exclusion from the trustee results in an unrestricted right to the immediate possession or enjoyment of property or the income from property that qualifies as a present interest in property. Under the provisions of the trust in Answer (A), all contributions made by Trevor to the extent of the annual exclusion amount per beneficiary can be excluded from gross gifts under IRC § 2503(b). (It should be noted that because the child is the only beneficiary of the trust, there is no possibility of a deemed gift by the child due to lapse of the demand right.)

As acknowledged above, one or more of the children may exercise the demand right, and may take possession of the amount of the contribution. Trevor should be advised that there is no way to stop the child from exercising his or her right. Of course, Trevor is not obligated to make a contribution to the trust in the future. However, it is important to note that the court in *Estate of Cristofani v. Comm'r*, 97 T.C. 74 (1991), determined under similar facts that there was no agreement or understanding between decedent, the trustees, and the beneficiaries that the grandchildren would not exercise their right of withdrawal following a contribution to the trust. Trevor should be warned that he cannot have a separate understanding in which his children are not allowed to exercise their right of withdrawal. Such an understanding would prevent the contribution from being a present interest qualified for the annual exclusion. However, in the absence of any agreement, if one or more of the children exercise their right of withdrawal, Trevor is not prevented from deciding that he will not make any more contributions to the trust. This unspoken threat generally prevents an exercise of the demand power.

**Answer (B) is incorrect.** Answer (B) is incorrect because the trustee has the power to deny a beneficiary's request for annual withdrawal. By authorizing the trustee to deny a request for withdrawal, the beneficiaries have lost their legal right to elect to presently enjoy and possess the contributed property as required by the reasoning of both courts in *Crummey* and *Cristofani*. The inability to presently possess the contributed property causes the contribution to be treated as a future interest not qualified for the annual exclusion.

**Answers (C) and (D) are also incorrect.** IRC § 2503(c) generally provides that all or any part of a transfer for the benefit of a minor under the age of 21 will be considered a gift of a present interest if three conditions are met. First, both the property and income from the property may be expended by or for the benefit of the donee before he or she reaches 21 years of age. Treas. Reg. § 25.2503-4(a). Second, any remaining portion of the property and its income not disposed under the first condition must pass to the donee when he or she reaches 21 years of age. *Id.* Finally, if a donee dies prior to reaching 21 years of age, any portion of the property and its income not disposed under the first condition must be payable either to the donee's estate or as the donee appointed under a general power of appointment. *Id.* Where a trust contains provisions that satisfy each of the three conditions, contributions to the trust qualify for annual exclusion. Moreover, the three conditions will remain satisfied even though a trustee is given discretion in determining the amount and purpose for which trust expenditures are to be made. Treas. Reg. § 25.2503-4(b)(1).

The trust provisions in Answers (C) and (D) each satisfy the three requirements qualifying contributions to the trusts for the annual exclusion. Further, the trust provisions in Answers (C) and (D) providing that the trustee may distribute net income and principal to the beneficiary for maintenance, education, health, or support during the life of the beneficiary will not prevent the annual contributions from satisfying the three IRC§ 2503(c) conditions. *See, e.g.*, Rev. Rul. 67-270, 1967-2 CB 349. However, with respect to Answer (C), the trust provisions require the trustee to distribute trust principal and accrued income when the beneficiary attains 21 years of age. Similarly, in Answer (D), the trust beneficiary may elect to receive any and all trust income and principal upon attaining the age of 21. Both of these provisions are designed to satisfy the requirement that all the trust property including any remaining income must pass to the donee when he or she attains the age of 21. But neither provision satisfies Trevor's preference that his children not receive any of the trust corpus until they reach the age of 40.

164. **Answer (A) is correct.** The Tax Court addressed this issue under similar facts in the *Estate of Cristofani v. Comm'r*, 97 T.C. 74 (1991). In *Cristofani*, taxpayer decedent had two adult children and five minor grandchildren. Taxpayer's estate argued that the right of the decedent's grandchildren to withdraw an amount equal to the annual exclusion within a 15-day period after contribution constitutes a present-interest gift in property qualifying for the full amount of the annual exclusion. The Commissioner argued that the annual exclusions should be disallowed on the grounds that the grandchildren had only contingent interests in the trust. The court responded: "We do not believe, however, that *Crummey* requires that the beneficiaries of a trust must have a vested present interest or vested remainder interest in the trust corpus or income, in order to qualify for the" annual exclusion. Thus, withdrawal rights for both children and grandchildren can result in annual exclusion gifts. **For this reason, Answer (C) is incorrect.**

Because withdrawal rights are general powers of appointment, a lapse of the right in excess of the greater of $5,000 or 5% of the trust property will be treated as a release of a general power of appointment and will result in a taxable transfer by the holder of the withdrawal right if the trust has multiple beneficiaries. IRC § 2514(e). Thus, the withdrawal right should be limited to $5,000 to avoid any gift by a holder of the withdrawal right. For this reason, **Answers (B) and (D) are incorrect.**

165. **Answer (A) is the correct answer.** For purposes of the gift tax, any contribution to a qualified tuition program on behalf of an individual is treated as a completed present-interest gift. IRC § 529(c)(2). In general, a "qualified tuition program" includes any state program under which a person may purchase credits that entitle the beneficiary to waive payment of qualified higher education expenses. *See* IRC § 529(b). Such expenses include tuition, fees, books, supplies, and equipment required to attend or enroll in an eligible education institution. IRC § 529(e)(3). With certain restrictions, costs in relation to room and board are also included as qualified expenses. *See* IRC § 529(e)(3)(B). Virtually every state college or university is an eligible education institution. *See* IRC § 529(e)(5). In Answer (A), with respect to the $50,000 contributed by Kyle this year to the 12 separate IRC § 529-qualified tuition programs, no gift tax is due. As here, if the aggregate contribution made by Kyle exceeds the annual gift exclusion amount for the year, Kyle may make an election to treat the gift as being made ratably over the succeeding five-year period. Thus, given the

proper election, Kyle is allowed to make a $50,000 contribution to each of the 12 qualified tuition programs and, for gift tax purposes, it will be treated as if Kyle had made $10,000 annual contributions to each of the tuition programs for each of the next five years. While no specific limitation is placed upon the amount of the contribution, the Code disqualifies a tuition program unless it implements safeguards against contributions in excess of the amount necessary to cover beneficiary's qualified higher education expenses. IRC § 529(c)(2)(B). Further, by making a gift of $50,000 in the first year ($600,000 total), Kyle will avoid inclusion of any appreciation on that amount that would have occurred during the five years in his estate. From an income tax perspective, Kyle may also avoid paying income tax on any of the investment income that may result from holding the excess funds.

**Answers (B) and (C) are incorrect.** Answer (B) is very close to Answer (C). Because Kyle will have used his annual exclusion amounts with respect to gifts made to the 529 plans, any gifts to the *Crummey* trusts will be subject to gift tax.

**Answer (D) is also incorrect.** Answer (D) fails to take advantage of Kyle's ability to make $600,000 of gifts in year one and, thus, avoids tax on any appreciation that would have been associated with the additional amount of gift in Answer (A).

166.  **Answer (C) is correct.** Any amount of tuition paid to an educational organization "on behalf of an individual" is excluded from treatment as a gift. IRC § 2503(e). Under the rule, the payment must be made to an educational organization that maintains a regular faculty and curriculum and normally has a regularly enrolled student body in a particular place. Treas. Reg. § 25.2503-6(b). The amount of the exclusion for tuition expenses is unlimited. Tuition specifically does not include "books, supplies, dormitory fees, board, or other similar expenses which do not constitute direct tuition costs." *Id.* In addition to the exclusion allowed under IRC § 2503(e), an annual exclusion may also be taken for the outright cash gift to the student in the amount of the annual exclusion.

**Answers (A) and (B) are incorrect** because the check is made to the student or to the trust, and not to the educational organization. Contribution to a trust, as proposed in Answer (B), that contains provisions requiring the use of the funds for tuition results in a completed gift for federal gift tax purposes. Treas. Reg. § 25.2503-6(c)(example 2). **Answer (D) is not the best answer** because the IRC § 2503(e) exclusion is allowable only for tuition, and not room and board.

167.  In addition to annual exclusion gifts, Hannah may also take an exclusion for gifts made directly to medical providers for qualifying medical expenses. IRC § 2503(e). Qualifying medical expenses include "diagnoses, cure, mitigation, treatment or prevention of disease, or for the purpose of affecting any structure or function of the body or for transportation primarily for and essential to medical care. Treas. Reg. § 25.2503-6(b)(3). Thus, amounts paid directly to the orthodontist treating the grandchild qualify for the IRC § 2503(e) exclusion. As with tuition expenses, the payment for medical expenses cannot be made to the patient, but instead must be made directly to the provider.

168. **Answer (B) is the correct answer.** Georgia may transfer in the aggregate up to her applicable exclusion amount, which the problem indicates in 2012 is $5,120,000. IRC §§ 2505, 2010(c). She may also make an annual exclusion gift of a present interest in an amount up to $13,000 person during 2012. IRC § 2503(b). Absent a split gift election under IRC § 2513, Georgia may not apply any of Arthur's applicable exclusion amount or annual gift tax exclusion to offset the taxable amount. Thus, Georgia may give an equal amount to each child equal to one-half of the available applicable exclusion amount of $5,120,000 plus the amount of the annual gift tax exclusion of $13,000, for a total gift to each child of $2,573,000. **Answer (A) is incorrect** because it does not take advantage of the gift tax annual exclusion amount. **Answer (D) is also incorrect** because Georgia may not apply Arthur's applicable exclusion amount to offset gift tax owed on her transfers to the children absent the split gift election, which has not been made on our facts.

    **Answer (C) is incorrect.** Georgia has made the transfer to Arthur conditioned on a further transfer by Arthur to their children. The Service would see a gift subject to such a condition as an indirect transfer to the children from Georgia and would attribute the gift to her for purposes of determining Georgia's gift tax. Because Arthur has insufficient assets to make a gift in excess of $2 million, it would not be possible to argue that the funds for the gift came wholly from his assets. The Service has taken a similar position in Technical Advice Memorandum 9729005 addressing payment of gift tax under IRC § 2035 when the spouse, who had received a gift from the donor spouse, could not pay gift tax absent the gift from the donor spouse because he lacked sufficient assets.

169. **Answer (D) is correct.** When a couple elects to split gifts, the election is made for all gifts during the calendar year. Transfers made by either spouse are deemed to be made one-half by each spouse. IRC § 2513(a)(1). Thus, Georgia may transfer up to $5,146,000 to each child. The annual gift tax exclusion available to Georgia of $13,000 and that available to Arthur of $13,000 will shelter up to $26,000 of the gift to each child. The applicable exclusion amount of each spouse will shelter the remaining $5,120,000 transfer to each child. For this same reason, **Answers (A), (B), and (C) are incorrect.** In order to effectively make the election, both spouses must consent to the election. The consent generally is made on the gift tax return for the year in which the election is made. IRC § 2513(a)(2).

170. **Answer (A) is correct.** If Heidi and Roger elect to split gifts each will be deemed to make one-half of each transfer by either spouse. The election once made applies to all transfers by either spouse during the year. Thus, the maximum transfer that either spouse can make to a child is $26,000, one-half will deem to be made by each spouse, thus, allowing allocation of each spouse's annual gift tax exclusion amount. **Answers (B), (C), and (D) are incorrect.** To the extent a transfer exceeds the annual gift tax exclusion, each dollar in excess of the annual gift tax exclusion will be subject to tax in Heidi's hands because she has fully used her applicable exclusion amount.

171.  **Answer (B) is correct.** Gift tax is imposed on the transfer of any property by gift during such year by any individual who is either a citizen or a resident of the United States. *See* Treas. Reg. § 25.2501(a)(1). The gift tax will apply to gifts of cash made by David, who is a citizen of the United States, to his children. However, Antonia is neither a citizen nor a resident. Therefore, in general, the gift tax will not apply to gifts made by Antonia to the children. The issue then becomes whether a gift made by David and Antonia can qualify for split gift treatment under IRC § 2513. Under IRC § 2513, a gift made by one spouse to any person other than his spouse is considered to be made one-half by him and one-half by his spouse. However, the general rule is only applicable if at the time of the gift each spouse is either a citizen or a resident of the United States. If either spouse was a nonresident and not a citizen of the United States during any portion of the year, the consent is not effective. Treas. Reg. § 25.2513-1(b)(2). Antonia is neither a citizen nor a resident of the United States, and this prevents the couple from making a valid consent to split gifts. Lack of valid consent by both spouses results in the failure to qualify for split-gifts and precludes the election. **Answers (A) and (D) are incorrect** because it is U.S. citizenship or residence that is required in order to make an election to split gifts. **Answer (C) is incorrect** because the statute clearly requires "each spouse [to be] a citizen or resident of the United States." IRC § 2513.

172.  **Answer (B) is correct.** A gift made by one spouse to a person other than his spouse generally may be treated as a split gift if both spouses elect split gift treatment. Such gift splitting is only allowed between "spouses." The statute clarifies the use of the term "spouse" by providing that "an individual shall be considered as the spouse of another individual only if he is married to such individual at the time of the gift and does not remarry during the remainder of the calendar year." IRC § 2513(a)(1). If a spouse dies after a transfer is made, the deceased spouse's executor may consent to a split gift election. Treasury Regulation 25.2513-1(b)(1), however, specifies that "[w]here the consent is signified by an executor or administrator of a deceased spouse, the consent is not effective with respect to gifts made by the surviving spouse during the portion of the calendar period that his spouse was deceased." Only the January 15, 2012 transfers were made by Allie at a time when she was married to Tom. Thus, it is only with respect to the January 15 gift that the split gift election is effective, and Allie will be treated as transferring $6,500 to each of her children on that date. She may allocate the remaining annual gift tax exclusion amount of $6,500 to the November 5, 2012 gift so that only the $6,500 over and above the $13,000 otherwise allowed in 2012 as an annual gift tax exclusion will be deemed a taxable gift by Allie. Because Tom is deceased at the time of the November 5, 2012 gift, it is not possible to allocate any portion of the annual exclusion that would have been available to Tom had he been alive in November. **Answer (A) is incorrect** because Allie will be deemed to transfer $19,500 to each child in 2012.

**Answers (C) and (D) are incorrect.** As indicated, treasury regulations contemplate the possibility of a spouse dying during the calendar year in which the couple anticipates making the election to split gifts. The regulations provide that so long as the surviving spouse does not remarry prior to the end of the year, gifts made while both spouse's were alive may benefit from the split gift election. Thus, the election can still be made even if transfers are made after the death of a spouse, with only those transfers made prior to death eligible for split gift treatment.

**173.**   **Answer (C) is the correct answer.** IRC § 2512 governs the valuation of property for gift tax purposes. The regulations under IRC § 2512 closely mirror (but are not as complete as) the regulations under IRC § 2031, which governs property valuation for estate tax purposes. The basic valuation principles of IRC § 2031 apply equally for both gift and estate tax purposes. The gift tax regulations provide that the amount of a gift of property is the value of the item of property on the date of the gift. Treas. Reg. § 25.2512-1. *See also* Treas. Reg. § 20.2031-1(b). The value is defined as "the price at which such property would change hands between a willing buyer and a willing seller, neither being under any compulsion to buy or to sell, and both having reasonable knowledge of relevant facts." Treas. Reg. § 25.2512-1. In applying this standard, price is not determined by reference to a forced sale or a market in which such a piece of property would not commonly be sold. *Id.* Rather, fair market value is the price at which a comparable item would be sold at retail. *Id.*

The retail price or "value" of an automobile is equal to the price for which an auto of same description, make, model, age, and condition could be purchased by a member of the general public from a retail seller. Treas. Reg. § 25.2512-1. The price is not determined by the amount that a dealer in used autos might pay for the same auto. *Id.* Answer (C) provides the best comparative value because several retail sellers are attempting to sell similar cars in the same geographical area for $25,000. Given that the price is determined by reference to the retail market, the value for gift tax purposes should be set at $25,000, the retail price in the location where Benny made the gift to Joseph.

**Answer (B) is incorrect.** Answer (B) sets the value at $18,000 or the price at which a local auto dealer would purchase the car. This price would be more akin to a wholesale price that a dealer in property might pay for inventory. As noted, the regulations distinguish between the price at which something might be purchased versus the price for which the property would be sold. Valuation is based specifically on the price at which a similar item is sold at retail and not the wholesale purchase price. Thus, although a donor might prefer to value something at the lower price a dealer in such property might offer, the lower price is not "value" contemplated by the statute for gift tax purposes.

**Answers (A) and (D) are also incorrect.** Answer (A) presents only the original cost that Uncle Benny paid for the car. That may once have been the retail value but, after 40 years, the retail value of the Mustang has fluctuated immensely. Of course, $2,500 is not the value of the car today. Answer (D) does not represent the value at which a 1964 ½ Mustang could be purchased by a member of the general public. Note that if such an offer could affect value, then an opportunity would arise in every valuation event to support an artificially low value based upon possibly spurious offers.

**174.**   Where consideration is provided by the donee, the exchange is classified as a transfer that is in part a gift and in part a sale. Consideration paid by the donee affects the value of the gift given and can affect the basis that the donee ultimately retains in the property.

Uncle Benny and Joseph are related, and Benny's obvious intent to give a gift operates to take the exchange out of the definition of a transfer in the ordinary course of business. *See* Treas. Reg. § 25.2512-8. Because the transfer was not free from donative intent, the payment of $7,000 for the car cannot be considered its value. Inasmuch as the $25,000 value of the Mustang exceeds $7,000 given by Joseph in consideration for receiving the car, there is a gift of $18,000. *Id.* The $18,000 represents the excess of the $25,000 value of the car over the $7,000 of consideration given therefore.

175.    **Answer (B) is the correct answer.** For gift tax purposes, the value of a share of stock is the fair market value of the share on the date of the gift. Treas. Reg. § 25.2512-2(a). If the stock shares that are the subject of the gift are traded on a stock exchange or in an over-the-counter market, the mean between the highest and lowest quoted selling prices on the date of the gift is deemed to be the fair market value of such share of stock. Treas. Reg. § 25.2512-2(b). The regulation's use of the word "mean" between the highest selling price and the lowest selling price on the date of gift is an average that is equal to the arithmetic mean or the amount obtained by adding the highest selling price to the lowest selling price and dividing by two.

On date of the gift of Big Inc. stock to Nancy, it sold at a high of $10.00 and a low of $7.00. The mean selling price and the value of one share of Big Inc. is $8.50, derived by adding the highest selling price of $10 to $7, the lowest selling price to obtain $17.00, and then dividing $17.00 by two to arrive at the mean of $8.50 per share. The per-share value is then multiplied by 1,000, the number of shares that Helen gave to her niece Nancy to arrive at the deemed value of the gift of $8,500.

**Answers (A), (C), and (D) are incorrect.** Answer (A) reflects the lowest trading value of all the shares, and Answer (C) reflects the highest trading value, neither of which is correct as it is the mean of these two values that provides the fair market value of the shares for federal gift tax purposes. Answer (D) is not correct as it is the high and low values added together, without taking the mean, as is required by the regulations.

176.    Closely held business valuation, whether it is valuation of a corporation, partnership, limited liability company or other non-publicly traded business is an art. Often disputes with the Service come down to a battle of expert appraisers, as there is a lack of objective evidence of value in contrast to publicly traded entity interests where interests are frequently bought and sold. Treasury regulations § 25.2512-3(a) indicate the appraiser should determine fair market value based on "the net amount which a willing purchaser . . . would pay for the interest to a willing seller, neither being under any compulsion to buy or to sell and both having reasonable knowledge of the relevant facts." In order to gather and analyze all the relevant facts and circumstances, taxpayers often rely on the opinions of an expert or qualified appraiser to substantiate the fair market value of many types of gifted property. *See, e.g., Estate of Jones v. Comm'r*, 116 T.C. 121 (2001) (valuation of partnership interests). In general, courts and the IRS will evaluate the opinions of the experts and appraisers based upon their professional qualifications. *See Estate of Jones v. Comm'r*, 116 T.C. 121, 131 (2001); *Estate of Davis v. Comm'r*, 110 T.C. 530, 536 (1998). It is important to note that neither the courts nor the IRS are bound by an opinion provided by an expert. *Id.* at 131.

Often the appraised value is a combination of factors which include the value of the individual assets and the earning capacity of the business. Regulations provide: "the net value is determined on the basis of all relevant factors including — (1) A fair appraisal as of the date of the gift of all the assets of the business, tangible and intangible, including good will; (2) The demonstrated earning capacity of the business; and (3) the other factors . . . relating to the valuation of corporate stock to the extent applicable." *Id.* The other relevant factors include: "the good will of the business; the economic outlook in the particular industry; the company's position in the industry and its management; the degree of control of the business represented by the block of stock to be valued; and the values of securities of corporations engaged in the same or similar lines of business which are listed on a stock exchange." Thus, different methods of business valuation have developed and continue to evolve taking into account these factors. The methodologies factor in the assets owned by the business, the earnings capacity of the business and the value of comparable publicly traded companies. The appraisal attached to the gift tax return should include complete "financial and other data upon which the valuation [was] based."

177.   **Answer (D) is the correct answer.** A gift of property is valued as of the date of the transfer. *See* IRC § 2512(a). Again, the fair market value of the transferred property is the price at which the property would change hands between a willing buyer and willing seller, neither being under a compulsion to buy or to sell and both having reasonable knowledge of relevant facts. *See United States v. Cartwright*, 411 U.S. 546 (1973); Treas. Reg. § 25.2512-1. It is assumed within this basic standard that the hypothetical willing buyer and seller will seek to maximize economic advantage to the benefit of both. *See Estate of Jones v. Comm'r*, 116 T.C. 121, 130 (2001); *Estate of Davis v. Comm'r*, 110 T.C. 530, 535 (1998). Guidance on the specific process of determining a fair market value between a hypothetical buyer and seller is done in different ways. As was seen in the prior problems, the regulations specifically address the manner in which stock values and business values are arrived at. *See* Treas. Reg. § 25.2512-2. The regulations also specifically address, among other things, valuation of cash on hand, notes, annuities, insurance contracts, business interests, and household effects. *See* Treas. Regs. §§ 25.2512-2 through 25.2512-6. With respect to certain assets such as certain types of securities, the rules are specific. However, the estate and gift tax regulations provide only general guidance on the manner in which certain property interests are valued. For example, valuations of business interests and personal effects are to be done with reference to all relevant facts and circumstances. *See* Treas. Regs. §§ 25.2512-3; 20.2031-3; 20.2031-6.

With respect to valuing Dick's Branford, Connecticut home, there is only general and no specific guidance in the regulations. Certainly the value of the home will require Dick to report the fair market value of the home on a gift tax return. Therefore, he is required to determine the value at which the property would change hands between a willing buyer and willing seller. Without experience of his own, he is best advised to substantiate the value that he reports on the gift tax return by relying on the opinion of an expert appraiser. Because a qualified expert appraiser is most likely to arrive at a reasonable determination of the value of the home, Dick should report $600,000 as the value of the gift. Of course, the value of the home as determined by the appraiser can always be challenged by the IRS.

**Answer (A) is incorrect.** The gift tax valuation provisions do not contain a parallel provision to the IRC § 2032 alternate valuation rules that apply for federal estate tax purposes, and allow under certain circumstances the estate to value property included in the gross estate six months after decedent's date of death. The gift must be valued as of the date of the gift. There is no chance to reduce value if the value of the transferred asset depreciates after the date of the gift. **Answer (B) is incorrect** because it is pegged to the wrong valuation date.

The correct valuation date is the date of the transfer of the property, and not the date of purchase of the property. **Answer (C) is incorrect** because the assessed value of Dick's home as reflected on the county tax rolls does not necessarily reflect fair market value as is required by the estate and gift tax Code and Regulations. Indeed, the gift tax regulations specifically indicate that the value of property shall not be reported at the value at which it is assessed for local tax purposes unless that value accurately represents the fair market value of the property on the date of the gift. Treas. Reg. § 25.2512-1. It is clear in this case that $450,000 is substantially less than the appraiser's estimate of fair market value and that the value for property tax purposes is not representative of the fair market value of the house.

## Actuarial Concepts

178.   **Answer (B) is the correct answer.** Benny's goal is to give a life estate in the Colorado home to his brother Brett with a remainder interest equally to nephew and niece, Joseph and Katie. Benny's immediate issue is which actuarial table is the correct one to use. Benny's overriding issue is to value the gifts, which we will address in the next several questions. There are actually three gifts here. One gift is the life estate, and there are two gifts, one to Katie and one to Joseph, associated with the remainder.

The fair market value of a life estate or remainder is equal to the present value of the interest. Treas. Reg. § 25.2512-5(a). Determination of the present value of gifts given after May 1, 2009, is governed by Treasury Regulation § 25.2512-5T(d). (The actuarial valuation tables are updated every 10 years following the prior census.) In general, the fair market value of a specific interest in a life estate or remainder is obtained by reference to the appropriate interest rate and a standard actuarial factor. Treas. Reg. § 25.2512-5T(d). The regulations refer to the factors derived and the mortality components provided under IRC § 7520 and the gift tax treasury regulations thereunder.

In this question we are concerned only with which table the appropriate standard actuarial factor comes from. The IRS Publication 1457, refers to actuarial values for remainder factors for one life, two lives, and terms certain. The website http://www.irs.gov/retirement/article/0,id=206601,00.html includes actuarial factors for an interest for the life of one individual in Table S. Further, Table S applies only where property is gifted after May 1, 2009. Treas. Reg. § 20.2031-7T(d). Because Benny gave the Colorado home to Brett "for life" as of July 15, 2012, Benny must refer to Table S, which provides the factor for determining the value of a remainder interest.

While not necessarily intuitive, Benny has given 100 percent of the home away, but he has given it away in parts. It is important to note that the value of the remainder interest in the home is based upon the expected duration of Brett's "single" life. The shorter the life interest holder's expected lifespan, the sooner the remainder interest holders, here Joseph and Katie, will take the home. In general, the sooner they are expected to get the home, the more the remainder value of the home is worth in Joseph's and Katie's hands. Because Brett's life is the measuring life for determining the remainder factor, reference to Table S will allow Benny to obtain the appropriate single life remainder factor that, as expanded upon in the following questions, will allow him to calculate both the value of Brett's life estate and the value of Joseph's and Katie's remainder interests.

As a final note and from a practical standpoint, Table S is also provided to a limited extent in the regulations under Treasury Regulation § 20.2031-7T. Students can sometimes become frustrated with edited versions of the Code and Regulations that do not contain all of the available actuarial tables. Reference to the website indicated above is common in practice.

**Answers (A), (B), and (D) are incorrect.** For reasons explained above, the remaining answers are not correct. Table B contains factors for determining the value of a remainder interest after a term of years' interest in the property has expired. Answer (B), suggesting Table R(2), Two Life Last-to-Die Factors, applies when a life estate is measured by two lives and the value sought to be calculated is a remainder interest after the second life holder dies. This table might have been used in this problem if, hypothetically, Benny had given the home to Brett and his wife and it was to be passed to Katie and Joseph upon the death of either Brett or his wife, whichever was the last to die. Finally, Table K applies to valuation of annuities. Neither the life interest held by Brett nor the remainder interests held by Joseph and Katie qualify as annuities. In general, an annuity is a contract whereby one party is guaranteed to receive an amount of money on a regular interval (e.g., monthly or annual) for a defined period of time.

179. **Answer (B) is the correct answer.** Now that you have assisted Benny in identifying the appropriate actuarial table, it becomes apparent that in order to use Table S to identify the specific standard valuation factor, Benny needs to know Brett's age and the applicable federal rate ("AFR") of interest that applies. *See* Treas. Reg. § 20.2031-7(d). Brett's age is obtained from Benny; as the problem tells you, he is 52 years old.

Obtaining the appropriate AFR is a little more technical. Use of Table S to determine the fair market value of the gifted property requires reference to IRC § 7520 interest rates for the month in which the gift occurs and the appropriate actuarial tables. Treas. Reg. § 25.2512-5(d)(2)(iii). The value of any interest for life or remainder interest must be determined by using an interest rate (rounded to the nearest two-tenths of 1 percent) equal to 120 percent of the annual federal midterm rate in effect for the month in which the valuation date falls. IRC § 7520(a)(2); Treas. Reg. § 1.7520-1(b).

Each month the Secretary of the Treasury is directed to determine the federal short-term, mid-term, and long-term rates that apply for the following calendar month. IRC § 1274(d). The IRS publishes revenue rulings near the end of each month, and each revenue ruling has tables that contain the applicable federal rates for the following month for purposes of IRC § 1274(d). As a practical matter, the rates can be found on the Internet in many places. Historically, the IRS has published the rulings at http://www.irs.gov/businesses/small/article/0,id=112482,00.html.

Benny's gift of the home was made on April 15, 2012. Therefore, in order to determine the appropriate rate, Rev. Rul. 2012-11 must be referenced and 120 percent of the mid-term AFR rate for April 2012 must be cross-referenced. For purposes of valuing Joseph and Katie's remainder interests after Brett's life estate, the appropriate AFR rate is 1.38 percent.

**Answers (A), (C), and (D) are incorrect.** For reasons already explained, the values reflected in Answers (A), (C), and (D) are incorrect. Answer (B) is incorrect because it is 120 percent of the annual AFR rate for short-term instruments (as opposed to mid-term rates). Answer (C), 1.40 percent, reflects the unadjusted IRC Section 7520 rate. Finally, Answer (D) at 3.27 percent is the 120 percent of the long-term rate. All the wrong options represent common errors made after obtaining the correct revenue ruling.

180.   **Answer (D) is the correct answer.** We are now asked to calculate the value of Brett's life interest in Benny's Colorado home. We have determined that Table S is the appropriate actuarial table to use. We have also identified the appropriate AFR rate for use in Table S to be 1.38 percent, and we know Brett is 52 years of age as indicated in the problem. The Code and Regulations are specific in requiring that 120 percent of the annual mid-term rate rounded to the nearest two-tenths of 1 percent. Rounding 1.38 percent to the nearest two-tenths of 1 percent requires us to round up, producing a result of 1.40 percent. Cross-referencing 1.40 percent with 52 years of age on Table S, we arrive at a single-life remainder factor of 0.72127. Multiplying the remainder factor of 0.72127 by $2,000,000, which is the stated fair market value of Benny's Colorado home, results in Joseph's and Katie's remainder interest value of $1,442,540.

It is important to note that Joseph and Katie's remainder interest is proportional to Brett's life interest. By gifting a life interest in the home to Brett and a remainder interest to Joseph and Katie, Benny has gifted the full value of the home away. Brett's life interest is equal in value to the full $2,000,000 value of the home reduced by Joseph and Katie's combined remainder interest valued at $1,442,540. Thus, Brett's life interest is worth $557,460.

Alternatively, one can arrive at the same answer by first deriving Brett's life interest factor from Joseph and Katie's Table S single-life remainder interest factor. Mathematically, one minus the remainder factor of 0.72127 results in Brett's life interest factor of 0.27873, as indicated in Table S. Multiplying Brett's life interest factor by $2,000,000 yields a life interest of $557,460.

**Answers (A), (B), and (C) are incorrect.** Answer (A) is incorrect, as it represents the full value of the home. Brett's interest is only a partial interest for life. In general, a remainder interest must have some positive value. Answer (B) reflects the value of Joseph's and Katie's combined remainder interests. Finally Answer (C) reflects one-half of the value of Katie's and Joseph's combined remainder interest.

181.   **Answer (C) is the correct answer.** As indicated in the answer to Question 180, the appropriate single-life remainder factor is 0.72127. Application of this factor results in a determination that the present value of Joseph and Katie's remainder interest in the home as being worth $1,442,540. Since Joseph and Katie each have an equal interest in the home after Brett's death, their individual interests equal one-half of the full remainder value or $721,270.

**Answers (A), (B), and (D) are incorrect.** Again, Answer (A) is incorrect, as it represents the full value of the home. Answer (B) reflects the full value of Katie and Joseph's combined remainder interest. Finally, Answer (D) reflects the value of Brett's life interest in the home.

182.   The issue here is how to determine the value of Brett's term interest in the home. Whereas previously we referred to Table S to identify the specific single-life remainder factor, we now must refer to Table B, which can be found at http://www.irs.gov/retirement/article/0,id=206601,00.html. Again, reference to Publication 1457, and the website will provide access to Table B. Table B contains term certain remainder factors that apply to gifts made after May 1, 2009. In general, Table B is used in a manner similar to Table S. However, with respect to a term interest, Table B requires the donor taxpayer to cross-reference the number of years that the interest in the gifted property lasts with the

appropriate AFR rate for the month in which the gift is made. The AFR rate is the same rate that was used in the preceding problems for remainder interests. Thus, the AFR rate is the published rate for the month in which the gift was given.

Benny gifted use of the home to Brett for a term of 10 years. As determined above, the applicable AFR rate is obtained from Rev. Rul. 2012-11. The relevant rate is 120 percent of the mid-term AFR rate for April 2012, which is stated as 1.38 percent. Rounding up to the nearest two-tenths of 1 percent, we arrive at 1.40 percent and cross-reference this rate with the 10-year length of the term, to obtain a term certain remainder factor of 0.870203. The $2,000,000 value of the home is multiplied by the 0.870203 remainder factor to arrive at $1,740,406. This dollar amount represents the present value of Katie's remainder interest in the home. Again, the call of the question targets the value of Brett's term interest. Therefore, since the value of the term interest plus the remainder interest equals $2,000,000, the full value of the home, we must subtract the value of Katie's remainder interest from the full value. Subtracting $1,740,406 from $2,000,000 we arrive at $259,594, the present value of Benny's gift to Brett of the 10-year term interest.

183.    **Answer (D) is the correct answer.** Congress enacted IRC § 2702 to ensure that transfers in trust for the benefit of family members more accurately reflect the realities of the transfer. Section 2702 effectively terminates the planning benefits of a grantor retained income trust or GRIT as between certain family members (except for those trusts holding a qualified personal residence). Prior to enactment of IRC Section 2702 it was possible to create a GRIT, in which grantor retained an income interest with remainder to children, where the income interest was valued for gift tax purposes pursuant to the actuarial tables, but the property was invested in growth assets. The actuarial tables contemplated that income at the imputed interest rate would be distributed to the income beneficiary. The trust assets in reality, however, would be invested more heavily in growth stock causing most appreciation to benefit the remainder and less than the assumed rate of interest to be paid to the income beneficiary. Recognizing the difficulty in accurately valuing the income actually distributed under the actuarial tables, Congress enacted IRC § 2702 to require that only annuity interests or unitrust interests, and their corresponding remainder interests, would be capable of valuation for purposes of determining the value of any gift. Section 2702 forces any retained interest to be quantified and in fact paid out in the form of an annuity or unitrust interest. Planning benefits under Section 2702 now accrue only if the assets held in trust actually outperform 120 percent of the applicable federal midterm rate.

Essentially, IRC § 2702 requires a transfer in trust "to . . . a member of the transferor's family" where the transferor retains an interest other than a "qualified" annuity or unitrust interest (or a remainder interest following an annuity or unitrust interest) to be valued for gift tax purposes as if the interest retained by the trustor equals zero. IRC § 2702(a)(2), (b)(1). In this fact scenario, Frank has retained an income interest, as opposed to an annuity or unitrust interest, and, thus, his interest is not a qualified interest. Not only does Frank fail to retain a qualified interest, but he also passes the remainder to a "member of the transferor's family." Section 2702 defines "member of the transferor's family" by cross reference to IRC § 2704(c)(2). Member of family under that section includes "an individual's spouse, any ancestor or lineal descendant of such individual or such individual's spouse, . . . any brother or sister of the individual, and . . . any spouse of any" such individual. Thus, as a "descendant," Samuel is a member of Frank's family. As a result the interest retained by Frank is given a zero value, and the entire $1 million transferred to the trust is subject to reporting on Frank's gift tax return.

**Answers (A), (B), and (C) are incorrect.** Answer (A) is incorrect because it is Frank's retained interest that has a zero value, and not the gift. The gift is deemed to be the full $1 million. Answers (B) and (C) are incorrect because neither the retained interest nor the gift are subject to valuation under the actuarial tables.

184.    **Answer(C) is the correct answer.** Because in this fact scenario Nicholas does not fall within the definition of "a member of [Frank's] family for purposes of the special valuation rules under IRC Section 2702 as discussed in the previous answer, Frank's retained interest can now be valued actuarially. Thus, to determine the value of the remainder interest passing to Nicholas, the value of Frank's retained interest, with an actuarial valuation of $300,000, is subtracted from the full $1 million value transferred to the trust. This yields a remainder interest of $700,000 attributable to Nicholas' remainder interest. The only completed gift is the remainder to Nicholas, and so the gift tax return reports a gift of the remainder interest to Nicholas of $700,000. For the reasons stated, **Answers (A), (B), and (D) are incorrect.**

185.    **Answer (C) is the correct answer.** In this question, Frank retains a qualified interest, specifically a qualified annuity interest as defined in IRC § 2702(b). A qualified annuity or unitrust interest avoids the concerns enunciated in the 1990 Senate Report accompanying enactment of IRC § 2702. The committee "reasons" for enactment of IRC § 2702 are as follows: "[T]he committee is concerned about the undervaluation of gifts valued pursuant to Treasury tables. Based on average rates of return and life expectancy, those tables are seldom accurate in a particular case, and therefore, may be the subject of adverse selection. Because the taxpayer decides what property to give, when to give it, and often controls the return on the property, use of Treasury tables undervalues the transferred interests in the aggregate, more often than not. Therefore, the committee determines that the valuation problems inherent in trusts and term interests in property are best addressed by valuing retained interests at zero unless they take an easily valued form as an annuity or unitrust interest." Thus, even though the remainder passes to "a member of transferor's family" the annuity interest, defined as a right to receive a fixed amount at least annually allows Frank to subtract the actuarial value of the retained annuity interest from the amount transferred to the trust to arrive at the value of the gift. The gift is $700,000 or the amount transferred to the trust of $1,000,000 less the $300,000 retained annuity interest. **Answers (A), (B), and (D) are incorrect** because none of the answers attributes the correct value to Frank's retained annuity interest.

186.    **Answer (B) is the correct answer.** In Ellie's hands each share of Tech Corporation has a fair market value of $20.00 ($10,000,000 total value divided by 500,000, the total number of outstanding shares). If, for example, Ellie were to sell all 1,000,000 shares to a single buyer for $10,000,000, each share would have a value of $20.00. This is true because the 1,000,000 shares represent all of the value of the assets of the corporation.

However, the valuation of shares of stock in a closely held company must take into account all relevant facts and circumstances of the particular corporation at issue. *See Northern Trust Co. v. Comm'r*, 87 T.C. 349, 384 (1986); Treas. Reg. § 20.2031-2(f). One relevant fact in valuing corporate shares is the number of shares given. Shares of stock of a corporation that represent a minority interest are normally worth less than a proportionate share of the value of the assets of the corporation. *See Estate of Bright v. United States*, 658 F.2d 999 (5th Cir. 1981). The reduction in value associated with a minority of shares is referred to as a minority discount. The minority discount applies because, among other things, the holder of a minority interest has no control over corporate policy, is not capable of authorizing a corporate dividend, and cannot compel liquidation or other corporate actions that require a vote of the shareholders. *See Harwood v. Comm'r*, 82 T.C. 239, 267 (1984), *aff'd*, 786 F.2d 1174 (9th Cir. 1986); *Estate of Andrews v. Comm'r*, 79 T.C. 938, 953 (1982).

Ellie initially owned 100 percent of the company, and each share of stock in Ellie's hands had a $20.00 value. Upon receipt of the 7,500 shares from Ellie, Nate became merely a minority shareholder. A minority shareholder does not have sufficient voting rights to cause the corporation to take any action. Unlike Ellie, Nate lacks any control over corporate actions. Having only a minority interest, Nate cannot direct the board of directors to resolve to pay dividends or compel the corporation to take any action requiring a vote of the shareholders. Without such rights, Nate's shares have little value.

**Answer (C) is incorrect.** A control premium operates to increase the per-share value of stock where the amount of stock gifted represents a controlling interest in the corporation. The amount of stock ownership in a particular corporation that represents a "controlling interest" can vary from corporation to corporation. For example, in a simple setting where a majority vote is all that is required under the corporation's articles of incorporation for corporate action to be ratified, a greater than 50 percent share interest would represent "control" of the company. Where a super majority vote is required to induce corporate action, a greater than 50 percent interest may be required to maintain control. Ellie has only given Nate a 1.5 percent interest in Tech Corporation. Under these circumstances, Nate does not have a controlling interest, and no control premium adjustment would be required.

**Answer (A) is incorrect.** A blockage discount, also sometimes referred to as an absorption discount, generally applies, for example, where an owner of stock traded on a public market owns such a large proportion of a corporation's stock that selling all or a substantial portion of the block of stock would likely operate to depress the stock price on the public exchanges. A blockage discount would not apply to a 1.5 percent interest in a privately held corporation. **Answer (D) is incorrect** as it is a red herring.

187. **Answer (C) is the correct answer.** When determining the value of closely held stock, a discount is allowed in order to reflect lack of marketability. A lack-of-marketability discount is applied under the theory that there is no recognized market for closely held stock. *See, e.g., Mandelbaum v. Comm'r*, T.C. Memo. 1995-255. The Tax Court has summarized the factors that impact a marketability discount as follows: (1) financial statement analysis, (2) dividend policy, (3) outlook of the company, (4) management of the company, (5) control factor in the shares to be purchased, (6) company redemption policy, (7) restriction on transfer, (8) holding period of the stock, and (9) costs of a public offering. *See Estate of Jelke v. Comm'r*, T.C. Memo 2005-131; *Mandelbaum v. Comm'r*, T.C. Memo 1995-255.

While an extensive analysis of each of the factors elucidated in *Mandelbaum* is beyond the scope of this answer, a weighing of the list of factors assists courts in establishing the amount, if any, of a marketability discount. For example, the availability of regular financial statements reviewed by a qualified certified public accountant (CPA) firm showing strong financial performance from year to year would lean in favor of increased marketability of the stock and, therefore, reduced marketability discount. *See Mandelbaum v. Comm'r, supra.* Similarly, the outlook of the company, including its history, its rank in the industry, and its economic forecast, are also relevant factors for determining the stock's marketability or value. If, for example, a company is not the leader in its industry, an increased marketability discount may be appropriate. *Id.* Restrictions on transfer also impact the marketability of stock. If a shareholders' agreement restricts a shareholder's ability to freely transfer stock in the corporation, such restrictions may warrant a decrease in value and, therefore, an increased marketability discount. *Id.* Further, an interest in closely held stock is less marketable if an investor must hold it for a long period of time in order to profit. *Id.* Thus, market risk tends to increase (and marketability tends to decrease) the lengthier the holding period becomes. *Id.*

Here, Nate's shares are subject to an enforceable shareholder's agreement. The shareholder's agreement restricts Nate's ability to sell the shares to a third party under certain circumstances. Such a restriction makes Nate's shares less marketable, and these facts support an increased marketability discount.

**Answers (A), (B), and (D) are incorrect.** For reasons already explained, Answers (A) and (B) are incorrect. Answer (D) refers to a capital gains discount, which generally applies in valuing a corporation's stock where the corporation holds assets that are appreciated and are subject to built-in capital gains. When a corporation holds appreciated assets, sale of the assets will result in taxable capital gains. Prior to sale of the assets, the entity will accrue a deferred tax liability associated with the built-in (but as yet unrealized) capital gains. In *Estate of Davis v. Comm'r*, 110 T.C. 530 (1998), the Tax Court held that in determining the fair market value of closely held corporate stock, built-in capital gains discounts are appropriate under certain circumstances. *Id.* at 547. There is no indication in the fact pattern that Tech Corporation holds a material amount of appreciated assets. Under these circumstances, it would not be appropriate to apply a capital gains discount.

188.   No, the transfer of the shares will not take into account a minority interest. In fact, a premium may instead apply. Under the arm's-length standard, a willing buyer will logically pay more for a block of shares that results in the purchaser acquiring a majority or controlling interest. In general, federal tax law has isolated control as a separate element for purposes of determining the fair market value of corporate stock. *Philip Morris, Inc. v. Comm'r*, 96 T.C. 606, 628 (1991). In *Philip Morris*, the Tax Court indicated payment of a premium for control is based on the notion that the per-share value of a controlling interest is higher than one would pay per share for a minority interest. *Id.* at 629.

The Tax Court has indicated that a discount will not apply in situations where a minority block of stock has "swing vote characteristics." *Estate of Magnin v. Comm'r*, T.C. Memo. 2001-31. A "swing vote premium" may be assigned to the value of a minority block of shares that if sold may result in another shareholder gaining control. In *Estate of Winkler v. Comm'r*, T.C. Memo 1989-231, three shareholders held stock interests of 50 percent, 40 percent, and 10 percent. The issue addressed was whether a minority discount applied for estate tax purposes of valuing the 10 percent interest. The Tax Court determined that because a third hypothetical buyer would be able to combine with one of the two remaining shareholders to either effect or block control of the company, the 10 percent interest possessed "swing vote characteristics." As such, an unrelated willing buyer may be willing to pay a premium for a 10 percent block of voting stock.

Here, Nels owns 40 percent of the shares prior to receiving an additional gift from Jenna. An additional 20 percent block of Hometown Inc. stock would result in Nels holding a majority interest in the corporation. Similar to the outcome in the *Estate of Winkler*, a willing buyer would likely pay a premium for the additional 20 percent of the shares due to the fact that such shares would represent a swing vote. Thus, rather than a discount for a minority interest, the Service will likely assert that a valuation premium should be assigned.

189. **Answer (D) is correct.** A minority discount reflects the inability of a person holding a minority interest in the company to impact key decisions in a closely held entity. *See Estate of Bright v. United States*, 658 F.2d 999 (5th Cir. 1981). A lack of marketability discount, on the other hand, reflects the lack of a ready market for purchase of the entity interest or the existence of some other factor that makes sale difficult. *See Furman v. 'Comm'r*, T.C. Memo. 1998-157. Both discounts often can be taken with respect to entity interests in a closely held family entity, especially in light of the Service's 1993 ruling, Revenue Ruling 93-12, rejecting family attribution in the valuation of entity interests. The minority discount and the lack of marketability discount are especially appropriate when valuing membership interests in a family limited liability company (LLC) or limited partnership interests in a family limited partnership (FLP). Under most states' laws it is the manager of the LLC and the general partner in a FLP that control management of the respective entities. Neither a member, who is not a manager, or a limited partner exercises control over the underlying entity. (It should be noted that a member of a member-managed LLC, however, does have management duties.) Likewise, because of the fact that there is no ready market for closely held entities, a marketability discount is also appropriate. For the reasons stated a membership interest in a limited liability company often is valued after taking a minority and a marketability discount. For the same reason, **Answer (C) is incorrect** because a minority discount is not appropriate in valuing the interest of a general partner. **Answer (A) is incorrect** because the sole proprietor owns all assets of the business, and holds control over the use and management of each asset. As a result, a minority interest discount is not appropriate with respect to the assets of a sole proprietorship. On the estate tax return it is the assets of the sole proprietorship that are included. **Answer (B) is incorrect.** Because there is a ready and active market for publicly traded stock, by definition, a lack of marketability discount is not appropriate for such stock.

Historically, FLPs have been used by taxpayers to accomplish a number of business, estate tax, and gift tax goals in addition to provision of minority and marketability discounts. Prior to the advent of the LLC, FLPs were purportedly formed by many taxpayers for, among other things: consolidation of financial interests with a goal of improving investment opportunities while minimizing their risks through diversification; centralized management of assets; orderly succession of the family assets; allowing family members to become equity holders through gifting of FLP (or LLC) interests; and assuring long-term business continuity by restricting sales of FLP interests outside of the family.

Limited partnerships generally provide the flexibility to allow these goals to be accomplished. Importantly, unless an election is made otherwise, a limited partnership is treated as a partnership for federal income tax purposes. *See* Treas. Reg. § 301.7701-3(a). A partnership is generally not subject to income tax on items of income, gain, loss, or deduction. Rather, partnerships are treated as "pass-through" entities in which the individual partners are subject to income tax. Tax is imposed on each partner's ratable share of the partnership tax items passed through to each partner. A taxpayer may contribute assets to a limited partnership in return for general partner units, limited partner units, or both. Under state law, a general partner is authorized to manage assets held by the limited partnership. Limited partners are not allowed to participate in management decisions. In this fashion, a taxpayer who is also a general partner in a limited partnership can maintain control over the assets he or she contributed. Limited partners remain liable only for the amount contributed to a limited partnership whereas general partners remain individually liable. In order to shield the general partner's personal assets from liabilities arising from the limited partnership, a taxpayer general partner may form a wholly or partially owned corporation to act as the general partner of the limited partnership. After formation of a limited partnership and pursuant to the terms of the partnership agreement, a taxpayer may choose to gift general or limited partner units (or both) to various family members (or unrelated third parties), thereby taking advantage of various valuation discounts. See the previous topic for a detailed discussion of the types of discounts and how they may apply.

With the advent of the LLC in the 1980s and its increasing popularity as an accepted business entity, LLCs are also used for the same general purposes as FLPs. As in a corporation, all the equity holders of an LLC are shielded from individual liability. However, like a general or limited partnership, LLCs are also treated as partnerships for federal income tax purposes. There is no managing general partner in an LLC. Rather, LLCs are managed either by one or more members who are appointed by the other members (manager-managed) or managed by all the members in unison (member-managed). In order to retain control of assets contributed to a family limited liability company (FLLC), a taxpayer may initially appoint himself or herself as the sole manager. As a manager, a taxpayer who creates an LLC may maintain control over assets contributed to the LLC. Retaining such an interest, however, may cause inclusion in a taxpayer donor's gross estate under IRC § 2036(a)(2).

190.   **Answer (D) is correct.** Teresa has dual planning goals, as do most clients. She would like to maximize use of her applicable exclusion amount, and obtain sound management of her assets. The choice of placing her assets in an FLP, will maximize use of her applicable exclusion amount as the value of the entity interests reflect a minority and lack of marketability discount that would not be available if the full value of the underlying assets were transferred by gift. Minority and marketability discounts often exceed a combined 35 percent discount. *See Estate of Nowell v. Comm'r*, T.C. Memo. 1999-15. The discounts, thus, essentially result in the transfer of the underlying FLP assets at a substantially reduced value reflected in the entity interests.

**Answer (A) is incorrect** because outright transfer of stock in the family ranch, while likely eligible for discounts, will not provide the centralized management of the stock itself by her child Amanda that is preferred by Teresa. With an FLP, the stock can be transferred to the FLP, with Teresa acting as the general partner of the FLP. **Answers (B) and (C) are incorrect** because a transfer of the property to a trust, while placing management in Amanda's hands as trustee, does not achieve the discounts associated with the transfer of limited partnership interests. Thus, transfers to trust will not maximize use of Teresa's applicable exclusion amount in the same way that a transfer of the property to an FLP, with a subsequent transfer of the general partnership interest to Amanda, and the limited partnership interests to others,

**191.** Whether or not Carol may take an annual gift tax exclusion for transfers of the membership interests in the LLC depends on whether or not the "present interest" requirement of IRC § 2503(b) is met. In order to qualify as a "present interest" the United States Supreme Court indicated that the beneficiary must be able to enjoy a "substantial present economic benefit" in the transferred property. *Fondren v. Comm'r*, 324 U.S. 18, 20–21 (1945). Building on this notion the Tax Court in *Hackl v. Comm'r*, 118 T.C. 279 (2002), *aff'd*, 335 F.3d 664 (7th Cir. 2003), addressed taxpayer's ability under similar facts to take an annual exclusion for gifts of LLC interests, and held the gifts failed to qualify as present interests. The Tax Court looked to see if the beneficiary was entitled to income in an ascertainable amount. In *Hackl* the LLC operated at a loss with its major asset being timberland, and the parent as manager of the LLC controlled the flow of income and the ability of the beneficiary to sell the LLC interest. The Seventh Circuit affirmed the Tax Court holding in *Hackl*. The Seventh Circuit found that "restrictions on the transferability of the shares meant that they were essentially without immediate value to the donees. In a more recent case, the Tax Court similarly denied an annual exclusion for transfers of limited partnership interests in *Price v. Comm'r*, T.C. Memo. 2010-2. In *Price*, the court noted that the partnership agreement precluded withdrawal of the partner and did not provide for distribution of income to the partners. In fact, income was not distributed for a period of two years. If the taxpayer wants to obtain an annual gift tax exclusion for the transfer of entity interests, it would be important to structure the entity so that the limited partner could sell the limited partnership interests and/or obtain income from the partnership interest, often two things that donor's are reluctant to allow.

**192.** **Answer (A) is correct.** It is correct because the structure of the transaction avoids the pitfalls of Answers (B), (C), and (D) which have led courts to apply the step transaction doctrine, and thereby eliminate the ability of the transferor, here Teresa, to apply minority and marketability discounts in valuing the transfer of limited partnership interests to the beneficiaries. In Answer (A) Teresa forms the partnership with her children, and waits six months prior to transferring limited partnership interests to her children. Waiting for a substantial period of time to transfer limited partnership interests avoids the possibility of a court applying the step transaction doctrine, or an indirect gift argument as happened in the cases discussed below.

In the last decade, the IRS has more aggressively challenged valuation discounts attributed to gifts of interests in FLPs. The IRS has proceeded under a number of theories with some success and some failure. Among other things, the IRS has argued: an indirect gift occurs upon formation of an FLP; the taxpayer improperly retained an interest under IRC § 2036(a); and the formation of an FLP, contribution of assets, and gifting of units constitutes a tax-motivated transaction. Under the facts of Answer (B), Teresa is likely to be deemed to have made an indirect gift of the assets contributed to the FLP to her children. A transfer to a partnership for less than full and adequate consideration may represent an indirect gift of the contributed assets to the other partners. *See Shepherd v. Comm'r*, 115 T.C. 376, 389 (2000), *aff'd*, 283 F.3d 1258 (11th Cir. 2002). In *Shepherd*, the taxpayer contributed land and stocks to a limited partnership. 115 T.C. 376, 377 (2000). Taxpayer's two children each received a 25 percent interest in the partnership upon taxpayer's initial contribution. The taxpayer took the position that the transfers of partnership interests represented two separate gifts and that these gifts should each be subject to minority and marketability discounts. *Id.* at 384. The Commissioner argued that the discounts were inappropriate because the taxpayer gave his sons gifts of the contributed assets rather than an interest in the partnership. *Id.* Further, it was argued that the taxpayer completed the two gifts prior to the formation of the partnership. *Id.* The Tax Court agreed with the Commissioner, holding that the transfers were indirect gifts to the sons of a ratable share of the assets contributed and that no valuation discounts applied. *Id.* at 389.

The facts in Answer (D) bear some similarity to the facts in the *Shepherd* case. None of Teresa's children contributes assets to the partnership, and Teresa's contribution is credited to the partnership accounts and on the same day the limited partnership interests are transferred to the children. Thus, Teresa's contribution is likely to be treated as an indirect gift of a ratable share of the contributed assets. It is important to note, however, that the *Shepherd* court made it clear that not every capital contribution to a partnership will result in a gift to the other partners. *Id.* at 389. This is especially true where the contributing partner's capital account reflects the full amount of his or her contribution. Thereafter, the contributing partner may gift an interest to other persons. *Id.* The other reason that **both Answers (C) and (D) are incorrect** is that a partnership requires two investors, and one person may not form a partnership. In Answers (C) and (D) Teresa contributed 100 percent of the partnership assets, thus, the partnership was not formed in either instance until the transfer of the limited partnership interests to the children causing options (C) and (D) to mirror the facts of *Shepherd*.

Questions have also arisen regarding the proximity of a gift of limited partnership units in relation to the formation of the limited partnership. **Answer (B) is incorrect** because it mirrors the facts of *Senda* in that the transfer of limited partnership interests occurred on the same day as formation of the limited partnership. In *Senda v. Comm'r*, T.C. Memo. 2004-160, *aff'd*, 433 F.3d 1044 (8th Cir. 2006), the taxpayer was unable to prove that the contribution had been made before a gift of limited partnership units. The taxpayer made an initial contribution to the partnership and then on the same day made a gift of limited partnership units to his children. The Eighth Circuit Court of Appeals affirmed the Tax Court's finding that the taxpayer failed to prove that the contribution was made prior to the gifts of the partnership interests. 433 F.3d 1044, 1047 (8th Cir. 2006). The Court of Appeals then went on to indicate that the taxpayer overlooked the ultimate finding of the tax court, stating that "[a]t best, the transactions were integrated (as asserted by respondent) and, in effect, simultaneous." *Id.* at 1048. The Court of Appeals further noted that even if the taxpayer's contribution would have first been credited to his capital account, this extra step would not have had an impact on the determination that the transaction was integrated. The Court then implicated the step transaction doctrine by stating that "formally distinct steps are considered as an integrated whole, rather than in isolation, so federal tax liability is based on a realistic view of the entire transaction." *Id.* at 1049. Under the reasoning in *Senda*, the formation of the partnership by Teresa as set forth in Answer (B) could be viewed as a single transaction in which the assets contributed by Teresa to the limited partnership (as opposed to those contributed by her children) are treated as indirectly transferred to the children rather than a contribution by Teresa followed by separate gifts to the children of limited partnership interests in excess of the 5 percent reflecting the children's contributions.

Following the holdings of *Senda* and *Shepherd*, the courts in two cases, *Holman v. Comm'r*, 130 T.C. 170 (2008) and *Gross v. Comm'r*, T.C. Memo. 2008-221, found that formation of a partnership with a lapse of six and 11 days respectively between formation and the transfer of limited partnership did not implicate the step transaction doctrine. The Tax Court in both cases held for the taxpayer and respected the substance of the transaction. Answer (A) is

**correct** because it mirrors closely the facts of *Gross*, where taxpayer formed a limited partnership interest, with her daughters, who also made a small contribution to the partnership. The court viewed the lapse of time, as creating real economic risk because the underlying assets of the limited partnership were shares of publicly traded stock. It warned in footnote 5: "The real economic risk of a change in value arises from the nature of the [limited partnership] securities as heavily traded, relatively volatile common stocks. We might view the impact of a 11-day hiatus differently in the case of another type of investment; e.g., a preferred stock or a long-term Government bond." The fact that in Answer (A) six months elapse between formation and contribution should be sufficient time for a court to acknowledge economic risk, and to respect the later transfer of limited partnership interests to the children.

193.     **Answer (A) is correct.** The Service has successfully included the undiscounted value of the assets of FLPs and FLLCs on the theory that there was an implied agreement that the donor would retain the right to use and enjoy the assets distributed to the limited partnership during her life. In the Service's first big win in the limited partnership arena, it argued in *Estate of Schauerhamer v. Comm'r*, T.C. Memo. 1997-242, the taxpayer used the limited partnership as her personal piggy bank, and took disproportionate distributions in relation to the other limited partners. In Answer (A), although Brianna retained only a 10 percent interest in the FLP, she received more than 80% of the income, clearly a disproportionate distribution. Under the facts of Answer (A), as under the facts of *Schauerhamer*, the IRS agent should include the undiscounted value of the limited partnership assets under IRC § 2036(a)(1) on the basis that Brianna impliedly retained an income interest in the transferred assets.

For purposes of section 2036(a)(1), enjoyment of property is retained if there is an express or implied agreement at the time of the transfer that the transferor will enjoy present economic benefits of the property. *See Estate of Reichardt v. Comm'r*, 114 T.C. 144, 151 (2000). In *Reichardt*, the decedent taxpayer failed to limit his enjoyment of property transferred to a partnership. The Tax Court found that notwithstanding that taxpayer transferred actual legal title of property to the partnership, the taxpayer's relationship to the assets was the same both before and after the assets were contributed. *Id.* at 153. Therefore, the value of the assets held by the partnership were included in the taxpayer's gross estate at fair market value. *Id.* As support for its conclusion, the Tax Court found, among other things, that the taxpayer-decedent commingled partnership funds with personal funds, depositing some partnership income in his personal account. Taxpayer also used the partnership's checking account as his personal account and resided in a residence held by the partnership without paying rent to the partnership. *Id.*

Although the Service has successfully included the undiscounted value on the theory that decedent has retained the power to control who is to receive the income from the assets transferred to the partnership by virtue of being the general partner pursuant to IRC Section 2036(a)(2), the facts do not indicate that Brianna retained a general partnership interest. If she had, as did the taxpayer in *Estate of Strangi v. Comm'r*, T.C. Memo 2003-145, Section 2036(a)(2) would have included the undiscounted assets in Brianna's gross estate by virtue of her retained power over the assets. In a later case, *Estate of Turner v. Comm'r*, T.C. Memo. 2011-209, the Tax Court found that a retained right to amend the partnership agreement constituted a prohibited power under IRC § 2036(a)(2), and included the undiscounted value of the assets transferred to the family limited partnership in that decedent donor's gross estate. For the reasons stated, **Answer (B) is incorrect.**

**Answer (C) is incorrect** because it references inclusion of the undiscounted value of the partnership interests as opposed to the value of the assets contributed to the limited partnership. Upon application of IRC § 2036, it is the property contributed to the partnership as opposed to the partnership interests that is included. **Answer (D) is incorrect** because as indicated IRC § 2036 applies to cause inclusion of the underlying assets for the reasons stated above.

194. Section 2036 of the Code does not apply if taxpayer makes a bona fide transfer for adequate consideration. If taxpayer can demonstrate a "significant non-tax reason" for creating the family limited partnership that is in fact supported by the facts, the courts will apply the "bona fide sale for full and adequate consideration" to IRC § 2036. If the exception applies, assets will not be included in the gross estate under IRC § 2036. Several courts have recognized significant non-tax reasons precluding application of IRC § 2036. For example, in *Estate of Shurtz v. Comm'r*, T.C. Memo. 2010-21, the fact that it would be too cumbersome to obtain the signatures of all 14 owners of timberland served as a sufficient "significant non-tax reason" to deem the formation of the limited partnership a bona fide transaction. Also, for example, in *Estate of Schutt v. Comm'r*, T.C. Memo. 2005-126, the taxpayer's pursuit of a specific investment strategy rose to the level of a significant non-tax reason. In the fact pattern, the fact that the LLC was created a number of years before with the intent of operating an active business should be sufficient to meet the requirement of a significant non-tax reason, and thereby exempt the LLC assets from inclusion in Zach's gross estate.

195.   **Answer (C) is the correct answer.** Section 2053 of the Code allows the deduction of certain claims and expenses. The types of deductible expenses include funeral expenses, administration expenses and claims against the estate, and certain unpaid mortgages. In order for a deduction to be taken pursuant to IRC § 2053, the item deducted must fall within one of these general categories. A loss in the value of stock as enunciated in Answer (C) does not fall within any of these enumerated categories, and, thus, (C) is the correct answer.

   **Answers (A), (B), and (D) are incorrect.** Each of the items listed in those answers falls within one of the categories of deductible expenses and claims. The cost of a cemetery plot as outlined in Answer (A) may generally be deducted as a funeral expense. Because it is necessary to value assets for purposes of preparing the estate tax return, the appraiser's fees in Answer (B) fall within the definition of administration expenses. Treasury regulations specifically reference appraiser's fees as being a deductible miscellaneous administration expense. Specifically it provides: "Miscellaneous administration expenses include such expenses as court costs, surrogates' fees, accountants' fees, appraisers' fees, clerk hire, etc." Treas. Reg. § 20.2053-3(d)(3). The medical expenses in Answer (D) were incurred prior to decedent's death and remained outstanding as of decedent's death. Thus, the medical expenses fall into the category of claims against the estate. As such they are deductible under IRC § 2053. Keep in mind that under certain circumstances medical expenses may be taken on decedent's income tax return instead of decedent's estate tax return.

196.   **Answer (C) is the correct answer.** The issue here is whether the expenses incurred for decedent's family to have one last family gathering in Hawaii to celebrate decedent's life qualify as funeral expenses deductible under IRC § 2053. Treasury Regulation § 20.2053-2 does not specifically define funeral expenses. The regulations indicate only that "[a] reasonable expenditure for a tombstone, monument, or mausoleum, or for a burial lot, either for the decedent or his family, including a reasonable expenditure for its future care, may be deducted under this heading, provided such expenditure is allowable by the local law. Included in funeral expenses is the cost of transportation of the person bringing the body to the place of burial." The Tax Court, however, in *Estate of Davenport v. Comm'r*, T.C. Memo. 2006-215 indicates that reception expenses for the purpose of recognizing and thanking third parties for their support during decedent's life do not fall within the definition of funeral expenses. The court indicated that to be deductible as a funeral expense, the expense should be one traditionally connected with a funeral in eulogizing and laying to rest the deceased. *Id.* In addition, the regulations imply that the expense to be deductible is subject to a standard of reasonableness. *Id.* Travel expenses to Hawaii in order to celebrate decedent's life, like the expenses in *Davenport*, generally do not fall under the umbrella of "eulogizing and laying to rest the decedent." In addition, travel expenses to Hawaii for decedent's entire family might not meet the reasonableness standard that seems to underlay the treasury regulation. *Id.* **Answers (A) and (B) are incorrect** because it is unlikely as indicated that a court would find the expenses reasonable and would disallow the expense under reasoning

similar to *Davenport*. Both answers characterize the family's travel expenses to Hawaii as reasonable. Answer (A) also is incorrect for the reason that an expense is not made reasonable simply due to a request of the decedent as to burial and funeral expenses. **Answer (D) is incorrect.** There is no requirement in the regulations that the expense be paid within a "reasonable time." The only reference is to the reasonableness of the expense itself.

The facts indicate that the travel expenses are deductible for state law purposes. Nevertheless, Answer (B) is incorrect because allowability under state law is not the only requirement for deductibility under IRC § 2053. While expenses must be allowable under state law, in order for a funeral expense deduction to be taken, the majority of courts hold that the expense also must meet federal requirements. *See Estate of Millikin v. Comm'r*, 125 F.3d 339 (6th Cir. 1997). Thus, the issue under these facts focuses not on state law, but on compliance with the regulation requirement that the expense incurred be a "funeral" expense as contemplated by the Code and accompanying Treasury Regulations.

197.      **Answer (C) is the best answer.** Executor fees fall within the category of deductible administration expenses provided the fee is allowable by state law, and is paid, or if unpaid at the filing of the return, is reasonably ascertainable. Treasury Regulations amended in 2009, generally limit any deduction to the amount "actually paid." Treas. Reg. § 20.2053-1(d)(1). The regulations, however, allow an exception to the "actually paid" requirement if an amount "is not yet paid, provided that the amount to be paid is ascertainable with reasonable certainty and will be paid. For example, executors' commissions and attorneys' fees that are not yet paid . . . [may be deemed] ascertainable with reasonable certainty and may be deducted if such expenses will be paid." Treas. Reg. § 20.2053-1(d)(4). Those same regulations note that if an "expense is contested or contingent, such . . . . expense cannot be ascertained with reasonable certainty." *Id.* Example 1 of Treasury Regulation § 20.2053-1(d)(7) on facts similar to those in the fact pattern indicates that the executor fees should be deductible up to the statutory amount allowable and not contested. Thus, the executor fees should only be deducted up to the $80,000 statutorily allowable amount on the estate tax return because the amount in excess is contested. In order to preserve the right to take a deduction for the excess $20,000 in the event it is actually paid, the example indicates the estate should file a protective claim for refund. With regard to executor fees, the Treasury Regulations further provide: "[T]he amount of the commissions claimed as a deduction must be in accordance with the usually accepted standards and practice of allowing such an amount in estates of similar size and character in the jurisdiction in which the estate is being administered, or any deviation from the usually accepted standards or range of amounts (permissible under applicable local law) must be justified to the satisfaction of the Commissioner." Treas. Reg. § 20.2053-3(b). Thus, the executor may still be allowed to collect the additional $20,000 in fees if justified and paid. **Answer (A) is incorrect** because as indicated the expense must either be actually paid, or reasonably ascertainable and not contested, in order to be deductible. It is not enough for the executor to simply assert the amount owed.

**Answers (B) and (D) are not the best answers.** While the regulations allow for the possibility of an executor fee deduction in excess of the statutory maximum in the event the executor can justify the fee, Answer (B) is not the best answer because the facts indicate that the amount in excess of the $80,000 statutorily allowed amount is contested, and the fact of contest precludes an immediate deduction. *See id.* Answer (D) is not the best answer because the uncontested portion of the fee can be taken even though it is not paid, on the basis that it is reasonably ascertainable.

198.  **Answer (A) is correct.** Treasury regulations acknowledge that sales expenses may qualify as an expense of administration. Treasury Regulation 20.2053-3(d)(2). However, IRC § 2053 provides a deduction for administration expenses only to the extent the expenses are "allowable by the laws of the jurisdiction . . . in which the estate is being administered." The question indicates that in fact the selling expenses are allowable under local law. In addition, Treasury Regulations specifically require that the underlying sale be necessary "to pay the decedent's debts, expenses of administration or taxes, to preserve the estate, or to effect distribution." The sale of Shirley's home is necessary to pay federal estate taxes. Thus, Answer (A) is the best answer as both requirements for taking a deduction for the selling expenses are satisfied.

It is important to note that there is a divergence of opinion as between the Seventh Circuit and all other circuits deciding the issue of whether expenses need only be "allowable" under applicable state law or whether an expense must be both "allowable" under state law and "necessary" as required by the federal treasury regulations in order for the expense to be deductible for federal estate tax purposes. Under similar facts, the Sixth Circuit in *Estate of Millikin v. Comm'r*, 125 F.3d 339 (6th Cir. 1997), upheld the Treasury Regulation, and stated: "We agree with the Commissioner that the phrase 'administration expenses' is neither self-defining nor unambiguous. Moreover we find that the Treasury Regulation's construction of that phrase to include only those expenses 'actually and necessarily incurred . . . is a permissible construction of the states." In the Seventh Circuit, an administrative expense may be deducted for federal tax purposes if local law allows the expense. *See Ballance v. United States*, 347 F.2d 419, 423 (7th Cir. 1965) (the definition of "administration expenses" in the Regulations including only such expenses as are necessary does not override the statutory provisions authorizing a deduction for administration expenses allowed by local state law under which the estate is being administered). *Compare Estate of Smith v. Comm'r*, 510 F.2d 479 (2d Cir. 1975) (determined commissions for the sale of artwork incurred to avoid flooding the market with artwork were not necessary). Thus, under the holdings *Estate of Millikin* and *Estate of Smith*, federal courts may reexamine a lower state court's allowance of administration expenses "to determine whether they were in fact necessary to carry out the administration of the estate or merely prudent or advisable in preserving the interests of the beneficiaries." *Estate of Smith*, 510 F.2d at 483. **Answer (D) is incorrect** because the regulations do not require a choice between selling property to pay estate taxes and taking out a loan to pay estate taxes with a corresponding deduction for interest payments on the loan. Courts apply the same "necessary" standard to deductibility of loan interest. *See Estate of Bahr v. Comm'r*, 68 T.C. 74 (1977).

**Answer (B) is incorrect** because selling expenses can be deductible regardless of whether incurred in administering probate or nonprobate property. Treasury regulations differentiate as between expenses paid from property subject to claims and those paid from property not subject to claims only with respect to the time within which the claim is paid. If the expense is incurred in the administration of property not subject to claims that is included in the gross estate, the expense must be paid within the limitations period for assessment of estate tax. Treas. Reg. § 20.2053-1(a)(2). If, on the other hand, the expense is incurred in the administration of estate assets, but paid from nonprobate assets not subject to claims, the expense must be paid within the time for filing the estate tax return plus extensions. Treas. Reg. § 20.2053-1(c)(2).

**Answer (C) is incorrect.** As a general rule, expenses incurred for the benefit of the beneficiary are not deductible. Typically these expenses do not meet the necessary requirement of the regulations. The Treasury regulations specifically state: "Expenditures not essential to the proper settlement of the estate, but incurred for the individual benefit of the heirs, legatees, or devisees, may not be taken as deductions." Treas. Reg. § 20.2053-3(a).

199.  **Answer (C) is the best answer.** Answer (C) states the actual reason the estate may not claim the deduction on the return. **Answer (D) while also correct is not the best answer.** Answer (D) does not state the specific reason for the estate being unable to deduct the appraised value of the claim as of decedent's date of death, it only acknowledges possible exceptions that are inapplicable to the facts of the question.

This question focuses on deductible amounts falling within the category of "claims against the estate." Treas. Reg. § 20.2053-1(a)(1)(iii). To be deductible a claim against the estate must be allowable under state law, and if "founded on a promise or agreement . . . [must be] contracted bona fide and for an adequate and full consideration in money or money's worth [except for certain charitable gifts]." IRC § 2053(a), (c)(1). The claim at issue is not subject to the last requirement because it involves a claim based in tort. Following amendments to the regulations in 2009, contested claims are also subject to the requirement that the claim in fact be paid, or be reasonably ascertainable. The malpractice claim is not paid at the time of filing the return, nor is it reasonably ascertainable. The Treasury Regulations specifically limit the deductible amount as follows: "To take into account properly events occurring after the date of a decedent's death in determining the amount deductible under section 2053 and these regulations, the deduction for any claim or expense . . . is limited to the total amount actually paid in settlement or satisfaction of that item." Treas. Reg. § 20.2053-1(d)(1). The 2009 regulations allow for the filing of a protective claim for refund in the event the dispute is not resolved prior to the running of the period of limitations. Treas. Reg. § 20.2053-1(d)(2). The regulations provide exceptions to this rule in the event a counterclaim is pending, Treas. Reg. § 20.2053-4(b), and also to the extent the full value of the aggregate claims to be deducted do not exceed $500,000, Treas. Reg. § 20.2053-4(c).

**Answers (A) and (B) are incorrect** because a contested or contingent claim may no longer be deducted until actually paid, and is limited to the extent of the amount paid. The Treasury Regulations reject deduction until the $10,000,000 is in fact paid, if at all, and also reject any notion that the contested claim should be valued as of date of death absent meeting the requirements of one of the exceptions to the general rule. The 2009 amendments to the Treasury Regulations were made in response to a split among the circuits as to whether a contested claim may be deducted at its appraised date of death value regardless of the amount actually paid.

Prior to enactment of the recent regulations, some courts hold as the Tenth Circuit did in *McMorris v. Comm'r*, 243 F.3d 1254 (10th Cir. 2001), where decedent's estate took a deduction for federal income taxes due as of the date of decedent's death. The IRS contested the amount that decedent reported as basis and gain in the stock, arguing that decedent's basis in the stock was lower than reported and that decedent owed tax on substantially higher gains. However, the decedent's estate was successful in proving that the decedent's basis in the stock was higher than originally reported by the decedent. As such, decedent's original sale of the stock resulted in a loss instead of gain and a refund (as opposed to a liability) arose. Notwithstanding that decedent's estate was due a refund, the decedent's estate sought to deduct the tax liabilities associated with the sale of stock that were thought to have existed as of the date of decedent's death and asserted by the Service and contested by the estate. The Commissioner argued that because there ended up being no tax due in relation to the stock (and indeed a refund), decedent's estate was no longer entitled to the deduction. Decedent's estate argued that post-death events are not considered in determining the amount of an estate tax deduction because the original income tax liabilities related to valid and enforceable claims against the estate at the time of decedent's death. The Tenth Circuit Court of Appeals agreed with decedent's estate finding that post-death events are not to be considered in valuing a deduction taken on an estate tax return several years before. The Tenth Circuit relied on the Supreme Court's holding in *Ithaca Trust v. United States*, 279 U.S. 151 (1929), where the Court held that the value of a charitable remainder interest for charitable deduction purposes must be determined as of date of death. Consistent with the holding in Ithaca Trust, a number of courts, such as the one ruling on the *McMorris* case have held that post-death events may not be considered in determining the value of a claim against an estate. On the other hand, in *Jacobs v. Comm'r*, 34 F.2d 233 (8th Cir. 1929), the Eighth Circuit distinguished Ithaca Trust, stating that "the claims which Congress intended to be deducted were actual claims, not theoretical ones." Under the *Jacobs* line of reasoning, only claims determined to be valid and actually paid as of the date of death may be deducted. *Id.* at 235. Thus, in some circuits, under the *Jacobs* line of reasoning, the amount deductible under IRC § 2053(a)(3) is the actual amount paid by the estate in satisfaction of the claim, and post-death events may impact the "value" of a deduction for estate tax purposes. *See Estate of Saunders v. Comm'r*, 136 T.C. 406 (2011); *Estate of Foster v. Comm'r*, T.C. Memo 2011-95 (appealable to the 9th Cir.).

200. **Answer (A) is the best answer.** The claim at issue in this question is one founded on contract. As noted above, in addition to being allowable under state law, a claim if "founded on a promise or agreement . . . [must be] contracted bona fide and for an adequate and full consideration in money or money's worth [except for certain charitable gifts]." IRC § 2053(a), (c)(1). Whenever a decedent's family member files the claim, the issue becomes whether the claim is bona fide. Because the son in fact rendered valuable housekeeping services at the same amount that his business offers the service to third parties, the issue is not one of adequate and full consideration in money or money's worth. Instead the issue is the bona fide nature of the claim.

The 2009 amendments to the Treasury Regulations provide a list of factors to be considered in determining whether a claim is bona fide as between family members (or a related entity) and the decedent. Among the factors to be considered are whether the claim (1) arose in the ordinary course of business and was negotiated at arm's length, (2) is in the nature of an "expectation or claim of inheritance," (3) originates pursuant to an agreement substantiated with contemporaneous evidence, (4) performance pursuant to the terms of the agreement, and (5) reporting of the transaction for income and employment tax purposes. Treas. Reg. § 20.2053-1(a)(1)(ii). While the Question does not provide facts addressing each of these factors, it does appear that the agreement between Jim and his Mom did arise in the ordinary course of Jim's business and that it was performed according to its terms. It can be inferred that because payment is made to Jim's business that he has been reporting the amounts properly for income and employment tax purposes. For this reason, Answer (A) is the best answer.

**Answer (B) is incorrect.** The question deals with a "claim against the estate" as opposed to an "administration expense" as referenced in Answer (B).

**Answers (C) and (D) also are incorrect.** Answer (C) suggests a lack of adequate consideration. In fact, the facts of the question indicate that Jim does perform services for the promise of payment. The performance of services should be considered by the Service to meet the adequate consideration requirement. Answer (D) acknowledges that the regulations call into scrutiny the bona fides of a claim asserted by a family member, however, the above discussion acknowledges that the ultimate answer relies on a weighing and balancing of factors.

201.   **Answer (A) is the correct answer.** This question reflects closely the facts of Treas. Reg. § 20.2053-4(d)(7) example 8. As in the facts of the question the claim at issue in the question involves a property settlement agreement on divorce to pay a continuing and recurring support obligation. Section 2043(b)(2) of the Code recognizes that an agreement meeting the requirements of IRC § 2516 also meets the adequate and full consideration requirement for deductibility of claims under IRC § 2053. The agreement between Imogen and Tom meets the requirements of IRC § 2516 as it was entered into within the requisite time of divorce (one year prior and two years after), and involved the division of marital property and support owed to the spouse. **Thus, Answer (C) is incorrect** because IRC § 2043(b)(2) causes the agreement to satisfy the adequate and full consideration requirement. **Answer (D) is also incorrect** for the same reason, and a written agreement in satisfaction of the support rights of a spouse falls under the protection of IRC §§ 2043(b)(2) and 2516. As between Answers (A) and (B), Answer (A) is correct as example 8 indicates: "to the extent the obligation to make the recurring payment is a claim that will be paid, E may deduct the amount of the claim (*measured according to actuarial principles*, using factors set forth in the transfer tax regulations or otherwise provided by the IRS) under the rule for deducting certain ascertainable amounts." Treas. Reg. § 20.2053-4(d)(7) example 8 (emphasis added). Thus, Answer (A) is correct and **Answer (B) is incorrect.**

202.   **Answer (A) is correct.** Section 2053(c)(1)(B) of the Code speaks to the deductibility of certain taxes and provides: "Any income taxes on income received after the death of the decedent, or property taxes not accrued before his death, or any estate, succession, legacy, or inheritance taxes, shall not be deductible under this section." Thus, **Answers (B) and (C) are incorrect** because each involves payment of an inheritance or estate tax. **Answer (D) is incorrect** because the income tax accrued following decedent's death. **Answer (A) is correct** because the income taxed accrued prior to Mac's date of death.

203.   **Answer (A) is correct.** Where the mortgage is a recourse mortgage, the full value of the home is included in Becky's gross estate, and the mortgage, for which Becky was personally liable, is deductible in full pursuant to IRC § 2053. Whereas, if the mortgage is nonrecourse, in other words, the decedent's other assets are not at stake as collateral, then only the "value of the equity of redemption (or the value of the property, less the mortgage or indebtedness) need be returned as part of the value of the gross estate." Treas. Reg. § 20.2053-7. Because the mortgage in this question is recourse Answer (A) is the correct answer and the full value of the home is included in the gross estate, with a corresponding full deduction under IRC § 2053. **For this reason, Answers (B) and (D) are incorrect. Answer (C) is incorrect** as it is irrelevant whether the mortgage is held as against a probate or nonprobate asset so long as the asset is included in the gross estate.

204. **Answer (A) is the correct answer.** This question involves expenses with regard to termination of a trust which holds nonprobate assets includible in the gross estate but not subject to claims. Treasury Regulation § 20.2053-1(a)(2) specifically indicates that "expenses incurred in administering property which is included in the gross estate but which is not subject to claims and which — (i) Would be allowed as deductions . . . if the property being administered were subject to claims; and (ii) Were paid before the expiration of the period of limitation for assessment [for collection of estate taxes]" are deductible. The period of limitation begins to run from the date of filing the return and extends for three years. *See* IRC § 6501. The question specifically indicates the administration expenses at issue are allowable under state law and ascertainable. Thus, as discussed in prior questions, the fact that the expenses are unpaid as of the filing of the return do not preclude taking a deduction so long as the expenses will be paid. **For these same reasons Answers (B) and (C) are incorrect.** The regulations make clear that expenses incurred in the administration of nonprobate property may also be deducted, thus, **Answer (D) is incorrect.** It should be noted that if property not subject to claims was used to pay expenses related to property subject to claims, the deduction to that extent would be limited to the amount of such property used to pay claims prior to timely filing the estate tax return, including extensions. *See* Treas. Reg. § 20.2053-1(c).

205. A deduction is allowed for a loss resulting from a fire or other casualty that is incurred during the settlement of an estate. IRC § 2054. The loss must occur following decedent's death and prior to distribution of the estate assets to a beneficiary. Treas. Reg. § 20.2054-1. The facts of this question indicate that the loss of the apartment building was due to fire, and that the fire occurred during administration of the estate and prior to distribution of any assets. A deduction, however, is not allowed if the loss is compensated for by insurance. In this fact pattern the estate was compensated by insurance for the value of the building. Typically the land has a value separate and apart from any building, and because the land itself was not impacted by the fire, the estate should not receive any reimbursement to the extent of its value. Thus, because the estate was fully reimbursed by insurance for the value of its losses from the fire, no deduction is allowable under IRC § 2054.

206. **Answer (B) is the correct answer.** The issue that arises in this problem is whether the person or organization that receives the bequest is a qualified recipient. A charitable contribution deduction from gross estate is allowed for all bequests, legacies, devises, or transfers to certain qualified recipients. IRC § 2055(a). In general, qualified recipients include governmental entities such as the United States, any state, any political subdivision of a state, or the District of Columbia. *Id.* Additionally, a religious, charitable, scientific, literary, or educational organization that qualifies under IRC § 501(c)(3) will qualify as a recipient. *Id.* A contribution to a state university such as the University of Wyoming would be deductible as a charitable contribution.

**Answer (A) is incorrect.** While a contribution to the Roman Catholic Church may be deductible as a charitable contribution to a church, a contribution to an individual priest for his own use would not be a contribution for religious purposes.

**Answers (C) and (D) are also incorrect.** Answers (C) and (D) result in contributions to organizations or trusts that are formed to either participate in a political campaign or that attempts to influence legislation. An estate may not deduct a bequest to an organization (or trust) if the organization does not meet the requirements outlined under IRC § 501(c)(3). IRC § 2055(a)(3). IRC § 501(c)(3) disqualifies organizations that attempt to influence legislation, participate in, or intervene in any political campaign on behalf of (or in opposition to) any candidate for public office. IRC § 2055(a)(3); *see also Buder v. United States*, 7 F.3d 1382, 1385 (8th Cir. 1993). Thus, neither a lobbying group nor the Democratic National Committee would qualify as an exempt organization under IRC § 501(c)(3) or for an estate tax charitable deduction under IRC § 2055(a).

207. **Answer (D) is the correct answer.** In general, a direct transfer to a qualified charity will be deductible for estate tax purposes. However, a failure on the part of a decedent to name a specific qualified recipient may result in a denial of a charitable bequest. In Answer (D), the executor of decedent's estate receives the amounts in trust to give to one of three qualified charities. The executor has a duty to distribute the bequest for purposes that are exclusively charitable within the meaning of IRC § 2055(a). Although the executor is not a qualified person, the $35,000 passing to the United Way is eligible for a federal estate tax charitable deduction. *See* Rev. Rul. 69-285. It is noteworthy to point out that in certain states, local law may have an adverse impact on this analysis. *See* Rev. Rul. 71-441, 1971-2 C.B. 335. However, the facts of the question specifically negate the impact of state law.

**Answers (A) and (B) are incorrect.** In Answers (A) and (B), the bequest is not made to a charity. Rather, the bequest is made to an executor who is not a qualified charity or decedent's widow who must consent. Thus, the bequest is conditional upon some third party giving consent. The regulations provide that unless the possibility of the condition occurring is highly remote, no deduction will be allowed where the charitable transfer is dependent upon some condition precedent. Treas. Reg. § 20.2055-2(b)(1). In *Delaney v. Gardner*, 204

F.2d 855 (1st Cir. 1953), the decedent bequeathed cash amounts to a decedent's executors, "not subject to any trust, but in the hope that they will dispose of it at their absolute discretion and according to their own judgment, but giving due weight to any memoranda I may leave or any oral expressions by me to them made during my life." *Id.* at 856. The executors made distributions to charities on the list provided in the memorandum. The Court disallowed a charitable deduction because the executors had discretion to withhold part or the entire bequest from the several charities. *Id.* at 859-860. Answer (A) mirrors the facts of *Delaney v. Gardner.* Similarly, in Answer (B), because the wife has discretion to prevent the charities from receiving the bequest, no charitable deduction is allowed. *See also First Trust Co. of St. Paul v. Reynolds*, 137 F.2d 518 (8th Cir. 1943). Thus, under the facts of Answers (A) and (B), either a trustee or a wife has discretion to prevent the bequest from going to a qualified charity.

**Answer (C) is also incorrect.** Answer (C) is incorrect because although it may be laudable that the decedent bequeathed money to an indigent person, Byron T. Watson as a private individual is not a qualified recipient.

208. **Answer (B) is the correct answer.** The issue in this problem is whether a disclaimer that results in a transfer to a charity will affect the estate's ability to obtain a charitable deduction. As was seen in the previous problem, under certain circumstances where a contingency must occur in order for a charitable bequest to occur, the estate may not be authorized to take the deduction under IRC § 2055. However, for decedents dying after 1976, if a charitable transfer results from either a qualified disclaimer or termination, the estate tax charitable deduction generally is allowed. Treas. Reg. § 20.2055-2(c). Answer (B) contemplates a situation whereby the decedent's son disclaimed property that the decedent had bequeathed to him. Because the son executed a qualified disclaimer, the property passed to the residuary, which thereafter was transferred to a qualified charitable recipient. Regardless of the fact that the transfer was contingent upon the disclaimer, the estate will be able to deduct the value of the bequest that the son disclaimed.

**Answers (A) and (C) are incorrect.** In Answers (A) and (C) there is no qualified disclaimer. In order for there to be a qualified disclaimer under IRC § 2055(a), there must be a complete termination of the power to consume, invade, or appropriate property for the benefit of an individual before such power has been exercised and before the filing of the estate tax return. IRC § 2055(a). In Answers (A) and (C), the daughter does not completely terminate her life income interest in the assets. Rather, she attempts to give only a portion of her interest to the Red Cross. Under the circumstances set forth in Answer (A), no amount is actually remitted to the Red Cross unless income from the assets exceeds $1,000,000 in a given year. In Answer (C), the daughter gives up the income only for the foreseeable future.

**Answer (D) is also incorrect.** In general, receipt of consideration for a disclaimer will prevent the disclaimer from being qualified under the rules. In PLR 7809043, a beneficiary proposed to disclaim an interest in a trust in exchange for a lump sum payment. The Service found that the proposed disclaimer did not constitute an unqualified refusal by the beneficiary. Instead the Service reasoned that the beneficiary would merely be engaging in a sale or exchange as opposed to a charitable contribution. *See* Priv. Ltr. Rul. 7809043. Although in Answer (D) the daughter disclaims all of her interest in the residual assets, it appears that she has received consideration in form of a job offer from the Red Cross. Like the beneficiary in the Priv. Ltr. Rul., the daughter's disclaimer is likely to be disqualified for charitable deduction purposes.

**209.** **Answer (A) is the correct answer.** What is the correct amount of the charitable deduction allowed where the charitable bequest is in-kind? IRC § 2055(a) indicates that an estate tax charitable deduction is allowed in "the amount" of all qualified bequests and transfers. The Regulations clarify that a deduction is allowed for the "value" of property included in gross estate at the time of death that is transferred to a qualified recipient. Treas. Reg. § 20.2055-1(a). So long as the sculpture was included in the decedent's gross estate, the date-of-death value of the property transferred to a qualified recipient may be deducted. In this case, the date-of-death value is $2,000,000 and, therefore, the deduction amount is also $2,000,000, consistent with Answer (A).

**Answers (B), (C), and (D) are incorrect.** For reasons explained above, the remaining answers are all incorrect.

**210.** Yes, the answer to Question 209, above, would change if an IRC § 2032 election was made. If an alternative valuation election is made under IRC § 2032 to value the assets of an estate six months after the date of death, then for purposes of the IRC § 2055 charitable deduction, an adjustment must be made for any difference between the date-of-death value and the value as of the date six months after the date of decedent's death. IRC § 2032(b). In this instance, the value of the sculpture decreased from $2,000,000 to $1,500,000, thereby reducing the amount of the deduction available by $500,000. As is displayed in the facts of this question, in addition to reducing the value of assets included in a decedent's estate, an IRC § 2032 election to report the value of gross estate six months after the date of death will cause a corresponding decrease in the IRC § 2055 charitable deduction.

**211.** **Answer (A) is the correct answer.** Here, IRC § 2522(a), pertaining to gift tax charitable deductions, is implicated rather than IRC § 2055, related to the estate tax. However the two rules operate similarly under the circumstances of the problem. A charitable deduction is allowed in computing total taxable gifts for a calendar year for gifts made to qualified recipients. The definition of a "qualified recipient" for gift tax purposes is essentially the same as the definition for estate tax purposes under IRC § 2055. Thus, because the National Museum of Art is an IRC § 501(c)(3) organization, it is a qualified recipient under IRC § 2522. For gift tax purposes, the amount of the deduction is set at the fair market value of the property on the date that it was transferred to the charity. IRC § 2522. Consistent with Answer (A), a gift tax deduction of $2,000,000 is allowed.

**Answers (B), (C), and (D) are incorrect.** For reasons explained above, the remaining answers are all incorrect.

**212.** No, the answer to Question 211 above would remain the same. With several exceptions not relevant here, a nonresident individual who is not a citizen of the United States is treated the same as a citizen who is a resident. IRC § 2522(b), *see also* Treas. Reg. § 25.2522(b)-1. It is also worth noting that if we assumed instead that Rose, a nonresident noncitizen, had passed away and had made a charitable bequest of the sculpture, an estate tax charitable deduction would be allowed in lieu of the gift tax deduction. Again, the rules pertaining to charitable deductions are not meaningfully different as between the gift tax and the estate tax.

**213.** **Answer (A) is the correct answer.** The various scenarios provided in the answer options require an analysis of transfers that have both private and charitable purposes. For decedents passing away after December 31, 1969, where property passes in part to a charity and in part to a private noncharitable party, no estate tax charitable deduction is allowed for the value of the portion of the interest that passes to the charity. IRC § 2055(e)(2). Under the facts of Answer (A), the decedent retained a present interest in the income from the property while leaving a remainder interest to the charity. During decedent's life a split interest in the property may have existed. However, by retaining a life interest in the rental property, the full value of the property is included in decedent's gross estate. *See* IRC § 2036. Thus, the decedent did not make a split-interest transfer as contemplated by IRC § 2055(e)(2). The bequest of the post-death interest in the rental property to a qualified charity will result in a IRC § 2055 charitable deduction.

**Answers (B) and (C) are incorrect.** Unlike the transfer described in Answer (A), the transfers in Answers (B) and (C) are split-interest bequests. In Answer (B), decedent's brother will receive a life estate in the rental property and the remainder will pass to a charity. As discussed above, no charitable deduction is allowed for the charitable portion of a split-interest gift. Therefore, decedent's bequest of the remainder interest in the rental property to the charity will not result in a charitable deduction. IRC § 2055(e)(2). Similarly, in Answer (C), the decedent's estate may not deduct the value of the bequest passing to the charity because the bequest is contingent upon decedent's brother surviving him. If decedent's brother survives decedent, then the charity will never receive a bequest.

**Answer (D) is also incorrect.** Because under the terms of the decedent's will no property will pass from decedent to a charity, no charitable deduction will be allowed.

Note: Although this question asks whether a charitable deduction would exist for the decedent's estate tax purposes, it is also relevant to ask whether a charitable deduction exists for gift tax purposes under the circumstances presented in Answer (A). Section 2522(c)(2) of the gift tax provisions provides a similar rule to that found in the estate tax sections of the Code. In general, where a split-interest gift is made after December 31, 1969, no deduction is allowed for the charitable portion of the gift unless specific conditions not present here are met. Thus, no gift tax deduction would have been available on creation of the trust.

**214.** **Answer (C) is the correct answer.** The Code allows an estate tax marital deduction for property passing to a U.S. citizen surviving spouse. Generally, property passing to a non-U.S. citizen surviving spouse cannot be claimed as a marital deduction under IRC § 2056(d) unless property passes to the surviving spouse in the form of a qualified domestic trust or QDOT. IRC § 2056(d)(1)(A),(2). With certain exceptions, the terms of the qualified domestic trust subject principal (as opposed to income) distributions made to the surviving spouse during life and property remaining in the trust at death to estate tax calculated based on the aggregate amounts subject to tax in decedent's estate. IRC § 2056A(b). In order to qualify as a QDOT, the trust instrument must require that at least one trustee be either a U.S. citizen or domestic corporation. The trust instrument must also provide that no distributions (other than income) may be made unless the trustee has the right to withhold taxes from the distribution. Thus, amounts that are contributed to a QDOT do not completely escape U.S. taxation. It is important to note that if the Code allowed the estate of a deceased U.S. resident to benefit from a marital deduction in relation to assets distributed to a noncitizen surviving spouse, the assets received by the spouse may escape U.S. estate taxes. Thus, Answer (C) is correct because Sonja, although a resident of the United States does not have U.S. citizenship. **Answers (A), (B), and (D) all are incorrect** because none of these answers provides for passage of the property to Sonja as part of a qualified domestic trust. Instead each contemplates either an outright transfer to Sonja or a transfer to a non-qualifying trust.

It is also important to note that a non-U.S. citizen may avoid the need to place property in a QDOT if the spouse becomes a U.S. citizen. Specifically, the Code allows a marital deduction if decedent's non-U.S. citizen spouse becomes a U.S. citizen before the date that decedent's estate tax return is filed, provided the surviving spouse was a U.S. resident at all times after decedent's date of death and prior to becoming a U.S. citizen. IRC § 2056(d)(4).

Note: Treas. Reg. § 20.0-1(a) provides that some of the provisions of the regulations may be affected by the provisions of an applicable death tax convention between the United States and other foreign countries. A death tax convention between the United States and another country may exempt certain transfers by means of a bequest. The United States does not have a treaty with Iceland. It has treaties with Ireland, Italy, Japan, Netherlands, Norway, Sweden, Switzerland, Union of South Africa, and the United Kingdom. It also has entered into a protocol with Canada.

**215.** Lifetime gifts to non-U.S. citizen spouses are not eligible for the gift tax marital deduction. IRC § 2523(i)(1) (a limited exception exists for certain joint and survivor annuities). The federal gift tax does not provide for the possibility of a qualified domestic trust. It instead provides for an annual gift tax exclusion for transfers made to a non-U.S. citizen surviving spouse if a marital deduction would have been allowable with respect to the transfer except for the fact that the spouse is not a U.S. citizen. The amount of the gift tax exclusion equals

$100,000, and is adjusted for inflation. IRC § 2523(i)(2). Thus, the outright transfer from Hal to Sonja does not qualify for the marital deduction. An amount up to the gift tax annual exclusion for transfers to non-U.S. citizen surviving spouses, or in other words $100,000 as that amount is adjusted for inflation, is excluded from gift tax. Any excess is subject to gift tax to the donor, and may be sheltered by the donor's applicable exclusion amount, if any.

216.    **Answer (D) is correct.** In order to take a marital deduction for property passing to the surviving spouse where the order of death is determinable, the spouse must in fact survive the decedent. IRC § 2056(a). *See Estate of Lee v. Comm'r*, T.C. Memo. 2007-371. A survival clause included in the will or imposed by state law, must also allow for the passage of property to the estate of the spouse, or if property passes pursuant to a marital deduction trust, to that trust. Under Answer (D) state law imposes a survival requirement of 120 hours. Because Wendy in fact survived for more than 120 hours, and the will passes property outright to Wendy, a marital deduction is allowable. **Answer (B) is incorrect.** Although Henry and Wendy die as a result of a common accident and Henry is deemed to survive pursuant to the terms of the will, the Code requires that Henry in fact survive for Wendy's estate to take a marital deduction, something he does not do. Thus, a marital deduction is not allowable under Answer (B). **Answer (A) is incorrect** because under the terms of the will neither spouse take under the other's will as neither survives for at least 30 days. As a result property does not pass to either as surviving spouse, and a marital deduction, thus, is not allowable. **Answer (C) is not the best answer** because it does not reflect the facts. Wendy and Henry do not die simultaneously as indicated in the answer.

It should be noted that this question assumes Henry and Wendy were married at the time of death. In order to qualify as a surviving spouse, the transferee must survive the decedent and the decedent must be married to the transferee at the time of death. *See* Rev. Rul. 79-354. If at the time of death the decedent is not married to the transferee, no marital deduction is allowed with respect to transferred property. *Id.*

217.    **Answer (D) is correct.** In order to take a marital deduction for an interest in property the following requirements must be met: (1) the value of the property interest must be included in decedent's gross estate, (2) it must pass from the decedent (3) to the U.S. citizen surviving spouse, and (4) it must be a deductible interest. IRC § 2056(a); Treas. Reg. § 20.2056(a)-1(b). If these elements are met, the marital deduction is allowed and it is unlimited in amount. The answers to this question focus on the first and second requirements. The property subject to Answer (D) is included in the decedent's gross estate, and it passes from decedent to the surviving spouse. Treasury Regulation § 20.2056(c)-1(a) specifically indicates that a "dower or curtesy interest (or statutory interest in lieu thereof) of the decedent's surviving spouse is considered as having passed from the decedent to his spouse." It also indicates that interests passing as joint tenants with right of survivorship, interests subject to decedent's power to appoint, life insurance proceeds, and property gifted, bequeathed, devised by or inherited from the decedent all meet the passing requirement. *Id.* Thus, Answers (A), (B), and (C) also satisfy the passing requirement, however, the property interests described in Answers (A) and (B) are not included in decedent's gross estate and for that reason do not qualify for the marital deduction. For this reason, **Answers (A) and (B) are incorrect.** Because only one-half the value of the joint with right of survivorship bank account is included in decedent's gross estate under IRC § 2040(b), only one-half the value is included in the gross estate. The question asks which interest is "deductible in full" and for this reason, **Answer (C) is not the best answer.**

**218.** **Answer (D) is correct.** This question focuses on whether the property interest passing meets the requirements of a deductible interest. A deductible interest is one that is not a nondeductible terminable interest or an interest subject to one of the exceptions listed under IRC § 2056(b). Treas. Reg. § 20.2056(b)-1(a). Terminable interests are defined as "an interest which will terminate or fail on the lapse of time or on the occurrence or the failure to occur of some contingency." Treas. Reg. § 20.2056(b)-1(b). Each of the Answers (A) through (C) are terminable interests — life estate, copyrights, and patents — are all examples of terminable interests cited in the treasury regulation. *Id.* Answer (D) involves a note. The treasury regulations specifically indicate that "a bond, *note*, or similar contractual obligation, the discharge of which would not have the effect of an annuity or a term for years, is not a terminable interest." *Id.*

Just because the interest is "terminable" does not mean that it is a "nondeductible terminable interest." A terminable interest is nondeductible if (1) another interest in the same property passed to someone else for less than adequate consideration, (2) the other person (or the person's heirs and assigns) can enjoy the property after the surviving spouse's interest terminates, and (3) one of the enumerated exceptions do not apply. Treas. Reg. § 20.2056(b)-1(c)(1). The exceptions to the nondeductible terminable interest rule include those listed under IRC § 2056(b), including the ability to condition receipt of the property on the spouse surviving decedent by six months, the passage of the property to a general power of appointment marital trust, a general power of appointment life insurance trust, a qualified terminable interest property trust or a charitable remainder annuity trust where the surviving spouse is the only other beneficiary. Answers (A) and (B) are deductible interests because no interest in the patent or the copyright passes to anyone other than the surviving spouse, and no one else can enjoy the interest after Sara's death.

The property interests in Answers (A), (B), and (C) all qualify for the marital deduction because the property interests pass under Sara's will to her surviving spouse Hank, each interest is a deductible interest, and each is includible in Sara's gross estate. Thus, **Answers (A), (B), and (C) are all incorrect responses** to the question asked. **Answer (D) is correct** as it does not qualify for the marital deduction because Hank's life interest in the undeveloped land is a nondeductible terminable interest, and would not qualify for any of the exceptions to the nondeductible terminable interest rule. Specifically it does not produce sufficient income to meet the requirements of IRC §§ 2056(b)(5) or 2056(b)(7), it is not life insurance so it does not meet the requirements of IRC § 2056(b)(6), and the facts do not indicate that it passes to a charitable remainder trust per IRC § 2056(b)(8).

**219.** **Answer (A) is correct.** Cindy wants to provide for her spouse Sampo during his life, and also wants any property remaining at Sampo's death to pass to their children. Cindy can best achieve this goal and at the same time assure her estate receives a marital deduction for the property so passing by using a qualified terminable interest property trust or QTIP trust. A QTIP trust requires that all income be paid at least annually to the surviving spouse, and that no person may appoint any part of the property to someone other than the surviving spouse, during the spouse's lifetime. The trustee also may be given discretion to distribute principal to the surviving spouse during his life. On the death of the surviving spouse, property may pass as designated by decedent or subject to a power to appoint, including to persons other than the surviving spouse. Thus, Cindy can provide for Sampo's benefit, and at the same time ensure that any property remaining at Sampo's death passes to her children by using a QTIP trust. **Answer (B) is incorrect** because the surviving spouse by exercising his general power of appointment could require trustee to distribute all property held in the general power of appointment trust to him and the property, thus, would not necessarily pass to Cindy's children on Sampo's death. **Answer (C) is incorrect for similar reasons.** An estate trust is not one of the enumerated exceptions under the Code. A marital deduction is nevertheless allowed because the interest of the spouse by definition is not a nondeductible terminable interest. The surviving spouse may receive income or it may be accumulated for his benefit, and on his death, remaining property in the trust passes to the estate of the surviving spouse. Thus, on Sampo's death, the property in the trust will pass to his estate as opposed to Cindy's children. **Answer (D) is incorrect** because the remainder interest in a charitable remainder trust by definition must pass to a qualifying charity, and is not eligible to be distributed to Cindy's children.

220.   **Answer (D) is the correct answer.** In order to qualify for the marital deduction, the surviving spouse (or certain ESOPS) must be the only non-charitable beneficiary of the trust, and the remainder interest must pass to a qualifying charity. The spouse would receive either an annuity or unitrust interest, and the charity would receive the property remaining in the trust on the spouse's death. Thus, the surviving spouse receives only a life interest in the trust, and it is not includible in her gross estate. The decedent's estate obtains a marital deduction for the spouse's interest and a charitable deduction for the interest passing to charity. **Answers (A), (B), and (C) are incorrect.** Property held in a QTIP trust is includible in the surviving spouse's gross estate pursuant to IRC § 2044, and for this reason **Answer (A) is incorrect.** Property held in a general power of appointment marital deduction trust is includible in the surviving spouse's gross estate pursuant to IRC § 2041 and for this reason **Answer (B) is incorrect.** Property held in an estate trust is includible in the surviving spouse's gross estate under IRC § 2033, and for this reason, **Answer (C) is incorrect.**

221.   **Answer (B) is the correct answer.** The general power of appointment marital deduction trust may grant to the surviving spouse the power to require the trustee to distribute the entire property of the trust to her outright. Thus, this trust offers the greatest amount of control over the trust assets during the surviving spouse's life. A QTIP trust does not provide the surviving spouse the same control. While the surviving spouse receives all income and may receive distributions of principal, the spouse does not hold a general power of appointment. **Thus, Answer (A) is incorrect.** In a charitable remainder trust, the surviving spouse receives only an annuity or unitrust interest in the trust, and for that reason **Answer (D) is incorrect.** In an estate trust, the surviving spouse may or may not receive an income interest, and it is not until the death of the surviving spouse that the property in the estate trust passes to his or her estate. **For this reason, Answer (C) is incorrect.**

222.   **Answer (C) is the correct answer.** An estate trust is the only one of the four trusts that allows for accumulation of income. A QTIP trust and a general power of appointment trust require that all income be paid to the surviving spouse during the spouse's life time. This requirement can only be met by a showing that decedent in fact intended the surviving spouse receive income from the trust. Treas. Reg. § 20.2056(b)-5(f). If the trust property is not productive and decedent never intends for it to be productive, the trust is not eligible for a marital deduction under either IRC § 2056(b)(5) or IRC § 2056(b)(7). Treas. Reg. § 20.2056(b)-5(f)(5). However, if nonproductive property passes to a QTIP or a general power

of appointment marital trust, a provision allowing the surviving spouse to require the property be sold and made productive will cure any issue regarding the all income interest. *Id.* The treasury regulations make the all income requirement as set forth in Treasury Regulation § 20.2056(b)-5(f) applicable for purposes of the all income requirement under the QTIP trust. *See* Treas. Reg. § 20.2056(b)-7(d)(2). In light of the all income requirement, **Answers (A) and (B) are incorrect.** The beneficiary of a charitable remainder trust must receive an annuity or unitrust interest. This requires the trustee to distribute trust property to the spouse at least annually, and, thus, it would not be possible to ensure that the trustee would retain the undeveloped land in the trust for distribution to the remainder. For this reason, **Answer (D) is not the best answer.**

223.    **Answer (D) is the correct answer.** Absent an exception to the nondeductible terminable interest rule, property passing to a QTIP trust would be a nondeductible terminable interest because an interest in the property could be enjoyed by someone other than the surviving spouse after termination of the surviving spouse's interest. Also absent a special exception, only the property in which the surviving spouse had a beneficial interest would be deemed to "pass" to the surviving spouse. Treas. Reg. § 20.2056(c)-2. Finally, absent the specific inclusionary rule of IRC § 2044, the property of the QTIP trust would not be included in the surviving spouse's gross estate because it terminates at death. Because all three Answers (A), (B), and (C) state a reason why property passing to a QTIP trust would not be eligible for the marital deduction absent the IRC § 2056(b)(7) exception, Answer (D) is correct, and thus **Answers (A), (B), and (C) are not the best answers.**

224.    **Answer (B) is the correct answer.** In order for there to be a valid QTIP election, the trust property must pass from the decedent, decedent's executor must elect QTIP treatment, and the trust must provide a qualifying income interest for life to the surviving spouse. IRC § 2056(b)(7)(B)(i). A qualifying income interest requires that all income pass to the surviving spouse at least annually, and that no person have "a power to appoint any part of the property to any person other than the surviving spouse" during that spouse's life. IRC § 2056(b)(7)(B)(ii). Answer (B) allows the spouse to appoint property during the spouse's life to someone other than the surviving spouse, and, thus, violates the requirements of a qualifying income interest. For this reason, Answer (B) is the correct answer. Principal may be paid to the surviving spouse, it just may not be paid to someone other than the surviving spouse. **Thus, Answer (A) is incorrect.** Answer (C) mirrors the facts of *Estate of Clack v. Comm'r*, 106 T.C. 131 (1996), as incorporated into current Treasury Regulation § 20.2056(b)-7(d)(3). In that case, as in the regulation, the executor's ability to determine whether or not property should fund the QTIP trust does not cause a loss of the marital deduction. The contingent income interest is specifically approved by the court. **For this reason, Answer (C) is incorrect**, and does not disqualify the trust from a marital deduction. **Answer (D) is incorrect** because the provisions of IRC § 2056(b)(7) specifically allow appointment of property to someone other than the surviving spouse after the surviving spouse's death.

225.    **Answer (D) is the correct answer.** In order to qualify for the marital deduction pursuant to IRC § 2056(b)(5), the surviving spouse must have the power to appoint to herself or to her estate. It does not matter whether the power is exercisable only during life or only at death. The statute specifically allows for the spouse to appoint to someone other than the spouse. It does not, however, allow someone other than the surviving spouse to appoint to others. The statute specifically states that the surviving spouse must have a power to "appoint the entire

interest . . . (exercisable in favor of such surviving spouse, or of the estate of such surviving spouse, or in favor of either, whether or not in each case the power is exercisable in favor of others), and with no power in any other person to appoint any part of the interest . . . to any person other than the surviving spouse." For this reason, **Answers (A), (B), and (C) are incorrect.** Each of the powers stated in Answers (A), (B), and (C) are specifically approved by the plain wording of the statute as quoted above.

226.  Because payment of the life insurance proceeds in installments does not meet the definition of an "all income" interest, a special exception to the nondeductible terminable interest rule was required in order to qualify payment of life insurance proceeds in installments for the marital deduction. As a result, Congress enacted IRC § 2056(b)(6). The requirements of that section are essentially the same as the requirements for a general power of appointment marital deduction trust, except for the all income requirement which is replaced with the following: Installments or interest payments must commence within 13 months after the date of decedent's death, must be paid at least annually, and all installments must be paid only to the decedent's spouse. Pam may obtain a marital deduction for proceeds paid to Brent by complying with these requirements.

227.  **Answer (A) is correct.** Code Sections 2044 and 2519 were enacted specifically for the purpose of causing property held in a QTIP trust to be subject to wealth transfer tax either on the death of the surviving spouse, or in the event the surviving spouse transfers an interest in the QTIP trust during life, then at that time. The marital deduction only defers tax until the death of the surviving spouse. In effect it treats a married couple as one person for purposes of imposing transfer tax. The survivor is allowed the full benefit of the couple's property during his or her life without the necessity of subjecting the property to estate tax at the death of the first spouse to die. Without enactment of IRC § 2044, property held in a QTIP trust would avoid estate tax on the death of the surviving spouse.

Congress also enacted IRC § 2519 to ensure that property in the QTIP trust would be subject to tax on an earlier transfer by the surviving spouse of her income interest in the trust. The statute specifically provides that "any disposition of all or part of a qualifying income interest for life in any property . . . shall be treated as a transfer of all interests in such property other than the qualifying income interest." A gift of an income interest will trigger a deemed gift of the entire property held in the QTIP trust. Thus, IRC § 2519 works as a backstop to IRC § 2044 to ensure that a QTIP deduction merely defers estate (and/or gift tax) until the survivor's death (or if earlier gift of an interest in the trust). It should be noted that a gift of the income interest in a QTIP trust is also subject to gift tax at the time it is transferred.

**Answers (B) and (C) are incorrect.** Each of the Code sections referred to in these answers not only serves to include property in certain types of trusts subject to the marital deduction, but also include property in decedent's gross estate for other purposes as well. For this same reason **Answer (D) is incorrect.**

228.  The clause makes any interest to be received by the surviving spouse contingent on the spouse's survival for six months after the date of decedent's death. Absent the special exception to the nondeductible terminable interest rule as enunciated in IRC § 2056(b)(3), an interest passing to a surviving spouse contingent on his survival for six months would fail to qualify for the marital deduction. The IRC § 2056(b)(3) exception, however, allows such a contingency based on the spouse's survival to avoid classification as a nondeductible

terminable interest. Thus, if all the other requirements of the marital deduction provisions are met, such a contingency will not preclude the marital deduction. Six months is the longest period on which a gift may be made contingent. It is important to note that the contingency may only be that of survival and not of any other event. Treas. Reg. § 2.2056(b)-3(b).

**229.   Answer (B) is the correct answer.** A transfer from Hank to his son's daughter constitutes a transfer to a skip person, which is subject to the generation-skipping transfer (GST) tax. In order for a generation-skipping transfer to occur, there must be one of three types of transfers: (1) a direct skip, (2) a taxable termination, or (3) a taxable distribution. IRC § 2611. In each of the three types of transfers, there must be a transfer from a donor to a "skip person" either directly or to or from a trust. IRC § 2612(a). A skip person includes a natural person assigned to a generation that is at least two generations below the generation assignment of the transferor. IRC § 2613(a)(1).

While it may be obvious in this case that Miley is two family generations below Hank, reference must be made to the definitional sections of the generation-skipping transfer rules to support this conclusion. Generation assignments are made pursuant to two separate rules, including one for lineal descendants and another that serves as a catch-all for everyone who is not a lineal descendant. But that raises the question of what constitutes lineage. More narrowly, whose lineage is used to determine whether a recipient is appropriately related to the donor/transferor for purposes of the generation assignment rules? To be classified as a skip person, a transferee must be separated by two generations or more from a transferor. Family generation assignments are made by comparing (1) the number of generations between the grandparent and the transferor, with (2) the number of generations between the grandparent and the recipient. Here, a diagram is useful:

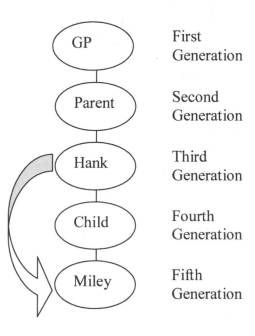

| | |
|---|---|
| GP | First Generation |
| Parent | Second Generation |
| Hank | Third Generation |
| Child | Fourth Generation |
| Miley | Fifth Generation |

Because Miley is a lineal descendant of Hank's grandparent (GP), family generation assignments must be made and compared. The comparison between generations is statutorily determined by comparing (1) the number of generations between Miley (e.g., fifth generation) and Hank's grandparent (GP) (e.g., first generation), which is three generations, with (2) the number of generations between the GP (e.g. first generation) and Hank (e.g., third generation), which is one generation of separation. Thus, comparing three generations to one generation, it is seen that there are two generations of difference.

Because there are two generations between Hank and Miley, Miley is a skip person under the rules. While the question does not inquire further, the next step would be to determine whether the transfer qualifies as a direct skip, taxable termination, or taxable distribution. These topics are explored more fully below.

**Answers (A) and (C) are incorrect.** Again, generation assignments are made by comparing the number of generations between the transferor's grandparent and the transferee with the number of generations between the grandparent and the transferor. With respect to the transfers to Hank's mother and grandfather, there is no possible comparison that will end up in more than one generation of difference. Note that all generational assignments are made by determining the number of generations away from the grandparent. Thus, any gift to a grandparent will always result in no generational difference.

**Answer (D) is also incorrect.** Referring to the diagram above, it can be seen again that Hank is assigned to the third generation, and Hank's daughter is assigned to the fourth generation. Thus, Hank's daughter is only one generation removed from Hank, and she is not a skip person.

230. **No, Answer (B) is still the correct answer.** For purposes of assigning generations to lineal descendants, a relationship by legal adoption is treated the same as a relationship by blood. IRC § 2651(b)(3)(A).

231. **Answer (D) is the correct answer.** Unlike the previous question, the answer options also include individuals who are lineal descendants of Hank's parents but not Hank. For purposes of determining whether the transferee is a skip person, a transferee who is a lineal descendant of Hank's grandparent but not Hank is still related in a manner that requires use of the lineal descendant rules. Here, Hank's grandniece ("Gniece") is a lineal descendant of Hank's grandparents. Grandniece must be separated by two generations or more from Hank to qualify as a skip person.

Generation assignments are made by comparing (1) the number of generations between the grandparent and Hank, with (2) the number of generations between the grandparent and Hank's grandniece. Again, a diagram substitutes for many paragraphs of explanation:

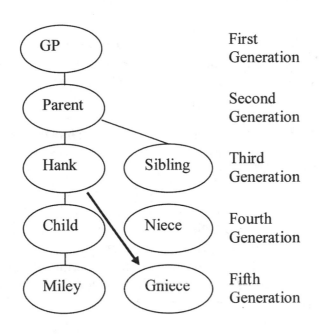

The comparison between generations is determined by comparing (1) the number of generations between Gniece (e.g., fifth generation) and Hank's GP (e.g., first generation), which is three generations, with (2) the number of generations between the GP (e.g., first generation) and Hank (e.g., third generation), which is one generation of separation. Thus, comparing the three generations to one generation, it is seen that there are two generations of difference.

Because there are two generations between Hank and Gniece, Gniece is a skip person under the rules.

**Answers (A) and (B) are incorrect.** Hank, his brother, and his cousin are each in the third generation. Since they are all the same number of generations away from Hank's grandparents, there is no generational difference.

**Answer (D) is also incorrect.** Using the diagram above, it can be seen again that Hank is assigned to the third generation and that Hank's daughter, as his child, is assigned to the fourth generation. Hank's daughter is only one generation removed from Hank, and, therefore, his daughter is not a skip person.

232. Yes, a transfer from Hank to Harley's grandson is a transfer to a skip person. For purposes of determining generation assignments, a relationship by half-blood is treated the same as a relationship by whole blood. IRC § 2651(b)(3)(B).

233. **Answer (C) is the correct answer.** The answer options here include individuals that, while commonly perceived as family members and friends, are not lineal descendants of either Hank or his grandparents. Transferees who are not lineal descendants of the transferor's grandparents are assigned to a generation on the basis of age under the nonlineal descendant rules. IRC § 2651(d). A transferee who is born not more than 12 and a half years after the date of the transferor's birth is assigned to the same generation as the transferor. *Id.* A transferee born more than 12 and a half years but not more than 37 and a half years after the date of birth of the transferor is treated as being one generation younger than the transferor. *Id.* A transferee born more than 37 and a half years but not more than 62 and a half years after the transferor is treated as being two generations younger that the transferor. *Id.* Hank's second cousin is a descendant of Hank's great grandparents, but the second cousin is not a descendant of Hank's grandparents. Therefore Hank's second cousin's generation is assigned under the nonlineal descendant rules. Hank is 57 years old, and his second cousin, who is 17 years old, is 40 years younger than him. Being 40 years younger, the second cousin is deemed to be two generations younger than Hank and is also deemed to

be a skip person under the rules.

**Answers (A), (B), and (D) are incorrect.** Each of the individuals described in Answers (A), (B), and (D) are not descendants of Hank's grandparents. However, each of the individuals is less than 37 and a half years younger than Hank. Therefore, none of these individuals qualifies as a skip person.

234. The fact that Hank married his friend's daughter prevents the daughter from being a skip person. An individual who has been married at any time to the transferor is deemed to be assigned to the transferor's generation. IRC § 2651(c)(1). Regardless of the fact that Hank's spouse is 40 years younger than he is, she is not a skip person, and transfers to her avoid the GST tax. The same principles applied to the now infamous marriage between the late J. Howard Marshall and Anna Nicole Smith, also deceased. On June 27, 1994, 26-year-old Anna Nicole Smith married J. Howard Marshall, then 89 years old. After only 13 months of marriage, Marshall died. It is notable that even though Smith was approximately 63 years younger (three generations younger by age) than Marshall, Smith was not deemed to be a skip person, and no amounts that Smith may have received through Marshall's will would have been subject to the generation-skipping tax.

235. **Answer (A) is the correct answer.** A transfer to a trust may also be subject to the GST tax. A trust qualifies as a "skip person" if all interests in the trust are held by skip persons. Treas. Reg. § 26.2612-1(d)(2)(i). In general, an interest in a trust exists if a person has a present right to receive trust principal or income. Treas. Reg. § 26.2612-1(e). If a person merely has a future right to receive income or principal, then such person is treated under the rules as having no interest at all. IRC 2652(c)(1)(A). Hank's granddaughter has a present interest for 10 years in the trust income. Granddaughter is a skip person under the family generation assignment rules and, by having a present right to trust income, all interests in the trust are held by skip persons. Thus, the trust itself is treated as a skip person under the rules. Why is it that the remainder interest held by Hank's wife has no impact on the outcome? It is true that "all" interests in trust must be held by skip persons, and it is also true that Hank's wife, a non-skip person, owns a remainder interest. However, Hank's wife's interest is merely a future right to receive the remainder of the trust assets. As a future interest, Hank's wife is treated as having no interest at all for purposes of determining whether the trust is a skip person.

**Answers (B), (C), and D are incorrect.** In Answer (B), Hank's son has an interest in the trust income for life. Because Hank's son is assigned to the first generation below Hank, he is a non-skip person. Further, because as a non-skip person the son has a present interest in the trust, "all" of the interests in the trust are not held by skip persons, and a transfer to the trust is not a transfer to a skip person. Similarly, Hank's wife and his son, both non-skip persons, have a present interest in Answers (C) and (D), respectively. Note that the creation of the trust inter vivos or as a testamentary trust is not decisive.

236. **Answer (C) is the correct answer.** Beginning in 2011, the generation skipping transfer tax exemption is equal to the basic exclusion amount, which is adjusted for inflation. IRC § 2631(c). (This assumes this provision does not sunset in 2013.) The GST exemption is limited to the basic exclusion amount, and, thus, differs from the applicable exclusion amount allowed for gift and estate tax purposes. The applicable exclusion amount as of 2011 is the aggregate of the basic exclusion amount and the deceased spousal unused exclusion amount (if any). **For this reason, Answers (A) and (D) are incorrect** as they reference an amount

other than the basic exclusion amount, as indexed for inflation. Answer (A) is the base amount of the basic exclusion amount prior to being indexed. Answer (D) references the applicable exclusion amount which is incorrect.

The GST exemption is allocated to generation-skipping transfers pursuant to a complicated set of allocation rules that are beyond the scope of this topic. The rules include automatic allocation rules in the event the donor fails to make an allocation of GST exemption to a GST transfer. The calculation of GST tax depends in part on the allocation of GST exemption.

In addition, outright transfers, not in trust, that are eligible for the gift tax annual exclusion and that are direct skips are not subject to GST tax. Thus, the outright transfers such as those being made by Hank, have an inclusion ratio of zero, and thus a GST tax rate of zero. IRC §§ 2642(c)(1), (3)(A); 2641(a). As a result, in addition to using his GST exemption amount, Hank can make outright annual exclusion gifts to each donee. For this reason, Answer (C) is correct and **Answer (B) is incorrect.**

237.    **Answer (B) is the correct answer.** In order to determine the GST tax owed, the character of the transfer (i.e. direct skip, taxable termination or taxable distribution) and the inclusion ratio must first be determined. When calculating the inclusion ratio for a direct skip (not in trust) begin with a calculation of the "applicable fraction." IRC § 2642(a)(1), (2). The applicable fraction for a direct skip is a fraction with (1) a numerator equal to the GST exemption allocated to the property transferred in such direct skip, in our case $1 million, and (2) a denominator the value of the property involved in the direct skip, in our case $2 million. (Because no charitable deduction is taken in our fact pattern, the denominator does not need to be adjusted.) Thus, the applicable fraction is one-half or 50%. For this reason, **Answers (A), (C), and (D) are incorrect.**

238.    **Answer (D) is the correct answer.** The amount of GST tax owed is determined by multiplying the "taxable amount" by the "applicable rate." IRC § 2602. Thus, the rate of tax on the GST transfer is the "applicable rate" and Answer (D) is correct. The applicable rate is determined under IRC § 2641(a), and it is equal to the maximum Federal estate tax rate of 35% multiplied by the inclusion ratio with respect to the direct skip, determined in the answer to Question 237 as 50%, which yields an applicable rate of 17.5%. **Answer (B) is not the best answer** because while the marginal tax rate is the highest estate tax rate of 35%, the applicable rate which applies to the direct skip to Hank's granddaughter takes into account allocation of Hank's remaining GST exemption to the transfer. For the same reasons **Answers (A) and (C) are not correct.**

239.    The GST tax is calculated by multiplying the "taxable amount" by the "applicable rate." IRC § 2602. The taxable amount depends on the type of transfer (i.e., direct skip, taxable termination, and taxable distribution). Hank's gift to his granddaughter is a direct skip, and as such the taxable amount is "the value of the property received" by the granddaughter, or in this case $2 million. IRC § 2623. The applicable rate as determined in the answer to Question 238 is 17.5%. Multiplying the taxable amount of $2 million by the applicable rate of 17.5 % yields a GST tax of $350,000. In the case of a direct skip the transferor pays the GST tax. Hank must pay a GST tax of $350,000.

240.    Hank makes a taxable gift to his granddaughter of $2 million. In addition to that amount, IRC § 2515 increases the amount of the taxable gift by the amount of the GST tax imposed on the taxable gift. As calculated in the answer to Question 239, the GST tax paid on the $2

million transfer to Hank's granddaughter is $350,000. Thus, Hank is deemed to have made taxable gifts in 2012 of $2,350,000, and the tax owed on that amount assuming Hank has no available applicable exclusion amount is $822,500. Thus, total transfer tax, gift and GST, that Hank pays on the $2 million taxable gift to this daughter is $1,172,500.

241.    **Answer (A) is the correct answer.** A taxable termination occurs when an interest in a trust terminates and immediately after the termination only a skip person (or persons) has an interest in the trust. IRC § 2612(a)(1)(A); Treas. Reg. § 26.2612-1 (b). Prior to Mona's death, Mona has an interest in the trust. Mona is a non-skip person because, as Hank's child, she is assigned to the generation immediately beneath Hank (e.g., one generation apart). During Mona's life, the trust is not a skip person, and a contribution to the trust is not a direct skip. Upon Mona's death, only Miley has an interest in the trust. Since Miley is assigned to the second generation below Hank, she is a skip person. After Mona's death all interests are held by skip persons, and a taxable termination occurs.

   **Answers (B), (C), and (D) are incorrect.** With respect to Answers (B) and (C), Mona, a nonskip person, continues to hold an interest in the trust. Therefore, no taxable termination has occurred. Note that Answer (C) describes a taxable distribution that is discussed more fully below. Answer (D) is incorrect for reasons already explained.

242.    **Answer (D) is the correct answer.** Notwithstanding that when Mona dies (as is the case in Answer (A)) a termination of an interest in trust occurs, where the resulting transfer is subject to federal estate or gift tax, there will be no taxable termination for GST tax purposes. Treas. Reg. § 26.2612-1(b). Because Mona had a general power of appointment over the assets, the value of the assets will be included in Mona's estate upon her death. *See* IRC § 2041. Upon including the assets in Mona's estate under the power of appointment rules, the value of the assets are taxed in Mona's estate. Thus, because the transfer from Mona to Miley was subject to estate tax, no taxable termination occurs and the transfer is not subject to GST tax.

   **Answers (A), (B), and (C) are incorrect.** Again, because the transfer was subject to the estate tax, no GST tax can be imposed when Mona dies in Answer (A). In Answer (B), Mona continues to be a non-skip person and continues to hold an interest in the trust. Therefore, no taxable termination has occurred. Again, Answer (C) describes a taxable distribution, which is discussed more fully below.

243.    **Answer (C) is the correct answer.** The term "taxable distribution" means any distribution from a trust to a skip person (other than a taxable termination or a direct skip). Miley continues to be deemed a skip person because she is assigned to the second generation below Hank under the lineal descendant rules. When the trustee distributes one-half of the principal to Miley on her eighteenth birthday, the distribution is a taxable distribution to Miley. *See* Treas. Reg. § 26.2612-1(f)(example 10). Note also that the distribution does not qualify as either a direct skip or a taxable termination. *Id.* If the distribution qualified as either a direct skip or taxable termination, the distribution could not qualify as a taxable distribution. *See* IRC § 2612(b) (parenthetical).

   **Answer (A) is incorrect.** Answer (A) describes a situation under which the original contribution would have been a direct skip. In Answer (A), Miley has a present interest in the trust while Mona, Hank's child, has merely a future interest. Because Miley has a current interest, a contribution to the trust will be a direct skip subject to GST on the date of contribution.

**Answer (B) is also incorrect.** The facts of Answer (B) describe a taxable termination. Again, even though there is a distribution to Miley at the end of Mona's life, meeting the requirements of a taxable termination prevents the distribution from qualifying as a taxable distribution under the rules. *Id.*

**Answer (D) is also incorrect** for reasons already explained above.

# PRACTICE FINAL EXAM: ANSWERS

1. **Answer (C) is correct.** As of January 1, 2010, the applicable exclusion amount for federal gift tax was set at $1 million and the federal gift tax was calculated based on an applicable credit amount of $345,800. IRC §§ 2505(a)(1), 2001(c). Under the Tax Relief, Unemployment Insurance Reauthorization, and Job Creation Act of 2010 ("TRA"), the applicable exclusion amount for federal estate tax purposes tops out at $5 million. The $5 million exclusion translates to an applicable credit amount of $1,730,800. IRC §§ 2010, 2001(c); *see also* TRA § 302(b). Thus, the applicable exclusion amounts and the applicable credit amounts for the federal estate and gift tax differ. Note that practitioners often refer to the applicable exclusion amount as the "credit shelter amount" or the "exemption equivalent."

    **Answers (A), (B), and (D) are incorrect.** For the reasons stated above, none of these answers is entirely correct.

2. **Answer (A) is correct.** As of January 1, 2011, with the TRA of 2010, the applicable exclusion amount for both federal estate and gift tax purposes tops out at $5 million in 2011, which translates to an applicable credit amount of $1,730,800. IRC §§ 2010, 2001(c). Thus, the applicable exclusion amounts and the applicable credit amounts for the federal estate and gift tax are once again the same. The TRA of 2010 generally sets the estate, gift and Generation Skipping Tax exemption at $5.0 million. *See* TRA § 302(a)(1), Beginning in 2012, the $5.0 million exemption is required to be indexed from 2010, and sets the maximum rate at 35%. *See* TRA § 302(a)(2). The $5 million exemptions generally apply in 2010. *See* TRA § 302(f). Note, however, that the gift tax exemption remained at $1.0 million only for 2010. *See* TRA § 302(b)(1)(B).

    **Answers (B), (C), and (D) are incorrect** for the reasons stated above.

3. Here, Clayton made a taxable gift of $950,000 in 2009. As previously noted, the applicable exclusion amount for federal gift tax was set at $1 million for 2009 and the federal gift tax was calculated based on an applicable credit amount of $345,800. IRC §§ 2505(a)(1), 2001(c). Gift tax is imposed on the transfer under IRC § 2501 and is computed under IRC § 2502(a) at the rates provided in IRC § 2001(c). Pursuant to the rate schedule, gift tax on the first $750,000 is $248,300. Gift tax is further imposed at a rate of 39% of the amount of the gift in excess of $750,000 which amounts to an additional $78,000 of gift tax ($950,000 - $750,000 = 200,000; 200,000 x .39 = $78,000). Adding the $248,000 to the $78,000 results in a tentative tax on the 2009 gift of $326,000. Applying the credit, results in no gift tax due as the credit of $345,800 exceeds the tentative tax of $326,000 by $19,800.

4. In 2011, Clayton gifts an additional $4,050,000 to his son. Between the 2009 and 2011 gifts, Clayton has transferred a total of $5,000,000. Gift tax on the $5,000,000 of gifts at the lower 35% rate that applies in 2011 results in a tax of $1,730,800. *See* IRC §§ 2502(a)(1), 2001(c). In order to arrive at the gift tax due on the $4,050,000 given in 2011, the tax imposed on the 2009 gift must be subtracted from the tax due on the total of $5,000,000. Note that gift tax

is now calculated on the $950,000 gift made in 2009 pursuant to the rate schedule provided in 2001(c) in 2011. This results in a gift tax of $313,300 [$155,800 (gift tax on the first $500,000 is $155,800) + $157,500 (.35 x $450,000) = $313,300]. Subtracting the $313,300 from the total tax of $1,730,800 results in gift tax due on the 2011 gift of $4,050,000 of $1,417,500. Finally the remaining credit available for use against the tax on the 2011 gift must be determined. Credit on the $5,000,000 exclusion amount is $1,730,800. The credit on the 2009 gift at the lower 35% rate is $313,300. Reducing the current credit of $1,730,800 by the $313,300, we arrive at $1,417,500 which offsets the full amount of the gift tax due on the 2011 gift of $4,050,000. The take away here is that the credit used on prior period gifts is calculated at the 35% rate.

5.     Federal estate tax is calculated under IRC § 2001. The formula for determining federal estate tax aggregates adjusted taxable gifts and the taxable estate to determine if decedent's taxable life time transfers exceed the $5 million applicable exclusion amount available to decedent's dying in 2012. *See* IRC § 2001(b). Aggregation also ensures application of the appropriate tax rate. In 2012, the top estate tax rate applicable to estates in excess of $5 million was 35 percent.

Adeline's taxable estate equals $3.7 million. Add to that amount adjusted taxable gifts of $2.5 million. Aggregate taxable transfers made by Adeline equal $6.2 million ($3.7 million taxable estate + $2.5 million taxable gift) as of her death in 2012. Note that Adeline's annual exclusion gifts of $2.2 million are not taxable gifts, and, thus, are not included in adjusted taxable gifts. Then determine the tentative tax on aggregate transfers of $6.2 million. The tentative tax based on the tax rate set forth in IRC § 2001(c) in 2012 is calculated as follows: $6,200,000 - $500,000 = $5,700,000; $5,700,000 × .35 = $1,995,000; $1,995,000 + 155,800 = $2,150,800. Thus the tentative tax on the aggregate amount of the taxable estate and adjusted taxable gifts is $2,150,800.

Next, subtract from the tentative tax of $2,150,800 the aggregate gift tax, which would have been payable on post-1976 gifts based on the estate tax rate effective as of Adeline's date of death. The tax that would have been payable on Adeline's $2.5 million dollar gift is zero, because the gift tax applicable exclusion equals $5 million. Thus, the tentative federal estate tax equals $2,150,800.

In order to determine the amount of federal estate tax owed by Adeline's estate, available credits must be subtracted. The only credit available based on our facts is the unified credit under IRC § 2010. The credit amount in 2012 equals $1,730,800. The credit is subtracted from the tentative federal estate tax of $2,150,800. Federal estate tax, thus, totals $420,000 or [$2,150,800 – 1,730,800].

6.     **Answer (B) is correct.** IRC § 2036 applies to include trust assets in the transferor's gross estate where transferor has retained an interest in trust assets "for his life or for any period not ascertainable without reference to his death or for any period which does not in fact end before his death." If Ally retains an interest for a term of years, which she outlives, then she has not retained an interest in the trust which satisfies the requirements of the statute. The term of 15 years is not for her life and is not a time period that requires reference to her death. Further, because Ally lives long past her normal life expectancy, the 15-year term does in fact end before her death.

**Answers (A) and (C) are incorrect.** On the other hand, the right to receive income or an annuity for life or the same combined with a right to principal fall into the proscribed language under IRC § 2036. With respect to a grantor retaining an income interest for life, at least a portion of the assets must be included in grantor's gross estate. Note that a life interest is only a partial interest in the whole. However, students should make note that Regulation § 20.2036-1(c) specifies how to determine the amounts included in a grantor's gross estate under such circumstances.

**Answer (D) is incorrect.** Because Answer (B) does not result in inclusion under IRC § 2036, Answer (D) is incorrect.

7. **Answer (D) is correct.** Although Ellen should have been entitled to only 20 percent of the income of the family limited partnership attributable to her 20 percent limited partnership interest, Ellen in fact received 100 percent of the income. The terms of the limited partnership were not respected by the parties. The facts indicate an implied agreement that Ellen retain the income to the transferred property. Thus, IRC § 2036(a)(1) requires gross estate inclusion of the value of all assets transferred by Ellen to the limited partnership because Ellen impliedly retained an income interest in the property transferred for a period that did not end before her death. *See Estate of Schauerhamer v. Comm'r*, T.C. Memo. 1997-242.

**Answers (A), (B), and (C) are incorrect** for the reasons stated above.

8. **Answer (B) is correct.** IRC § 2040 applies to determine the rental property value included in Heidi's gross estate. Treasury Regulation § 20.2040-1(c)(2) indicates that Heidi's gross estate will include that portion of the rental property value corresponding to the portion of the purchase priced furnished by Heidi. Thus, 50 percent of the rental property value is included in Heidi's gross estate. Because Heidi and Ingrid do not die simultaneously, the holding of Revenue Ruling 76-303, 1976-2 C.B. 266, does not apply in this situation. When Ingrid dies, IRC § 2033 will include 100 percent of the rental property value in Ingrid's gross estate because at the time of her death she owned the property and was able to transfer it pursuant to her will. For these same reasons, the remaining

**Answers (A), (C), and (D) are incorrect.**

9. **Answer (B) is correct.** IRC § 2013 allows a prior transfer credit for the purpose of avoiding double taxation when the transferor and the transferee die within 10 years of each other. The amount of the credit begins at 100 percent and decreases by 20 percent every two years. Because Ingrid died within two years of Heidi, Ingrid's estate may take 100 percent of the amount of the credit. In order to determine the credit, the estate must calculate two limitations. The first limitation determines the amount of estate tax attributable to the transferred property in the transferor's estate, and the second limitation determines the amount of the estate tax attributable to the transferred property in the transferee's estate. The transferee's estate is allowed the lesser of the two limitations as a credit. Thus, Ingrid's estate may take a $30,000 tax on prior transfers credit. For these same reasons, the remaining

**Answers (A), (C), and (D) are incorrect.**

10. **Answer (D) is correct.** During his life, Kyle can pay trust property only to himself for his support. A distribution standard limited to support falls within the list of ascertainable standards enumerated in Treasury Regulation 20.2041-1(c)(2). Because support is an ascertainable standard, Kyle's power to pay property to himself does not fall within the

definition of general power of appointment. Answer (A) is incorrect because the concept of a legal obligation of support is not applicable to payments to oneself. It is applicable only to the extent a beneficiary must support someone else, such as a child. Thus, during his life, Kyle does not possess a general power of appointment. He also does not possess a general power of appointment at his death because he may not distribute property to his estate or to the creditors of his estate per the definition set forth in IRC § 2041(b)(1). A power to appoint only to one's descendants is a special power, and not a general power of appointment. *See* Treas. Reg. § 20.2041-1(c)(1)(a) and (b). For this same reason,

**Answer (B) is incorrect. Answer (C) is incorrect** because the fact of exercise is irrelevant for federal estate tax purposes with respect to powers created after October 21, 1942.

11. **Answer (D) is correct.** IRC § 2035 includes in the gross estate those transfers made by decedent during the three-year period ending at death that otherwise would have been included in decedent's gross estate under IRC §§ 2036 through 2038 and 2042. Here Lannie transferred the insurance policy in 2008 and died the following year, well within the three-year time period. Had Lannie retained ownership of the insurance policy, she would have held incidents of ownership at her death that would have caused inclusion in her gross estate under IRC § 2042(2). Thus, the full value of the policy proceeds will be included in Lannie's gross estate. For these same reasons, Answer (A) is incorrect. The value included is not limited to the amount of the gift or of the taxable gift, and for that reason,

**Answers (B) and (C) are incorrect.**

12. Lannie could have avoided application of IRC § 2035 by transferring cash in the amount necessary to purchase the life insurance policy and pay the first premium to her child. If the child had purchased the policy instead of Lannie, IRC § 2035 could not apply because Lannie would then never have held incidents of ownership over the policy that could have caused IRC § 2042 inclusion of the proceeds.

13. **Answer (D) is the only correct answer.** Property taxes are deductible as claims against decedent's estate if they accrue and become due and owing prior to decedent's death so that they are an enforceable claim as of the date of death. Treas. Reg. § 20.2053-6(b).

**Answer (A) is incorrect** because the expense for the reception was not one ordinarily incurred as part of a funeral that entails the burial and eulogizing of the decedent. In a case, *Estate of Davenport v. Comm'r*, T.C. Memo. 2006-215, the court disallowed reception expenses. Treasury Regulation § 20.2053-2 allows as funeral expense deductions only those (i) actually incurred and (ii) those allowable under local law. In addition, if paid out of property not subject to claims, the regulation requires the expense be paid within nine months after the date of death.

**Answer (B) is incorrect** because the administration expense was not actually paid. To be deductible, Treasury Regulation § 20.2053-3(a) requires administration expenses to be (i) actually and (ii) necessarily incurred. The expense must also be allowable under local law. Treas. Reg. § 20.2053-1(b). The first element is not met.

**Answer (C) is incorrect** because to be deductible a claim generally must be "contracted bona fide and for an adequate and full consideration in money or money's worth." Marvin failed to receive consideration "in money or money's worth" in exchange for the promissory note. Courts scrutinize transactions between family members, and would likely find the "loan" to be in fact a gift to child.

14.     **Answer (A) is correct.** In order to obtain a marital deduction, the property subject to the deduction must be included in the decedent's gross estate. IRC § 2056(a); Treas. Reg. § 20.2056(a)-2(b)(1). The patent rights owned by Nancy would be included in her gross estate pursuant to IRC § 2033. The patent rights must pass from Nancy to Omar. If the patent rights pass to a qualified terminable interest property trust, the patent rights will be considered to have passed from Nancy to Omar under Treas. Reg. § 20.2056(c)-2(a)(2) and (b)(2). The interest passing must be a "deductible interest," or in other words, it cannot be a nondeductible terminable interest. Treasury Regulation § 20.2056(b)-1(b) specifically states that patent rights are not a terminable interest simply because they last for only the specified number of years allowed by federal law. Treasury regulations also indicate that property passing to a qualified terminable interest property trust qualifies as a deductible interest under an exception. Treas. Reg. § 20.2056(b)-1(d). Thus, the question becomes whether a qualified terminable interest property election can be made with respect to the trust created for the benefit of Omar. Here, Omar has a qualifying income interest for life because he is entitled to receive all trust income at least annually, and the facts indicate the patents pay substantial royalties. Thus, the exec   r can obtain a marital deduction for the patent rights passing to the trust by making an   C § 2056(b)(7) QTIP election.

        **Answer (B) is incorrect** because Omar does not hold a general power of appointment over the trust assets. He holds only a limited or special power of appointment to direct trust property on his death to Nancy's children.

        **Answer (C) is incorrect** because IRC § 2056(b)(3) permits the spouse's interest in trust to be conditioned on up to six months survival. For the reasons stated above, Omar's interest in trust is a deductible interest and, thus,

        **Answer (D) is incorrect.**

15.     **Answer (B) is correct.** In order to make a taxable gift, the donor must relinquish all "dominion and control." Treasury Regulation § 25.2511-2(b) indicates a gift is complete when "the donor has so parted with dominion and control as to leave in him no power to change its disposition, whether for his own benefit or for the benefit of another." To the extent Peter retains the right to change who will receive trust income or principal, the gift remains incomplete. This is the case in Answers (A), (C), and (D). In Answer (A), Peter retains the right to name who will receive income and principal. In Answer (C), Peter retains the right to revoke the trust. In Answer (D), as policy owner, Peter retains the right to name a different beneficiary. Only in Answer (B) is Peter precluded from exercising discretion to change who ultimately receives the property. In Answer (B), Peter at most may affect the timing of when property is received. Thus, Peter makes a completed gift in Answer (B).

16.     Quincy will have made a completed gift because, although he retains the power to pay income and principal for his friend's support, support is a fixed and ascertainable standard. As such, Quincy upon making the gift has relinquished dominion and control pursuant to Treasury Regulation § 25.2511-2(c).

17.     **Answer (D) is correct.** IRC § 2503(b) allows a taxpayer to transfer up to $10,000 per person per year, as that amount is adjusted for inflation, so long as the transfer is one of a present interest. In 2011 the gift tax annual exclusion amount is $13,000. Penelope transfers only

$10,000, so the entire amount will qualify for the annual exclusion provided it qualifies as a transfer of a present interest. The Ninth Circuit in *Crummey v. Comm'r*, 397 F.2d 82 (9th Cir. 1968), and the Tax Court in *Estate of Cristofani v. Comm'r*, 97 T.C. 74 (1991), acknowledged that a withdrawal right over property transferred to a trust is the transfer of a present interest. In this problem there is sufficient time for Rylan to exercise the withdrawal right, and it is assured that the trustee will notify Rylan of the withdrawal right. While the Service has made a substance-over-form argument, courts have consistently rejected this argument; thus,

**Answer (B) is incorrect.**

**Answers (A) and (C) are incorrect** because both answers focus on the impact of a lapse of the withdrawal right held by Rylan. An analysis of whether the withdrawal right lapses is irrelevant to an analysis of the transfer made by Penelope.

18.    **Answer (B) is correct.** Rylan's right to withdraw property from the trust amounts to a general power of appointment over the trust property. An exercise or release of a power of appointment is deemed a transfer of property for purposes of the federal gift tax pursuant to IRC § 2514(b). A lapse is treated as a release pursuant to IRC § 2514(e), but only to the extent that "the property which could have been appointed by exercise of such lapsed powers exceeds in value the greater of the following amounts: (1) $5,000, or (2) 5 percent of the aggregate value of the assets out of which, or the proceeds of which, the exercise of the lapsed powers could be satisfied." Thus, when Rylan allowed his power to lapse, the lapse is treated as a release to the extent of $5,000, or, in other words, the amount by which $10,000 exceeds $5,000. For these same reasons,

   **Answers (A), (C), and (D) are incorrect.**

19.    **Answer (B) is correct.** A skip person includes a natural person assigned to a generation that is at least two generations below the generation assignment of the transferor. IRC § 2613(a)(1). Whether a transferee, who is a lineal descendant of Jerry's grandparent but not of Jerry, is still related in a manner that results in a skip requires reference to the lineal descendant rules. *See* IRC § 2651. Here, Jerry's grandnephew Jason is a lineal descendant of Jerry's grandparents. Jason must be separated by two generations or more from Jerry to qualify as a skip person. Generation assignments are made by comparing (1) the number of generations between the grandparent and Jerry, with (2) the number of generations between the grandparent and Jason. The number of generations between Jason (e.g., fifth generation) and Jerry's grandparents (e.g., first generation) is three generations. The number of generations between the grandparent (e.g., first generation) and Jerry (e.g., third generation) is one generation of separation. Thus, comparing the three generations to one generation, it is seen that there are two generations of difference. Because there are two generations between Jerry and Jason, Jason is a skip person under the rules. Answers (A), (C), and (D) are incorrect for reasons explained above.

20.    **Answer (C) is the correct answer.** A taxable termination occurs when an interest in a trust terminates and immediately after the termination only one or more skip persons has an interest in the trust. IRC § 2612(a)(1)(A); Treas. Reg. § 26.2612-1 (b). Prior to Nancy's death, Nancy has an interest in the trust. Nancy is a non-skip person because, as Mary's child, she is assigned to the generation immediately beneath Mary (e.g., one generation apart). During Nancy's life, the trust is not a skip person, and a contribution to the trust is not a direct skip.

Upon Nancy's death, only Judy has an interest in the trust. Since Judy is assigned to the second generation below Mary, she is a skip person. After Nancy's death, all interests are held by skip persons and a taxable termination occurs.

**Answers (A), (B), and (D) are incorrect.** With respect to Answers (A) and (B), a non-skip person, continues to hold an interest in the trust. Therefore, no taxable termination has occurred. Note that Answer (B) describes a taxable distribution, which is discussed below. Answer (D) is incorrect for reasons already explained.

21.    **Answer (C) is the correct answer.** The term "taxable distribution" means any distribution from a trust to a skip person (other than a taxable termination or a direct skip). Einer continues to be deemed a skip person because he is assigned to the second generation below Frank under the lineal descendant rules. IRC § 2651(b). When the trustee distributes one-half of the principal to Einer on his eighteenth birthday, there is a taxable distribution to Einer. Note also that the distribution does not qualify as either a direct skip or a taxable termination. *Id.* If the distribution qualified as either a direct skip or taxable termination, it could not qualify as a taxable distribution. *See* IRC § 2612(b) (parenthetical).

**Answer (A) is incorrect.** Answer (A) describes a situation under which there would have been a taxable termination. In Answer (A), when Martine dies, a taxable termination occurs as opposed to a taxable distribution.

**Answer (B) is incorrect.** Answer (B) describes a situation under which the original contribution would have been a direct skip. In Answer (B), Einer has a present interest in the trust while Martine, Mary's child, has only a future interest. Because Einer has the only current interest, a contribution to the trust will be a direct skip subject to GST on the date of contribution.

**Answer (D) is also incorrect** for reasons already explained above.

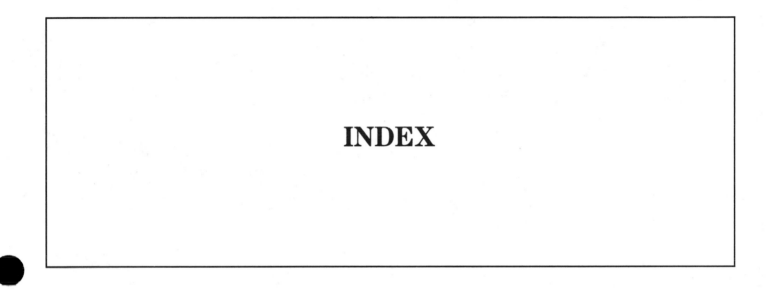

# INDEX

# INDEX

## TREASURY REGULATION INDEX